# The Habeas Corpus Manual

By: Raymond E. Lumsden

"[W]e fail in our primary duty of protecting the innocent and in punishing the guilty if we intentionally slam the courthouse doors against one who is, in fact, innocent of wrongdoing .... [If] the criminal justice system – even when its procedures were fairly followed – reaches a patently inaccurate result, which has caused an innocent person to be wrongly imprisoned for a crime he did not commit, the judicial system has an obligation to set things straight. Our criminal justice system makes two promises to its citizens: a fundamentally fair trial and an accurate result. If either of those promises are not met, the criminal justice system itself falls into disrepute and will eventually be disregarded."

Ex Parte Thompson, 153 S.W.3d 416, 421 (Tex. Crim. App. 2005)
(Cochran, J., concurring)

Freebird Publishers
www.FreebirdPublishers.com

## Freebird Publishers

Box 541, North Dighton, MA 02764
Info@FreebirdPublishers.com
www.FreebirdPublishers.com

Copyright © 2019
The Habeas Corpus Manual
By Raymond E. Lumsden

All Freebird Publishers titles, imprints, and distributed lines are available at special quantity discounts for bulk purchases for sales promotions, premiums, fundraising, educational, or institutional use.

ISBN-13: 978-1-7332826-1-1
ISBN-10: 1-7332826-1-0

Printed in the United States of America

# Dedications

To the four-corners of my heart and soul: Anthony, Alyssa, Joshua, and Rylee … my beloved children. You are my greatest accomplishments and sources of pride. My love for you is eternal.

To my grandchildren: Joe, Rysen, and Aniyah. I miss you! I love you!

To my beloved Chicago Bears – BEAR DOWN!!!!

"For whoever shut their ears to the cry of the poor
and the imprisoned will also cry themselves and not be heard"

Proverbs 21:13

# Foreword

My name is Raymond Lumsden. Currently, I am serving time in the Texas Department of Criminal Justice. Unlike the vast plethora of "writ writers" that flood the system with inadequate, ineffective, and frivolous motions, pleadings, and non-meritorious issues, I possess extensive legal training and experience in post-conviction relief.

I am a graduate of two highly accredited paralegal schools and have passed the State Bar Examination in an "inmate friendly" state. In the pages to follow, I will attempt to provide you with the most effective, sound, and universal steps in mounting an aggressive state post-conviction challenge to your sentence and conviction. Because the state of Texas does not allow inmates to maintain a law license or State Bar Number, I am unable to provide "legal advice." What I can legally pass along to you is knowledge based on my certified legal training and experience.

I will provide samples of letters, motions, and pleadings covering most of the scenarios you will encounter in your state *habeas corpus* and post-conviction efforts. I have paid little attention at this time to Federal post-conviction efforts and apply direct focus to state challenges. This is where most *pro-se* inmates and members of the public find themselves.

Without further talk, let's get to it. Time is of the essence.

Good Luck!

# Table of Contents

# How to Use This Book

This book will provide you with the tools to mount an aggressive and, hopefully, successful state post-conviction challenge. The forms, letters, instructions, etc. were all designed specifically for *pro-se* use, where the assistance of paid counsel is unavailable. That being said, it is always advisable to obtain paid counsel, if possible, in your efforts to challenge your conviction and sentence.

Everything in this book has been successful on at least one occasion where it was applied correctly. However, that certainly does not mean that each action will be successful every time, or even applicable to your situation. Facts win cases – not forms, motions, or pleadings. Yet how the facts are presented also play a role in your success. When using the enclosed forms, letters, and motions be sure to change them to best fit your case. Style, tone, idea, and direction should be made to fit your case specifically. There is no "one size fits all" when it comes to legal forms and pleadings.

Always double space your motions and pleadings. For the sake of space, where I have failed to double space those things, you must disregard the exception in my book. All courts require double-spaced filings, no matter what they are. Read your local court rules prior to filing any documents to learn what they expect specifically. This will grant you favor with that particular court, by showing them that you respect them enough to follow their rules.

You must use your common sense when bringing actions to the court. If it does not make sense to you, it will not make sense to the court. That is the fastest way to get your motions rejected without written order or denied in totality. I've tried to make it as easy as possible for you by including my general-purpose blank forms. However, if you still find them complicated or confusing, ask someone in your law library for help. Never file anything you don't understand. Everything else we will address as we go along.

*Notes:*

# Chapter One:
# Gathering What You Will Need

## Transcripts and Documents

Before you do anything else, you must gather every document that relates to your conviction and sentence. This includes the transcripts in your case that will help you analyze and discover issues related to your conviction. Whether it be ineffective assistance by your trial counsel, abuse of discretion, prosecutorial misconduct, or whatever, it will only come to light by researching your case. Then, and only then, can you begin to mount an effective post-conviction challenge.

Most states do not allow defendants to see or obtain copies of discovery documents and materials prior to their trial. In fact, some states will not allow you to see these documents at any time. That being said, you simply cannot mount any viable challenge to your conviction or sentence without your discovery material.

Below is a list of the items you will need to obtain and what purpose they will serve in your post-conviction challenge:

## Docket Sheet

This document is available to you by contacting the district clerk in the county where you were convicted. It will provide a detailed list of all documents, motions, letters, etc., that were filed in your case by your own trial attorney, as well as the state prosecutor. Most importantly, all the exhibits entered into the record in your case will be on the docket sheet. This is where you will uncover and discover a vast amount of information related to your case.

If your trial counsel was ineffective for failing to file motions during pretrial, especially to suppress evidence the state was intending to use against you, the docket sheet will show it. It is my own experience that what attorneys tell you they filed on your behalf never does get filed in the pretrial stage. The docket sheet will show you whether the jury in your case requested in writing any questions, or what they may have been thinking in their deliberations. It will show you the response to the jury questions or notes, and how your trial counsel addressed them. The docket sheet is the very first thing you need to obtain in your pursuit of post-conviction relief.

## Reporter's Record (Trial Transcripts)

This is where the "meat" of the post-conviction challenge rests. The Reporter's Record will contain almost every word said in every pretrial hearing, as well as in your trial. I say "almost" every word, because even the best court reporter cannot possibly get every single word said in a very fast-moving setting. However, they are usually pretty close. If there are errors and issues that directly caused your conviction, they will certainly be in the Reporter's Record, aka, your Trial Record.

A few examples are: (1) perhaps your trial counsel failed to object to hearsay evidence being allowed into the trial;(2) if you accepted a plea bargain, perhaps the trial court failed to properly admonish you to assure that you knowingly, willingly, and intentionally have accepted the plea; (3) perhaps your trial attorney "pulled the teeth" on extraneous offenses that would have been inadmissible but for his actions; (4) perhaps, your trial counsel admitted your guilt to the jury or failed to mount any meaningful adversarial challenge, failed to object to leading questions, failed to impeach lying witnesses, failed to present exculpatory and mitigating evidence on your behalf, failed to call witnesses, failed to object to an inaccurate indictment or charge, or any other mistake in the long list of ineffectiveness. It will all be in your Reporter's Record (Trial Record).

If you went through a trial, the Reporter's Record could possibly show that there was a question with jurisdiction in the court, or that there was inaccurate information in your indictment or jury instructions. It may show that there is a problem with identity, since the alleged suspect was white, 5'5" tall, and bald ... and you are 6'6' tall, African American, with a full head of hair. Whatever the issues that may provide relief in your case can more often than not be found in your Reporter's Record. Without it, your chances of success are greatly reduced. Later in this chapter, I will show you how to obtain the Reporter's Record in your case fairly easily and usually without cost, if you were indigent during your trial.

## Documents Needed

- Arrest warrants, search warrants, and the affidavits used to obtain the warrants;
- All investigation reports, police reports, CPS reports (or any other reports involved in your case);
- A copy of your indictment or charging papers;
- docket sheet;
- All pretrial motions, letters, or documents listed on your docket sheet, regardless of who filed it;
- Jury instructions;
- Jury charge;
- Reporter's Record, including *voir dire* (jury selection), opening arguments, trial, hearing held outside the presence of the jury during the trial, and closing arguments;
- All verdict forms;
- Motions for retrial;
- Sentencing, judgement, and conviction order;
- Notice of appeal;
- Appellant and Appellee briefs (direct appeal briefs);
- Court of Appeals opinion on direct appeal;
- Attorney Client file.

The above is a general list of the required documents necessary to mount an aggressive post-conviction challenge, if you went to trial on your case. Without the above documents, you have little chances of successful challenge to your conviction and sentence. So, stop procrastinating and get to work. Time is working against you.

If you accepted a plea agreement and announced your guilt without a trial, include any and all guilty plea transcripts, offers, pre-sentence investigation reports (PSI), or any objections to the Pre-sentence report. When accepting a guilty plea, your client file will hold an immense sum of valuable and important documents you are probably unaware of.

### Conclusion of Post-Conviction Gathering of Documents

At this stage, where you are investigating and gathering, important and necessary documents, it will resemble what should have been done by your trial counsel prior to your trial or guilty plea. The pre-trial investigation and the post-trial investigation should basically be identical. You must read and re-read everything, interview possible witnesses that weren't called at your trial or sentencing, seek expert opinions if possible, and obtain affidavits that could have helped you at trial or sentencing that your trial counsel failed to obtain. You must investigate all areas that may provide valid arguments to raise on your post-conviction relief attempts.

## Getting Your Docket Sheet

As I mentioned earlier, the docket sheet contains a detailed account of everything filed and done in your case. Motions, hearings, court entries, minutes, exhibits, etc. Generally, these things are recorded by the clerk as they happen, chronologically. The entry number and date the filed item was accepted will help you to follow the course of events prior to your trial and thereafter.

When you are ready to obtain a copy of your docket sheet, use the letter I have provided and customize the information to reflect your case. Form No. 1 is only for obtaining your docket sheet from your County of conviction. If you are trying to obtain a copy of your docket sheet from the Appeals Court that ruled on your direct appeal, you should use Form No. 2.

Sometimes the District Clerk's office will require a small fee for providing a copy of the docket sheet. However, if you were found to be indigent in your case and the court appointed an attorney to represent you for free, the District Clerk will usually waive any fees associated with obtaining a copy of the docket sheet. Just remember to inform them that you are still indigent and cannot afford any fee.

It is my experience that you may want to request a copy of your client file at the same time you request the docket sheet, so you can follow the contents of the client file with the dates listed on the docket sheet. Keep in mind, the docket sheet is not the trial transcript, but is a detailed list of everything that has been filed in your case both pretrial and post-trial.

FORM NO. 1

District Clerk
**Address**
**City, State, Zip Code**

Date

Re: Case Number_____

    Request for Docket Sheet

Dear Clerk:

I am respectfully requesting a copy of the Docket Sheet in the above case number. Additionally, I please ask that you waive any fee associated with this request due to my indigence and inability to pay.

If you are unwilling to waive any fee, please let me know in writing so that I may petition the trial court for a waiver of the fee required.

I appreciate your assistance in this matter.

Respectfully,


[Sign your name here]
_____
[Your Name]
[Address]

**FORM NO. 2**

Office of the Clerk
Court of Appeals
Address_____
City, State, Zip Code

Date

Re: Appeal Number_____
    Request for Docket Sheet

Dear Clerk:

I am writing to request a copy of the Docket Sheet in the above case number. If you require a fee for the Appellate Docket Sheet, I please ask that you waive it due to my incarceration and indigence.

I appreciate your assistance in these regards.

Respectfully,


[Sign your name here]

_____
[Your name]
[Address]


Cc: p/file

## Getting Your Client File

There simply is not any reason to begin to prepare a post-conviction appeal without your client file. You will need to obtain this from the trial attorney who represented you during that trial, in order to identify grounds for relief. This client file contains some documents and information I can guarantee that you are unaware of and will provide a great deal of insight as to how you were convicted in the first place. It all starts with your trial counsel.

The client file will usually consist of the following items: Discovery materials, motions filed, motions unfiled, responses, orders, exhibits, investigative reports, police reports, personal notes, written communication between your attorney and the prosecutor, research, case law related to your offense(s), plea offers, expert findings, and letters between you and your trial counsel. Every client file is different because attorneys are different in how well they prepare and defend you. Some client files are thick and filled with material and some are only a few sheets of paper.

### Request Your Client File

Initially, you will need to write a letter to your trial counsel and make a formal request for your client file. The same is true if you are trying to obtain a copy of your client file from your appeal counsel. You should sound confident in your request. You have the legal right to obtain the client file that was made during their representation of you.

The first letter that you send will be the only letter that you send. There is no rational reason to write additional letters requesting your client file, although numerous inmates make the mistake of doing so and waste valuable time. Send your letter to your trial counsel or appeal counsel requesting a complete copy of the client file in their possession that was created during the time in which they represented you (*see* Form No. 3). You should always send this letter Certified Mail, if possible, to leave a trail should proof become necessary. If sending the letter certified is not possible, make a photocopy of it before it is mailed.

### No Response from Attorney

As I said above, you are legally entitled to your client file. That being said, some attorneys will go out of their way to prevent you from obtaining your client file, because they are afraid of it proving just how incredibly ineffective, they were in representing you. When that happens – and it sometimes does – I do not waste time with State Bar letters. I immediately file a *Motion to Compel Attorney to Surrender the Case File*.

This motion is filed with the District Clerk in the County you were convicted in or the clerk of the sentencing court (*see* Form No. 4).

## FORM NO. 3

[Your Attorney's Name]
Attorney At Law
Address
City, State, Zip Code


Date


Re: **Client File**

    **Case No.**_____


Dear [Name of Attorney]:

I am writing in reference to the above case number in which you represented me. At this time, I am requesting a complete copy of my client file in your possession. This includes all discovery material, pretrial motions, responses, orders, etc.

I am entitled to the client file for several reasons. First, I am preparing to challenge my sentence and conviction in a habeas corpus petition. Lastly, I am entitled to my client file under federal law.

Hopefully, you will act accordingly, and not impede my rights, by providing me a copy of my client file within (14) days of this letter, by placing it in a large envelope, addressed to me, via certified mail to ensure its delivery.

I appreciate your assistance in this matter, and anxiously await receipt of the client file. If I haven't received it within the (14) days, I will be forced to file a Motion To Compel with the trial court.

Sincerely,



[Sign Name Here]


_____
[Your Name]
[Address]



Cc: p/file

FORM NO. 4

IN THE _____ DISTRICT COURT OF_____ COUNTY

STATE OF _____

| | |
|---|---|
| [Your Name Here]<br>_____,<br>　　　　Petitioner,<br><br>　　　　v.<br><br>STATE OF _____,<br>　　　　Respondent. | )<br>)<br>)<br>)　　Case No. _____<br>)<br>)<br>)<br>)<br>)<br>) |

### MOTION TO COMPEL ATTORNEY TO PRODUCE CLIENT'S FILE

COMES NOW [Your Name]_____, Petitioner, pro se, and moves the Court to issue an order compelling Attorney _____, to surrender the case file he created while representing Petitioner in the above case number. In support, Petitioner asserts the following:

1. Attorney _____, is currently employed at [Address]____, [City]_____, [State]_____, [Zip Code]_____.

2. Plaintiff has previously requested a copy of his client file in writing, on [Date]_____, [Year]_____, without response.

3. Plaintiff requires the client file in order to file a post-conviction challenge to both his conviction and sentence.

4. Plaintiff is entitled to his client file by law. See **Maxwell v. Florida**, 479 U.S. 972, 93 L.Ed.2d 418-420, 107 S.Ct. 474 (1986); **Spivey v. Zant**, 683 F.2d 881, 885 (5th Cir. 1982); **ABA Standards for Criminal Justice Defense Functions Standards and Commentary**. The right to effective and sound assistanc of counsel fully encompasses the client's right to obtain the work files created by the attorney.

5. Finally, it appears as though Attorney _____ is now

attempting to stall Petitioner's habeas challenge to his conviction and sentence based largely on the ineffective assistance of counsel received during his trial.

**WHEREFORE**, premised considered, Plaintiff respectfully urges this Honorable Court to issue an order compelling Attorney _____ to immediately provide the client file to Plaintiff within (10) days of receipt of this order, via registered mail.

**Respectfully** submitted on this_____day of _____, 20____.

[Sign Name Here]

_____
Your Name
Pro Se
Address
City, State, Zip Code

[CAPTION]

**ORDER**

Upon consideration of the defendant, _____[Your Name]_____, motion to compel attorney _____ to surrender the case file in the above captioned number the Court finds that the motion should be **GRANTED.**

**IT IS HEREBY** ORDERED that attorney _____ is directed to produce and release the client file to the defendant_____ in the above entitled action.

Done this _____ day of _____ 20_____ .


_____
PRESIDING JUDGE


(Include with Form F.4)

# Getting Your Reporter's Record

Obtaining your Reporter's Record, also known as your Trial Transcripts, is going to take a little work. That being said, without it you are unlikely to mount any effective post-conviction challenge. It is vital that you are able to review every word of your pretrial, trial, and post-trial hearings and events, so that you can cite issues in your appeal.

### Direct Appeal Still Pending

At this stage of the process, the court of Appeals will not allow you to obtain a copy of the trial record. If you are attempting to obtain the Reporter's Record/Trial Record from the court of Appeals, you must wait until the direct appellate procedure has concluded.

You can, however, attempt to obtain a copy of the Reporter's Record from the trial court you were convicted in, if you are indigent and unable to pay the ridiculous fees usually accompanied with the records (*see* Form No. 5). You will need to research case law relevant to obtaining free copies of your Reporter's Record/Trial Records in your state and adapt the form accordingly. Out of the dozens I have filed on behalf of myself and others, I can count on one hand the times the request has been denied by the trial court. In short, Courts are usually very generous in granting free copies of the trial record for indigent defendants.

### If You Lost Your Direct Appeal

At this stage of the proceedings, your Reporter's Record is with the court of Appeals that handled your direct appeal. If you want a copy of the Appellate Record, which includes the Reporter's Record, you can file a motion with the court of Appeals to obtain it. You can simply amend Form No. 5 to reflect the different court in the Caption of the motion.

### When You Get Your Transcripts

Once you have been successful in obtaining your trial transcripts, aka Reporter's Record, it is very important that you do not write or make any marks on it. This includes highlighting. If you ever need an additional copy of the record, you will be able to photocopy the one you already have. Additionally, you may need to submit your copy to the court, which they will not accept if it is not a true and accurate copy of the original.

### Do Not Lose Your Transcripts

If you are lucky enough to obtain a free copy of your transcripts from either the trial court or the court of appeals, do not lose them. If you do, you will not receive another free copy – even if you are still indigent and cannot afford to pay for a copy.

If, by chance, you do lose them you can purchase another copy from the trial court or the court of Appeals, for one dollar per page. The average trial lasts around 3 days, so that's around 1,000 pages of transcripts, depending on how effective your attorney was in defending you.

## Direct Appeal Counsel

Usually, if you were appointed indigent appeal counsel by the trial court, they were provided a copy of the Reporter's Record/Trial Transcripts. It is my experience that they will often provide you with a free copy upon your request. Simply write them a letter requesting a copy of your trial transcripts for future challenge to your conviction should it be necessary.

*Notes:*

FORM NO. 5

IN THE _____ DISTRICT COURT OF _____ COUNTY

FOR THE STATE OF _____

| | | |
|---|---|---|
| THE STATE OF _____ | § | |
| vs. | § | Case No. _____ |
| | § | |
| [Your Name] _____ | § | |
| Defendant | § | |

## APPELLANT'S MOTION TO HAVE
## THE APPELLATE RECORD FURNISHED WITHOUT CHARGE

TO THE HONORABLE JUDGE OF SAID COURT:

COMES NOW __[Your Name]__ , Defendant in the above-entitled and numbered cause, and pursuant to the Rules of Appellate Procedure, asks this Court to have the appellate record furnished without charge, and in support thereof would show unto the Court as follows:

I.

Defendant was sentenced on _____, _____, in the above referenced case number to _____ years imprisonment. (LIST ALL OF YOUR CONVICTIONS AND SENTENCES)

II.

Defendant filed a Notice Of Appeal on _____, 20_____.

III.

Defendant cannot pay or give security for the appellate record, and requests that the Court order the reporter to transcribe all of the proceedings in this case and to furnish the reporter's record without a charge to the defendant/appellant.

### IV.

Defendant is preparing to challenge his conviction and sentence in a habeas corpus writ, and requires the reporter's record to establish the merits of his case. Without the reporter's record, defendant will be greatly prejudiced.

### V.

Defendant/Appellant does not own any interest in real property and does not have sufficient cash on hand, or in a bank, to pay the cost of the reporter's record. Defendant/Appellant has no way to raise sufficient cash to pay for the reporter's record.

### VI.

Defendant's affidavit of indigence is attached hereto in support of this motion.

**WHEREFORE**, the Defendant/Appellant prays that this motion be granted, and that the Court order the Official Court Reporter to transcribe all of the proceedings in this case and to furnish the appellate record without charge to Defendant/Appellant.

Respectfully Submitted,

[Sign Here]
_____
[Your Name] pro-se
[Address]

Raymond E. Lumsden

## CERTIFICATE OF SERVICE

    I, hereby certify that a true and correct copy of the foregoing Motion To Have The Appellate Record Furnished Without Charge, was served upon _____, on the _____ day of _____, 20_____.


[Sign Here]

_____
[Your Name]
[Your Address]

24

[CAPTION]

### ORDER ON APPELLANT'S MOTION TO HAVE
### THE APPELLATE RECORD FURNISHED WITHOUT CHARGE

On the _____ day of _____, 20___, came to be heard the Appellant's Motion To Have The Appellate Record Furnished Without Charge, and the Court, after reviewing the motion, finds that it should be and is hereby: GRANTED / DENIED in the interest of justice.

The Official Court Reporter for this Court is hereby ORDERED to now transcribe all of the proceedings in this case, and to furnish the entire reporter's record to appellant without requiring payment.

IT IS FURTHER ORDERED that this be done within (15) days from the signing of this order.

SIGNED AND ENTERED on this _____ day of _____, 20____.


_____
PRESIDING JUDGE

(Include with Form No.5)

# Chapter Two:
# Investigating Your Case

Once you have obtained your client file from your trial counsel and received a copy of your docket sheet from the District court clerk of your convicting county, you are ready to begin the investigation.

The first thing you need to do is inventory your client file. Basically, you need to "trim the fat," so to speak. The client file will be full of blank sheets of paper, duplicate copies, and worthless clutter. So, I recommend you do the following:

Look at your docket sheet. It is organized by the date that each item was filed in the court. Now, go through your client file and arrange the contents as they appear on the docket sheet. This way you will quickly be able to see what your trial counsel filed, and failed to file, on your behalf.

For instance, if the prosecutor filed a motion to use DNA evidence against you at trial, the next thing filed should be a *Motion to Suppress* from your trial counsel. If the prosecution filed a motion to use an expert witness against you at trial, the next thing filed should be a motion from your trial counsel for a pretrial hearing to establish that person as an expert. In Texas, we call that a Kelly hearing.

In short, you can often learn more about what your counsel did and, more importantly, failed to do, while representing you. Pay close attention to what they failed to file on your behalf in the pretrial stage. Pretrial motions and hearings set the stage for the entire trial and have great weight on the outcome. Most of the ineffective assistance of counsel claims that win on post-conviction appeal, stem from pretrial failures by counsel. If the prosecution filed a Motion to use DNA, Ballistic, Medical, or any other type of expert evidence to convict you, your trial counsel should have filed a motion on your behalf to obtain the assistance of expert witnesses to assist him. See *Ake v. Oklahoma* (Supreme Court 1985).

During the investigation stage you should do the following:

- Locate your docket sheet, and match every entry with the documents received in your client file
- Remove the items from your client file that are useless to you, such as blank paper, dividers, duplicates, etc.
- Create a new "file" by numbering the remaining items on the docket sheet as they appear. This will be your new Master file.

You should familiarize yourself with the new "Master" file, and put it firmly into your memory. If you cannot detail every fact associated with your case, you will never be able to effectively translate it in a post-conviction appeal. *Recite. Remember. Repeat.*

## The Indictment

This is the notification that the state must provide to you that clearly states the exact charge(s) you are facing. It is absolutely required. The indictment is based on the statute or penal code you are alleged to have violated. The statute or penal code must be concise, clear, and unambiguous, and must be set out in the indictment.

If you do not find an indictment in your client file or listed on the docket sheet, it may be an indication that you were never officially indicted by a Grand Jury. It could also indicate that your counsel may have obtained your permission to waive the indictment process, without your understanding. If there isn't an indictment on the record, try searching for a filing on the docket sheet titled, "Information." This will likely be the same as the indictment but requires a signed waiver of indictment by you. Search the client file for a copy of that waiver. If there isn't a waiver of the indictment signed by you and there exists only an "Information" filing, you can file a claim against your trial counsel for ineffective assistance.

## Discovery Material

Discovery is probably the most important part of the client file. It contains all of the alleged evidence that the state intends to bring against you at trial. Though you will not be entitled to see some of these items in their original form, you are certainly entitled to obtain a photograph of them. Case in point, if you were convicted of murder for shooting someone, you will never be allowed to have the gun itself. But, you can certainly have a photograph of the gun. This is important, because the gun they have in evidence may not be the same caliber or type of gun alleged in the case. Therefore, the "evidence" does not support a conviction, based on the deficiency and inaccuracy of the evidence.

If there was a surveillance video, you can request photos of it. If there was bruising, conversations that were recorded, or whatever other evidence exists, you want to request photos of it. Otherwise, you cannot verify that the evidence used to obtain your conviction was not false. This happens more often than you think and is the cause of numerous recent exonerations across the country.

## Writings and Notes

In every case there will be writings and notes – police officers, CPS, private investigators, your attorney, etc. These usually reflect the very thoughts and ideas that pertain to the specific person writing them. In some cases, there may be both exculpatory and mitigating evidence that went unknown to the jury or judge, because your trial counsel overlooked them. It could also disclose that the prosecution knew about the existence of that evidence and overlooked it intentionally, because they knew it would destroy their case against you. This violates the *Brady* law and requires reversal of your conviction if proven to affect the outcome of your trial.

Notes can include, but are not limited to: warrants, affidavits, police reports, forensic experts, witnesses, alibis, etc. Give these writings and notes a thorough review, and you may be surprised what you discover.

## Witness Lists

In the pretrial stage, the prosecution probably files a motion to obtain a list of your proposed witnesses for trial. Respectfully, your trial counsel would have provided that list and filed his own motion requesting a list of the state's proposed witness.

This is normal procedure in a criminal matter. You should look on the docket sheet to uncover those motions from both sides. If you discover that your trial counsel failed to provide a list of proposed witnesses in your case, that means he was ineffective for failing to investigate possible witnesses to assist in your defense. If there were no witnesses in the guilt/innocence stage of trial, certainly there should have been in the punishment stage of trial. This would be a valid claim in a post-conviction appeal under the *Strickland v. Washington* standards.

Furthermore, where the prosecution intends to utilize expert witness testimony and evidence against you at trial, your counsel is obligated to seek out defense experts to provide opposition to those witnesses via the adversarial challenge criteria, as well as to assist the defense. See *Ake v. Oklahoma*, 470 U.S. 68, 105 S.Ct. 1087, 84 L.Ed.2d 53 (1985). Where a defendant is considered indigent and cannot afford to hire expert witnesses, trial counsel is required to seek additional funds from the trial court so that experts can be retained to assist the defense.

Where the prosecution provides the names of expert witnesses to your trial counsel in the pretrial stage, it becomes incumbent on your trial counsel to challenge the credentials and knowledge of those experts by filing a motion for a "Gatekeeper" hearing. There your trial counsel can cross-exam the qualifications, credentials, and experience of the state's alleged experts. Failure to do so could allow non-experts to testify as experts, which will greatly prejudice you in front of the jury.

Where trial counsel opposes the admission of a witness for the state at trial based on their alleged expertise, your trial counsel should have filed a motion to strike the witness at the conclusion of their testimony. This gives the courts another opportunity to rule in favor of excluding the state's expert witness and more importantly, preserves the error for appeal. Failure to file the motion to strike is ineffective assistance of counsel. Look for that motion on the docket sheet.

In conclusion, your trial counsel had a duty to seek out witnesses who would have established a defense for you at trial, as well as to challenge witnesses the prosecution intended to use against you.

## Motions and Court Orders

As I stated previously, everything that happens in a criminal procedure is recorded in the docket sheet. The court clerk is responsible for updating and maintaining the docket sheet. The entire docket sheet begins with the filing of motions. Then the opposing party will respond with a motion of their own. At that point, you will see the court settle the motion dispute by issuing a ruling or order on the matter.

If there wasn't a motion filed, then the issue was never presented – simple as that.

What you will likely discover in the client file you were provided by your trial counsel, is that they drew up motions they intended to file but forgot to file them, effectively failing to preserve the issue for appeal purposes. This again is ineffective assistance of counsel and is actionable in a post-conviction attack on the conviction and sentence.

## Accused Conduct

When you are accused of violating a statute or penal code, it will be written inside of the indictment. The indictment is the written statement of a grand jury accusing the person therein named of some act or omission in which, by law, is declared to be an offense.

Most state constitutions require that every defendant has a right to indictment by a grand jury for felony offenses. The fact that you are in prison right now assures that you were convicted of a felony offense. So, while reading your indictment as to the alleged conduct that violated the law, you should pay it very close attention. The focus is on the alleged "conduct" itself. In most all states the indictment must allege, in plain and intelligible language, all the facts and circumstances necessary to establish all the material elements of the conduct charged.

## Violated Statute or Penal Code

Here you need to give special attention to the statute or penal code you were alleged to have violated. Take a very in-depth look at the conduct the state asserts were illegal, and see if it is stated in the statute or penal code specifically. Review every single word of your indictment or charge.

Often when you compare the wording in the alleged conduct in the indictment, it is far different from the statute or penal code. This is a well-established practice for prosecutors, allowing them to charge you with a crime they can actually prove in court, instead of the alleged conduct you actually did. If you committed conduct in violation of the statute or penal code for simple assault, the prosecution can manipulate the wording of the statute or penal code to "upward depart" and charge you with rape.

It happens in almost every single case in America, because the state will then be able to "offer" you a lesser charge and sentence in exchange for a plea of guilt.

Once you have completed the investigation process, you are now ready to start determining the legal issues you will pursue in your post-conviction appeal. This is where you determine the grounds you want the appeals courts to overturn your conviction and sentence on.

So … let's dig for dirt.

*Notes:*

# Chapter Three:
# Establishing Your Claims

Here is where you determine what claims you intend to raise in your post-conviction attack on your conviction and sentence. The biggest mistake most appellants make is that they raise issues that lack merit or that were already determined on direct appeal, and therefore considered "dead" by the higher appeal courts. Additionally, you will need evaluate some issues you may be attached to and let them go because they simply won't bring success and will only serve to diminish the claims that will.

I know you want to bring up every single thing that happened to you, and you feel that they are important. This is a big mistake. What it tells the higher courts is that you are naming 10 claims because you aren't at all confident in any single claim. It's a guaranteed denial, so you must be willing to abandon a few of the "weaker" claims.

## The Docket Sheet

Ineffective assistance of trial counsel, prosecutorial misconduct, and sometimes abuse of discretion, is what you will likely find in the docket sheet. Most all of the ineffective assistance claims that are successful on post-conviction are based on pretrial failures. What your trial counsel did *not* do prior to trial is far more important that what he *did* do in most cases of ineffective assistance of counsel.

Did he request an investigator to seek out witnesses, obtain reports, and uncover exculpatory and mitigating evidence? Did he seek out the assistance of expert witnesses? Did he file motions requesting funds for these things? Did your trial counsel aggressively negotiate a plea agreement on your behalf? Did they even tell you about any plea offers? All of these things will be shown in the docket sheet.

If your trial counsel told you that he had filed certain motions in his defense of you, then they should be in the docket sheet. If they are not, then they were never filed, and the trial counsel was ineffective if it had any effect on the outcome of the trial.

Most importantly, look at the signature on every form you were asked to sign during the pretrial and trial stages. You would be shocked to discover how many attorneys will forge the names of their clients on forms just to accomplish the quick resolve of a case. Make certain that the signature is actually yours.

## Writings and Notes

This evidence is very full of helpful claims that can be used in a post-conviction attack on your conviction and sentence. More important than how your case was handled, is how your case *should have been* handled. The very first writings by your trial counsel usually reflect his actual thoughts, ideas, and opinions. This of course is before the prosecution gets to them and changes those impressions and ideas. Fear, manipulation, and false evidence are all reasons why attorneys will abandon their initial feelings and ideas of how they should defend you.

Notes written by attorneys during the first meeting with a defendant are usually written in haste and without bias. They only have a limited time to spend with you at the jail, or in their office, and they have not yet been poisoned by the prosecution, police officers, or anyone else. So what they write in that first interview is normally their honest opinions, ideas, and intentions. You will be able to prove their ineffectiveness by showing the appeals courts that they failed to take actions they initially intended to do, which would have changed the outcome of the trial had they done them.

It is my experience that most attorneys have the initial instinct to fight aggressively on your behalf, even where they are court appointed and receive little money to represent you. Then, at some point, the prosecutor, who yields far more power and can make your attorney's life very difficult, will effectively get your attorney to "lay down." Remember, the prosecutor is unlimited in his funding and can present a very difficult time for your trial counsel, who has limited funds. Additionally, the prosecution and your trial counsel more than likely work closely together on a daily basis. The ability for your trial counsel to "help" his other clients may in fact be determined by whether he will sacrifice your case (you) to the prosecution. Believe it or not, this kind of horse-trading happens every day, in almost every courthouse in America.

Let's say the prosecution intends to use blood evidence against you at trial, because they attest it is your blood. On your initial meeting with your trial counsel, he writes in his notes, "Get a DNA test on the blood to determine identity." At your trial, you discover that the state expert got up and testified that the blood in fact belonged to you, which was false because you were never at the scene of the alleged offense. You were then convicted based on the testimony of the expert and the blood evidence.

Here, had your trial counsel actually followed through with his written note to have the blood tested for DNA, you would have been proven innocent, and wouldn't be sitting in prison right now reading this book.

I think you can see how important those writings and notes are now.

## Trial Transcripts

At the time of your pretrial hearings, and especially during your trial, things were moving very fast. You were scared, nervous, angry, and uninformed as to what was happening. I assure you, reading the trial and pretrial transcripts will open your eyes to a plethora of things that you missed the first time around.

I recommend, however, that you wait to read the trial transcripts until after you have established a better understanding of criminal procedures and rules of a criminal proceeding. Without that understanding, you won't have any idea what to look for, and what the errors are.

My recommendation is that you read your state's rules of evidence and criminal procedure before you read your trial transcripts.

## The Plea Agreement

You will find an overabundance of issues that can be raised in a plea agreement in your case, if applicable. The biggest issue raised where a plea agreement was the basis of the conviction and sentence, was that it was agreed to "unknowingly, unwillingly, and unintelligently." These criteria are required when someone signs a plea agreement, and the court is required to admonish you (inform you) of your acceptance of the plea agreement before they take the agreement as accepted.

Furthermore, if you signed the plea agreement under duress, or while you were on psychiatric or pain medications, then it was not done so "willingly, intentionally, and intelligently." Therefore, it is void and must be overturned if you can prove it.

I will get much further into issues related to plea agreements in the later chapters of this book.

*Notes:*

*Notes:*

# Chapter Four:
# Analyzing Legal Issues

Every trial has error, omissions, oversight, testimony, ineffective assistance of counsel, bias, abuse of discretion, false testimony, and a plethora of other issues and imperfections.

Most courts, especially the United States Supreme Court, recognizes the numerous issues that plague the criminal justice system, focusing only on the idea that the trial process be fair, and not perfect. In fact, if you read *U.S. v. Hasting*, 461 U.S. 499. 509-510 (1983), you will uncover the feelings of the Supreme Court where Chief Justice Warren Berger said:

"Given the myriad safeguards provided to assure a fair trial and taking into account the reality of the human fallibility of the participants, there can be no such thing as an error-free, perfect trial, and …. the Constitution does not guarantee such a trial."

If you went to trial, especially through a Texas trial, then you are very much aware that errors – lots of errors – are made. The questions that need to be asked now are: What kind of errors occurred? How did those errors effect the trial? What is the standard of review for those errors? What burden of proof do you now require to prove the damage caused by those errors?

## Legal Considerations

1. What kind of error occurred?

- Constitutional Error – the error violated the U.S. Constitution
- Structural Error/Statutory Error – the error violated the state code or statutes
- Rule – the error violated state rules such as, Evidence Rule, Criminal Rule, Trial Rule, Jury Rule, Code of Judicial Conduct, etc.

2. How serious was the error?

- Fundamental Error – so prejudicial to the defendant that a fair trial was impossible
- Clear Error – an error that leaves the reviewing court with a definite and firm understanding that a mistake was made.
- Harmless Error – error that does not affect someone's substantial right.
- Abuse of Discretion – where the trial court makes a decision that is against logic, rule, or laws

3. What is the standard of review?

- Federal Courts' analysis of the issue related to the U.S. Constitution
- State Courts' analysis of the issue- applies to all issues

4. What is the burden of proof?

- Overwhelming evidence

- Evidence beyond a reasonable doubt
- Clear and convincing evidence
- By a clear and preponderance of evidence (easily to establish)

## Constitutional Violations

Every state has its own constitution that protects the rights of all citizens of that state. As well, the United States has its own Constitution that protects the rights of all citizens in every state.

When deciding which grounds for relief you are intending to bring in your post-conviction petition, you should raise the constitutional errors that you feel were violated as this will preserve the constitutional error throughout the federal appeals process in the event you are unsuccessful at the state level. The federal courts will quickly throw out any claims that were not brought before the state courts first.

As a state prisoner, the Constitutional Rights that have the greatest amount of impact on you specifically are as follows:

A. Amendment IV
- Unlawful search and seizure
- Warrants without a probable cause

B. Amendment V
- Indictments
- Double Jeopardy
- Right to remain silent
- Due process
- Compensation for property

C. Amendment VI
- Right to a speedy trial
- Right to an impartial jury
- Right to be informed of the charges against you
- Compulsory process for witnesses (subpoena)
- Confrontation of witnesses
- Effective assistance of counsel

D. Amendment VIII
- Excessive bailor bond
- Excessive fines (not applicable to state cases as of,2016)
- Cruel and unusual punishment

E. Amendment XIV
- State due process
- Equal protection

Most states have their own constitution that interprets your state rights far more liberally than the federal courts do. For that reason, you should always list both the federal and state constitutional violations when attacking your conviction and sentence on your state level post-conviction petition. It would be very wise for you to review your own state constitution, before raising issues in your post-conviction process. You stand a far better chance of success, if you do.

### Dual Constitutional Violations

As I indicated previously, sometimes your federal rights and your state rights will overlap on a constitutional level. When a criminal proceeding violates *both* your federal and state constitutional rights, you should cite that in your petition for post-conviction relief.

Be aware, however, that in some instances, you have a far higher chance of success in a state appeal, if you cite only the state constitutional violation. Confusing, right? That's how the system wants it to be.

For instance, the Texas Constitution affords far more protection for its citizens than does the United States Constitution Fourth Amendment. If you are expecting the federal review of search and seizure violations to be more in depth, that is a mistake. In *Kimmelman v. Morrison*, 477 U.S. 365, 375-377, 91 L.Ed. 2d 305, 106 S.Ct. 2574 (1986), state cases were sharply limited by the United States Supreme Court. What that means, is that in certain situations, focusing your attention to this issue based on the state constitution will be your best angle of attack. If no relief is won under the state constitution violation, it is very unlikely that you would have won on federal review of the same issue.

### Do Constitutional Violations Require Reversal?

Initially, it would seem that a constitutional violation would almost require a reversal of the conviction and sentence. However, and in spite of what the prison "writ writer's" will tell you, it's simply not so.

Constitutional violations can be held as "harmless" by appeal courts.

What matters most in situations where a constitutional violation has been raised in a post-conviction petition, are the facts associated with the error, as well as the type of constitutional error it was. Constitutional error – like all other error – carries different weight in the eyes of the appeals courts. So, let's talk about the different "kinds" of error.

## Different Kinds of Error

It is absolutely impossible for you to effectively raise the proper issues in your post-conviction petition, unless you know what kind of an error took place, and more importantly, how it affected your trial. Most *pro se* appellants attempt to argue every single violation that happened at their trial or proceeding as fundamental error, in desperate hope that the very sound of the word "fundamental" will convince the appeals courts to grant relief.

Truth be told, very few errors rise to the level of reversible error and are more than likely reviewed under the doctrine for harmless error by the appeals courts. Where appellants attempt to argue fundamental error where there isn't any, the result is a swift denial of the entire argument. So, what is fundamental error?

## Fundamental Error

Fundamental error is defined in the Black's Law Dictionary as an error "so prejudicial to the rights of a defendant as to make a fair trial an impossibility." Now, keep in mind that the courts look at a fair trial in a very broad manner, viewing the totality of the evidence in determination of how the error affected you. They call this the harmless error analysis.

The silver lining where fundamental error is concerned is that trial counsel isn't required to make an objection in order to preserve the error. The fundamental error doctrine provides a vehicle for the review of error not properly preserved for appeal.

In order to qualify as a fundamental error, the error must be so blatant of a violation of basic principles rendering the trial unfair to the due process rights of the defendant. The error must be so prejudicial as to make a fair trial impossible. The fact itself that the defendant was convicted does not constitute harm alone. Harm is determined by whether the defendant's right to a fair trial was detrimentally affected by the denial of procedural opportunities for the ascertainment of truth to which he would have been entitled.

The fundamental error doctrine is not directly applicable to ineffective assistance of counsel claims. In a post-conviction petition, you must prove ineffective assistance of counsel, while at the same time, proving the fundamental error also occurred. See *Arizona v. Fulminate*, 499 U.S. 279, 3IG, 113 L.Ed. 2d 302, III S.Ct. 1246 (1991), for a list of violations that rise to the level of fundamental error requiring reversal.

## Structural Error

The *Black's Law Dictionary* defines structural error as "a defect that effects the framework within which the trial proceedings, rather than simply an error in the trial process itself." An example of structural error is where the trial court fails to give the jury a mandatory instruction, such as guilt beyond "a reasonable doubt."

Even in cases where the person's guilt is overwhelming, a case is not always going to stand where a fundamental, structural error takes place. While these types of errors are rare, they require automatic reversal; see *Cage v. Louisiana*, 498 U.S. 39, 112 L.Ed. 2d 339, III S.Ct. 328 (1990) (per curium); and *Sullivan v. Louisiana*, 508 U.S.275, 282, 124 L.Ed.2d 182, 113 S.Ct. 2018) (1993).

In Texas, and possibly in your state as well, jury instruction error takes the lead in cases that required a reversal. Take a good look at the jury instructions in your case, especially the non-pattern instructions, to find fundamental errors. There have been numerous cases that were reversed due to jury instruction error on post-conviction petitions.

Remember, never raise a fundamental error claim on post-conviction petition unless you are certain that it rises to that level.

## Harmless Error

Harmless error is error that "does not affect the substantial rights of a party, given the error's likely impact on the jury in light of the other evidence presented at trial" *Chapman v. California*, 386 U.S. 18, 24, 87 S.Ct. 824, 828, 17 L.Ed. 2d 70S, 711 (1967).

Not all constitutional errors require a reversal. Only those errors of constitutional dimension which are "structural defects affecting the very framework within the trial proceeds" are reversible error. Harmless error that does not affect the substantial rights of a party given the error's impact on the jury in light of other evidence presented at trial, will most likely not be reversed.

## Clear Error

Clear Error is an error "that leaves a reviewing court with a firm idea or conviction that a mistake was made." In the state of Texas, and I assume the same is true in your state also, the court of Appeals will not reverse a trial court's factual findings and rulings unless an appellant is able to show that "clear error" occurred.

What that means, is that if you find yourself having to appeal a denial of your post-conviction petition, it's effectively the same as having to appeal the denial of the trial court findings. Therefore, you are going to have to convince the appellate court that the evidence supports a contrary finding as the one opined by the post-conviction court. In simple terms, the defendant must convince the appellate court that there is no way the trial court, or the direct appeal court, could have reached the verdict it did under the law.

That being said, citing "clear error" in your post-conviction petition isn't advisable. You raise it on appellate review where the court has made a determination on the wrong *facts*. You stand a far better chance of having your case reversed on "erroneous conclusion of law," which the court of Appeals will review *de novo* (as new), where the trial court or direct appeal court have erred in applying the law to the facts.

On a post-conviction petition, the Court of Criminal Appeals or Supreme Court in some states, focus largely on the conclusions of law. Rarely will they read the trial record and will rely heavily on the state's version of the facts. Is that fair? Of course not, but it is true. That is why it's very important to set the record straight, and get the facts straight, in response to the state's appellee brief. If you don't, the court of Appeals will consider them as "true" and will use them in their decision. Once that happens, those facts become what the courts consider the "actual facts." At that point, you will never be able to correct them.

If your direct appeal attorney failed to file a response brief in order to correct erroneous facts, you then have a claim of ineffective appeal counsel. Of course, you will have to prove that claim by showing the correct facts, as they are likely found in the trial transcripts.

## Abuse of Discretion

An abuse of discretion is where a judge's decision is against the logic and facts presented in a case, as well as the law or rules. Judges are presumed to know the rules and laws in which they are supposed to operate, however, they don't always follow them. For instance, if the judge allows hearsay evidence into a trial over the objection of a trial attorney, where the law clearly prohibits hearsay testimony, it's considered an abuse of discretion. Winning on an abuse of discretion claim is sometimes an act of pure futility. Trial courts have wide discretion in determining their rulings, and unless you can prove that the judge's ruling was contrary to the law (as in the Rules of Criminal Procedure, Rules of Evidence, United States Constitution, etc.) the higher appeals courts will not disturb the ruling.

That being said, don't be discouraged. Where it can be proven that the decision of the trial court violated statutory or constitutional law, the higher courts will reverse for an abuse of discretion. In these cases, you will more than likely have to make a showing that, but for, the abuse of discretion, the outcome of the trial would have been different. The same applies to any other court proceedings. *You must show prejudice.*

Proving that prejudice, however, will not be easy.

## Standard of Review

The authority by which a court makes its determinations is called the "standard of review." This outlines the law that dictates how they must review the issue. Often, it's simply referred to as the "standard."

An example of a standard review in a post-conviction argument looks like this:

### A. Standard of Review

In our due-process review of the sufficiency of the evidence to support a conviction, we view all of the evidence in the light most favorable to support a conviction found as the verdict to determine whether any rational trier of fact could have found the essential elements of the crime beyond a reasonable doubt. *Jackson v. Virginia*, 443 U.S. 307, 319, 99 S.Ct. 2781, 2789 (1979); Jenkins v. State, 493 S.W.3d 583, 599 (Tex. Crim. App. 2016)

Prior to raising any argument or issues on your post-conviction petition for relief, be sure to read the standard of review, so you can then argue the correct one. This will get you much further in the process and will bring you far better results. Citing the wrong standard of review on an issue will immediately get that issue disregarded by the reviewing court.

## Burden of Proof

The "burden of proof" is the evidence you will need to establish the issue you are raising in your argument. In almost every state, in a post-conviction petition for relief, the court's use a preponderance standard in reviewing the evidence presented. What is a preponderance standard? It's a standard of reviewing the evidence presented that originates from civil law practice. It means that the evidence is more favorable to you, than against you. The court is now required to apply the preponderance standard in the issues you raise in your post-conviction petition when weighing the evidence.

In all cases, the preponderance standard will be in the hands of the appeal court in determining where applicable. Truth is, judges are very hesitant to weigh evidence in favor of overturning a conviction, unless the evidence proves absolute error on behalf of the lower court. This doesn't mean that you don't have good issues, or that something bad didn't happen at your trial. It simply means that the "finality" of a conviction is the main focus of appeal judges in every court, in every state.

## Listing the Issues

The first rule of listing the issue(s) you wish to present in your post-conviction petition is this: *it only takes one good issue* to win a reversal of your conviction or to be granted some kind of relief.

This is where I spoke about having to "let go" of some issues that you may think are important. Your best chance of receiving relief from the court is to present your very *best* issues and to not be distracted by issues that aren't winners.

During an oral argument in a federal court, the attorney for the appellant began his argument with, "Good Morning, your honor. If it pleases the court, I would like to present four issues." At that point, the judge interrupted and said, "Just give me your best issue first." You are unlikely to be granted relief on the other issues if your best one doesn't do the job.

That being said, inmates will still make the big mistake of presenting too many issues in their post-conviction petitions. This is because they are unwilling to "let go" of their weaker issues, in belief that more is better. This is critical mistake. Simply throwing "stuff" at the wall and hoping that something sticks, doesn't work on post-conviction challenge and will get your petition rejected nearly every single time. Simply put ... *don't do it!*

What it demonstrates to the court when you raise too many issues in your post-conviction petition is that you simply don't have much faith in any particular issue. Weakness is what they see. Before you list your issues, you need to determine which is most likely to achieve success. In law school we are taught to do this by using the "Whirlybird" method.

Here, is an example of how to use the Whirlybird method in selecting your issue to present in your post-conviction petition.

## The Whirlybird Method

It begins looking like the drawing below:

The first thing you do is write the name of your Whirlybird in the center. Next, you begin writing down your ideas related to possible issues to be raised in your post-conviction petition. For every idea, use one of the branches from the center. For ideas that support the main idea, use a branch to support that as well. There are no right or wrong ideas; and there is no top or bottom. This will assist you in creating issues that have the best chance of obtaining relief.

Below is an example:

Once you have completed your Whirlybird, even if you felt the need to complete more than one, you can then begin to make an outline of the issues for better understanding and argument. It may look something like this:

1. Trial counsel provided ineffective assistance.
   (A) Trial counsel failed to perform an investigation that would have uncovered a witness who could have both provided an alibi for defendant and provided a description of the criminal.

      (B) Trial counsel failed to seek the assistance of expert witnesses to provide adversarial challenge, as well as DNA testing that could prove defendant's innocence.

      (C) Trial counsel failed to object to known perjured testimony of the prosecution witness, which prejudiced the defendant.

2. The conviction was secured by prosecutorial misconduct.

      (A) The prosecution used known false testimony when it allowed its witness to testify that she witnessed the crime, where record proves that she was out of town at the time of the crime.

      (B) The prosecution intentionally withheld "Brady" evidence when it failed to provide to the defense a statement from an eyewitness who identified a different person as the criminal.

      (C) The prosecution bolstered the testimony of its witness when in her closing argument she said, "Mary is not lying. Mary never lies. I have known her for 20 years. You should believe Mary."

      (D) Etc., etc. …

There are numerous reasons to utilize the Whirlybird technique as taught in most paralegal and law schools: (1) It encourages creativity, (2) It helps you to organize your thoughts, (3) It helps you choose your best issues, (4) It helps you to remember, and keep straight all of the issues.

Organization is just as important during the initial stages of your post-conviction petition as the issues themselves. Incoherent, disorganized, or multiplicious arguments will get you a fast denial on your petition.

Use the Whirlybird – it works.

*Notes:*

# Chapter Five:
# Ineffective Assistance of Counsel

There is reason I have chosen this issue to talk about before any other issues that can be raised in a post-conviction petition. This area constitutes the largest segment of claims raised in all state *habeas corpus* and post-conviction petitions.

Claims of ineffective assistance of counsel will *always* be considered by the courts. Therefore, whenever possible, you should *always* raise a ground for relief in the context of ineffective assistance of counsel. For example, you have very little chance to succeed in a post-conviction petition citing a Fourth Amendment claim, because it is not cognizable on post-conviction. However, your claim will be considered if you claim ineffective assistance of counsel for failing to object to a Fourth Amendment violation.

You see, it's not just what you argue; it's how you argue it.

In determining whether a defendant received ineffective assistance of counsel, courts shall use the standard set forth in *Strickland v. Washington*, 466 U.S. 668 (1984). Most states have adopted this standard in their own rulings, such as *Hernandez v. State*, 726 S.W.2d 53 (Tex. Crim. App_1986) here in Texas.

In *Strickland* the Supreme Court of the United States held, in the pertinent part:

"First, the defendant must show that counsel's performance was deficient. This requires showing that counsel made errors so serious that counsel was not functioning as the "counsel" guaranteed by the Sixth Amendment. Second, the defendant must show that the deficient performance prejudiced the defense. This requires showing that counsel's errors were so serious as to deprive the defendant of a fair trial, a trial whose result was reliable" (466 U.S. at 687, Id).

Most state appeals courts decide whether a defendant received claimed ineffective assistance of counsel by "the totality of the representation," rather than isolated acts or omissions of trial counsel. Courts do not consider an attorney to be ineffective simply because another attorney may have used different strategy than yours did. The following are also true:

1. Courts will consider the effectiveness of counsel's performance as of the time of trial, and not through hindsight.
2. The right to counsel is required at every stage of a criminal proceeding where the substantial rights of the defendant may be affected. Therefore, ineffective assistance can be raised at any of these stages.
3. A defendant must show that, but for the ineffectiveness of the trial counsel, the outcome would have been different. That is to say that the deficient performance of trial counsel caused the outcome.

## Commonly Used Ineffective Assistance Claims

1. Counsel deprived appellant of his right to a direct appeal
2. Counsel failed to notify appellant of his right to *pro se* petition for discretionary review
3. Involuntary guilty plea due to ineffective assistance of counsel
4. Failure to conduct a pre-trial investigation
5. Failure to call a witness
6. Failure to obtain experts to assist with the defense
7. Failure to object
8. Failure to investigate insanity at the time of offense due to voluntary intoxication (Involuntary intoxication is a defense to guilt. However, *voluntary* intoxication is not a defense to any guilt or innocence. It is, however, a defense as to punishment.)
9. Failure to impeach the testimony of an eyewitness
10. Failure to obtain a running objection as to the admission of hearsay evidence

These ten claims, although not the full extent of possible claims under the ineffective assistance of counsel issue, provide the greatest number of reversals across the country in state post-conviction petitions.

It is important to remember that when raising claims of ineffective assistance of counsel claims, you should get affidavits and secure an evidentiary hearing, if possible. Most courts will afford the attorney being accused of ineffective assistance of counsel by an appellant, an opportunity to respond to the claims before finding it to be true.

Now, being the issue of ineffective assistance of counsel is so very important as well as in-depth, I will address a few of those issues in a specific fashion. Here we go …

### Involuntary Pleas

In post-conviction *habeas* proceedings, there is a presumption of great regularity with respect to guilty pleas, and the applicant bears the burden of overcoming the presumption. A plea of guilty entered by an applicant fully aware of the direct consequences must stand unless the plea was induced by threats, misrepresentations, or perhaps by improper promises, as in *Brady v. U.S.*, 397 U.S. 742, 755 (1970).

The majority of involuntary pleas fit neatly into a claim of true ineffective assistance of counsel. Usually, these claims involve erroneous advice by counsel regarding the applicable punishment range, whether an applicant's sentence would run either concurrently or consecutively, or if the applicant believed he would receive a specific sentence in exchange for his plea of guilt. In some cases, many applicant's claim their pleas were involuntary due to some inaction, or action, on the part of the trial court.

For example, if an applicant is an illegal alien, as is quite common here in Texas, facing deportation could raise a claim that his plea was involuntary because he was not admonished of the deportation consequences of a conviction. See *Padilla v. Kentucky*, 559 U.S. 356 (2010).

Pleas may also be rendered involuntary when the State breaches a plea bargain agreement with an applicant. For example, the Court of Criminal Appeals of Texas has held that, given the ambiguity in the record, a waiver of appeal was not binding of a plea agreement and the State breached the plea agreement when it re-indicted applicant's brother, see *Ex parte DeLeon*, 400 S.W.3d 83 (Tex. Crim. App. 2013).

*Recantation* – Numerous Courts across the country have granted post-conviction relief based on involuntary plea, where the complainants have recanted. In a very recent case in Texas, the Court of Criminal Appeals granted relief to an applicant on a *habeas corpus* petition where he was not aware, at the time he entered the plea, that the complainants had recanted their allegations and would not have testified against him at trial. The applicant had learned of the recantations after entry of the plea, before sentencing. At the evidentiary hearing on the writ of *habeas corpus*, the applicant testified that he misunderstood his counsel and believed incorrectly that he could withdraw his plea at any time before sentencing, and that he fabricated the admissions of guilt in order to get a lenient sentence, see *Ex parte Zapata*, 235 S.W.3d 794 (Tex. Crim. App. 2013).

## Failure to Investigate

Also known as "failure to prepare," a failure to investigate claim is a very serious one where proven to have affected the outcome of the trial. A failure to investigate claim is brought under a violation of the Sixth and Fourteenth Amendments of the United States Constitution, as well as under your state constitution, which sometimes provides greater protection.

When you are alleging a failure to investigate, it is your obligation to prove what an investigation would have uncovered in assisting your defense. If you cannot do so, you will lose that issue. There simply isn't a court in the land that will assist you in "guessing" what an investigation would have or could have uncovered.

Your primary obstacle with this claim is that the trial counsel will cite "trial strategy" as their defense. With that, "strategic choices made after investigation is unchallengeable," as in *Strickland*, 466 U.S. at 686.

An example would be claiming that an expert witness should have been hired to assist the defense or a witness called to testify. For that claim, you *must* show the post-conviction court what evidence would have resulted had the expert or witness been called at trial, and you *must* show how it would have changed the outcome of the trial. It's that simple. Some failures by counsel are so extraordinarily bad, that they can't be explained away by the trial counsel, though I promise you they will try to do so. Here a few good cases to look at in support of your failure to investigate claim:

- *Sears v. Upton*, 561 U.S. 945, 130 S.Ct. 3259, 3264, 177 L.Ed. 2d 1025 (2010)
- *Gomez v. Beto*, 462 F.2d 596, 597 (5th Cir. 1972)
- *Porter v. McCollum*, 558 U.S.30, 40, 130 S.Ct. 447, 452-53, 175 L.Ed.2d 398 (2009)

The previously listed cases will give you a starting point to conduct research for cases in your particular state and circuit. By shepardizing them, you will uncover a plethora of legal authority to assist your claims.

## Failure to Obtain Experts to Assist the Defense

Trial counsel has a duty to see that necessary expert witnesses are available to the defendant for trial. This duty remains regardless of your financial position. Whether you are indigent and trial counsel was appointed to represent you or you hired your own trial counsel, the same duty remains. In either situation, where you cannot afford to hire expert witnesses, the trial counsel has three options: (1) Subpoena all of the experts who are involved in the case and introduced and elicit their opinions; (2) If trial counsel is convinced that the defendant cannot pay for experts to assist him in preparation for trial, withdraw from the case explaining to the court that applicant was now indigent, prove the indigence, and request the court to appoint new counsel; or (3) Remain as counsel, but request investigatory and expert witness fees from the trial court, pursuant to *Ake v. Oklahoma*, 470 U.S. 68, 105 S.Ct. 1087, 84 L.Ed.2d 53 (1985).

Indigent defendants have a right to a court-appointed expert under *Ake* in most circumstances. A defendant does not have the right to choose a particular expert witness; however, he does have the right to access a competent one.

Furthermore, that expert should be independent, not an expert who is required to report to the court or prosecution. The expert witness can then serve one or two objectives: (1) play a partisan role by providing defendant with the means to mount an adversarial challenge to the state's case; (2) testify in support of the defense theory, if the expert's opinion supports the theory.

The United States Supreme Court in *Ake* determined that:

"Access to expert assistance means more than an examination by a neutral expert. It also means the appointment of an expert to provide technical assistance to the defendant, to help evaluate the strength of his defense, to offer expert diagnosis if it is favorable to the defense, and to identify the weaknesses in the state's case by testifying or preparing counsel to cross-examine the opposing expert."

*Ake* applies to non-psychiatric experts also. The following are experts for the purposes of the argument:

- A chemist to evaluate controlled substances
- A Forensic expert to evaluate and address DNA issues
- A pathologist to investigate cause of death, etc.
- A ballistics expert to investigate gun powder residue, etc.
- A psychologist to investigate an insanity defense
- A jury consultant to assist in selecting a jury
- A Medical examiner to evaluate alleged abuse, assault, etc.

The above list isn't limited in nature. The type of expert isn't as important as what the expert witness could provide to the defense.

The important part is that trial counsel must make a showing of the compelling need for the assistance of the expert prior to trial. This is done by filing a motion in the trial court for funds, or appointment of a necessary expert witness. Without this specific showing, the courts will not grant the request for the assistance of an expert.

## Failure to Impeach a Witness

To prove that your trial attorney was ineffective for failing to impeach a witness, you must demonstrate a reasonable probability that, but for the counsel's deficient cross-examination of the witness on an issue, that you would have been found not guilty. Yep, that's a huge obstacle to overcome, which is why it's hard to prevail on – but certainly not impossible. And, if you are in fact able to prove that the witness was lying, a reversal is quite possible. The right to cross-examine is part of the Confrontation Clause of the Sixth Amendment, guaranteed to state defendants through the Fourteenth Amendment of the U.S. Constitution.

The right to cross-examination of witnesses, encompasses the right to the effective assistance of counsel on cross-examination in *Davis v. Alaska*, 415 U.S. 308 (1974).

In your petition for post-conviction relief, you must show exactly the kind of impeaching information could have been used to change the outcome of the trial. Of course, your trial counsel will simply say that they were already aware of that information, and it was "trial strategy" not to use it. Be prepared to argue against that in your petition, as well as at the evidentiary hearing, if you are successful in raising the issue.

A good practice tip is to search the client file for the information that was impeaching. If it's not in the client file, then that shows the trial attorney wasn't aware of it, and couldn't have used "trial strategy" regarding information he wasn't even aware of.

Cases to research on impeaching witnesses/Cross-examination are:

- *Douglas v. Alabama*, 380 U.S. 415 (1965)
- *United States v. Orr*, 636 F.3d 944, 951-52 (8th Cir. 2011)
- *Moore v. Marr*, 254 F.3d 1235, 1241 (10th Cir. 2001)

## Failure to Object

A claim for failure to object should be brought under the ordinary Fourteenth and Sixth Amendment constitutional claims of ineffective assistance of counsel. The standards for failing to object at trial are the same in nearly every state.

A wide assortment of things requires a trial attorney to object. The mission is to prove that an enormous harm occurred to your case, such that the outcome of the trial would have been different had your trial counsel made an objection. Inadmissible hearsay testimony, inadmissible evidence, leading questions, and speculation are some areas to consider.

The biggest mistake of most *pro se* petitioners on post-conviction appeals is that they attempt to raise this issue under prosecutorial misconduct. That is a very critical mistake, and one that will guarantee your claim being denied. Be very aware of how you raise the issue under a claim.

Where prosecutorial error arose, your trial counsel was obligated to make an objection. In some instances, he was required to seek a running objection in order to preserve the issue for appeal. However, if you cite prosecutorial misconduct on post-conviction petition, you will lose. Why? Because prosecutorial misconduct is not a cognizable claim on post-conviction. At the post-conviction stage, a free-standing claim of any prosecutorial misconduct is not allowed. Your trial attorney's failure to object to the prosecutorial misconduct at trial, waived it on appeal.

And so, you then raise the issue of ineffective assistance of counsel for failing to object to the prosecutorial misconduct. At that, the courts are required to review the error for prejudice. Some extremely narrow and complicated exceptions exist, where the claim may be raised as fundamental error, such as prosecutorial misconduct for newly discovered *Brady* evidence; see *California v. Trombetta*, 467 U.S. 479 (1984).

A few cases to review for failure to object are:

- *Victor v. Nebraska*, 511 U.S. 1 (1994)
- *Ward v. United States*, 995 F.2d 1317 (6th Cir. 1993)
- *United States v. Williams*, 358 F.3d 956, 962-64 (D.C. Cir. 2004)

## Failure to Suppress Evidence

In the pretrial stage of your proceedings, your trial counsel had the legal obligation to file a motion to suppress any evidence the state made intentions of using against you. Attorneys have an ethical and fiduciary duty to file motions in *limine*, particularly, motions to suppress.

Under the *Strickland* standard, the failure to suppress may be established by proving the two prong requirements. You must prove beyond a reasonable doubt (probability) that challenging the admissibility of the evidence would have:

(1) Led to its exclusion
(2) Led to his acquittal

Without meeting these, a defendant cannot establish that he was at all prejudiced. In addition to the Fourteenth Amendment claim and the Sixth Amendment claim for failing to suppress evidence, you should raise a Fourth Amendment claim. Harmless error analysis will be taken by the reviewing court; see *U.S. v. Cronic*, 466 U.S. 648 (1984).

Cases to look up related to the failure to suppress evidence are:

- *Martin v. Maxey*, 98 F.3d 844, 848 (5th Cir. 1996)
- *Ward v. Dretke*, 420 F.3d 479, 488 (5th Cir. 2005)
- *Kimmelman v. Morrison*, 477 U.S. 365, 375, 91 L.Ed.2d 305 (1986)

## Failure to Remedy a Conflict of Interest

A conflict of interest arises when your attorney is currently, or has, represented other parties adverse to your position. This sometimes happens when your trial attorney also represents a co-defendant in the same case. When you have a co-defendant, you are supposed to have separate attorney's appointed. Your trial counsel had an obligation to address the conflict and seek the appointment of separate counsel; see *Holloway v. Arkansas*, 435 U.S. 475, 485 (1978).

Prejudice will be presumed where there is an actual conflict, and not simply a potential conflict. An actual conflict arises when there is joint representation, and there are conflicting interests between the defendants.

When raised on a post-conviction petition, it will not be considered fundamental error. There, they are weighed under the *Strickland* and *Cuyler* standards.

Conflict of interest cases to review for your petition:

- *U.S. v. Morris*, 259 F.3d 894 (7th Cir. 2001)
- *Armienti v. U.S.*, 234 F.3d 820 (2nd Cir. 2000)

## Failure to Establish Competency

An accused must be competent to stand trial for a crime. Where a trial attorney knows, or should know, that the defendant has mental health or other deficiency in such a way as to inhibit his defense, the attorney is obligated to investigate these issues and bring them to the immediate attention of the trial court.

This includes mental retardation, psychiatric deficiency, or physical impairments. The United States Constitution, as well as most all state constitutions, forbid the trial of an individual lacking a rational and sufficient ability to consult with his lawyer, or understand the proceeding; see *Dusky v. United States*, 362 U.S. 402 (1960).

Where a defendant exhibits signs of mental incapacitation, or any type of psychiatric issues, it brings into question as to whether that person could have had the *men's rea* (intent) that is required to prove that an offense was "intentional." Something the state is required to prove in all criminal trials in this country.

Failure to establish competency cases for review:

- *Medina v. California*, 505 U.S. 437, 439, 112 S.Ct. 2572, 120 L.Ed. 2d 353 (1992)
- *Bouchillon v. Collins*, 907 F.2d 589, 592 (5th Cir. 1990)
- *McLuckie v. Abbott*, 337 F.3d 1193, 1199 (10th Cir. 2003)

# Conclusion

There are simply so many avenues under the ineffective assistance of counsel standard, that it would be nearly impossible to cite them all. I advise you to obtain a book specific to the ineffectiveness of trial counsel, as well as appeal counsel. A good one to read is *The Habeas*

*Citebook: Ineffective Assistance of Counsel*, written by Brandon Sample, whom I know personally. It is an amazing book of pure case law specific to claims of every kind of ineffective assistance of counsel under the sun, and it includes most all Supreme Court citings. I own a copy myself, and it has proven useful on many occasions.

*Notes:*

# Chapter Six:
# Newly Discovered Evidence

In every state, the discovery of new evidence will require a new trial where the appellant can establish that:

- the evidence has been discovered since trial
- the new evidence is material
- the new evidence is not cumulative
- the new evidence is not merely impeaching
- the new evidence is not privileged or incompetent
- the new evidence is trustworthy
- due diligence was used to discover it in time for trial, but failed
- it will likely produce a different outcome at a retrial

Anyone raising the claim of newly discovered evidence in a petition for post-conviction relief must overcome a very high standard of review in order to be entitled to relief. Specifically, the "new" evidence must such that would likely produce a different outcome at a new trial. In most cases, this is a higher hurdle than the prosecution is forced to meet where they intentionally destroy evidence.

If you believe you have a chance of success on a claim of newly discovered evidence and can satisfy the criteria listed above – *all* of the criteria – then raise it. Of course, each state has its own criteria you will need to overcome for newly discovered evidence, but most are very similar.

If the newly discovered evidence should have been discovered in time for trial but was not, then you would raise the new evidence under a claim of ineffective assistance of counsel for failing to obtain it. This will help avoid the issue being waived.

New evidence cases to review for your post-conviction petition:

- *United States v. Agurs*, 427 U.S. 97 (1976)
- *Mendez v. Brady*, 656 F.3d 126 (1st Cir. 2011)
- *U.S. v. Bartone*, 249 F.2d 156 (3rd Cir. 1957)

## Brady Violations and False Evidence

The state has an affirmative duty to disclose all material, including exculpatory evidence, to the defense prior to trial, under *Brady v. Maryland*, 373 U.S 83 (1963). Evidence is material only if there is a reasonable probability that, had the evidence been disclosed to the defense, the result would have been different. Favorable evidence includes impeachment evidence that could "make the difference between conviction and acquittal," *United States v. Bagley*, 473 U.S. 667, 676 (1985).

Applicants often allege that the state used perjured testimony to obtain the conviction. Usually, as part of their pleadings, applicants will point to various discrepancies in testimony given by witnesses. However, discrepancies in testimony alone do not make out a case for perjury. So, when raising these claims always stress that your allegations do not have any relationship in witness testimony, but actual perjury. Every attempt should be made to obtain affidavits from witnesses in question, or a live hearing should be requested where the witness is subjected to examination.

It is important to remember that there are some double jeopardy concerns when prosecutorial misconduct has occurred. The Court has held that double jeopardy bars retrial after a defendant has successfully moved for mistrial only when it shows that the prosecutor engaged in conduct that was intended to provoke the defendant into moving for a mistrial.

Over the past couple of years state appeals courts have experienced a dramatic shift in how they look at perjured testimony and false evidence claims. Review of perjured testimony claims are different that other more cognizable *habeas* claims. The first prong is whether the testimony was in fact false. The proper question in such a case is whether the testimony, taken as a whole, "gives the jury a false impression." The second prong is materiality, not harm. An applicant must show the court the false testimony was material and thus it was reasonably likely to influence the jury as to their judgement.

## DNA Evidence and Testing

Of all my legal training and education, my most extensive studies have been in this field. DNA "evidence" was used to convict me of a crime that I didn't commit – in fact, a crime that never happened at all. Because of it, I have studied DNA evidence in every manner possible, including an advanced paralegal course in Forensic DNA studies. That being said, let's jump right to it.

In some cases, DNA is used as evidence to gain a conviction, and in others the prosecution intentionally refrains from obtaining DNA testing. Ask yourself, why would the state intentionally "avoid" having something tested for DNA? Because finding innocence is not the nature of their business: They are paid to convict – simple as that.

Either way, wherever you find yourself on the issue as a post-conviction petitioner, you may be entitled to either DNA testing or re-testing.

There are two different kinds of DNA tests: STR and RFLP. STR testing stands for "Short Tandem Repeat." RFLP stands for "Restriction Fragment Length Polymorphism." Let's focus on the one most used by prosecutors, the Y-STR testing.

### Y-STR DNA Basics

Y-STR DNA profiles are derived from the Y chromosome, which is passed down largely intact from a father to all male offspring, generation to generation without changing. Every male in a paternal lineage – fathers, sons, brothers, uncles, first-, second-, third-, and fourth cousins;

and all the world-wide related male relatives – will share the exact same Y-STR DNA profile. If you are direct descendant of Moses on your father's side, a DNA test using Y-STR testing wouldn't be able to tell you apart.

Just as maternal lineage can be tracked with DNA, a Y-STR profile can be thought of as a "single genetic locus," as contrasted with the numerous independent loci available for traditional DNA typing. Because Y chromosome DNA does not undergo recombination at each generation, the discriminatory power of Y chromosome DNA also pales in comparison to traditional nuclear DNA.

Yep – very confusing. But I'm just getting started, so stay with me.

## Defending Against Y-STR DNA

Y chromosome DNA, from which Y-STR forensic markers are derived, differ from traditional nuclear DNA on a number of counts that should be the very central defense challenge at a trial. Just as with DNA, a well-planned challenge to Y-STR DNA evidence should zero in on those differences, in addition to following the general guidelines for DNA cases generally.

Y-STR DNA that can be developed through admissibility challenges under *Daubert*, and *Frye*, or other evidentiary standards governing expert given testimony and scientific evidence, or as a basis for challenging the expert directly through cross-examination.

DNA typing kits used by law enforcement and prosecutors have been in development to only respond to markers present on the Y chromosome, therefore eliminating the presence of female DNA. For that reason, this is the most used DNA testing kit in sexual assault cases.

The problem is that Y-STR DNA cannot be used to distinguish one male from another. It simply cannot identify a particular person as the only contributor.

## Forensic DNA Evidence is Not Infallible

Despite what the prosecution would like everyone to believe, DNA used to convict is not infallible. The newest form of DNA testing used to do a great deal of convicting, is called "Touch DNA." From as few as 3 skin cells, a genetic profile of the suspect is determined. Here's the problem: The term "Touch DNA" conveys to a jury that biological material found on an object or person is the result of "direct" contact. In fact, the forensic community has no way of knowing whether the DNA was left behind through such direct contact or by secondary transfer.

Fact is, if I shake your hand, I could then transfer your skin cells to whatever (or whomever) I touch next, without you ever having touched it. Interestingly, this fact is never explained in court by the prosecutions' DNA experts and never uncovered by defense attorneys who are not DNA or forensic experts themselves. Instead, the jury is told that there is a one-in-a-quadrillion chance that the evidence retrieved from the item or person does not belong to the defendant. Basically, saying that it's their DNA, and it could have only gotten there through direct contact with the defendant.

*Notes:*

In a study at Harvard University in 2016, 12 people were asked to hold and shake the hands of each other. Then, they were asked to touch their genitals and etc. In 85 of the cases tested from that group, the DNA of multiple people was found on the genitals of people they had never shaken hands within the test. It was purely from secondary and intermediate DNA transfer.

## DNA Testing on Post-Conviction

As of 2018, every state has statutes that allow for DNA testing. In most every state, the prosecutor must consent for the testing of the trial evidence; however, courts may order DNA testing over the prosecutor's objection. In all states, before testing is allowed, the petitioner is now required to show that a favorable test result would most likely change the verdict and/or establish the innocence of the defendant.

If the identity of the assailant was not an issue at trial, then the DNA testing would likely prove nothing and will likely be denied. If your state does not currently have a statute allowing DNA testing, you can still possibly obtain it under a claim of newly discovered evidence. For your convenience, I have provided a list of the DNA statutes where applicable.

Federal – Title 18 USC § 3600
Ariz. Rev. Stat. § 13-4240
Ark. Code Ann. § 16 112-201
Cal. Penal Code § 1405
Colo. Rev. Stat. § 18-1-411
Conn. Gen. Stat. Ann. § 52-582
Del. Code Title II, §4504
D.C. Code Ann. § 22-4133
Fla. Stat. Ann. § 925.11
Ga. Code Ann. § 5-5-41(c)
Haw. Rev. Stat. § §844D, 121-133
Idaho Code § 19-4902 725 III, Compo Stat. Ann. 5/116-3
Ind. Code § 35-38-7
Iowa Code § 81.10
Kan. Stat. Ann. § 21-2512
Ky. Rev. Stat. § 422.285
La. Code Crim. Proc. Ann. 926.1
Me. Rev. Stat. Ann. Title 15, §2137
Md. Code Crim. Proc. § 8-201
Mich. Compo Laws § 770.16
Minn. Stat. Ann. § 590.01
Mo. Rev. Stat. § 547.035

Mont. Code Ann. §46-21-110, 53-1
Neb. Rev. Stat. § 29-4120
Nev. Rev. Stat. § 176.0918
N.H Rev. Stat. Ann §651-D:1-D:4
N.J. Stat. Ann. § 2A:84A-32A
N.M. Stat. Ann § 31-1a-2
N.Y. Crim. Proc. Law § 440.30(1-a)
N.C. Gen. Stat. § 15A-269
N.D. Cent. Code Ann. § 29-32.1-13
Ohio Rev. Code Ann § 2953.71
Or. Rev. Stat. § 138.510, *et seq*
Pa. Stat. Ann. 42 § 9541 *et seq*
S.C Code Ann. §§17-28-10
R.I. Gen. Laws § 10-9.1-11
Tenn. Code Ann. § 40-30-403
Tex. Code Crim. Proc. Ann. 64.01 *et seq*
Utah Code Ann. § 78.35a—301
Vt. Stat. Ann. Title 13, §5561 *et seq*
Va. Code Ann. § 19.2-327.1
Wash. Rev. Code §10.73.170
W.Va. Code Ann. § 15 2B 14
Wi. Stat. Ann. § 974.07
Wyo. Stat. Ann. 7-12-302-315

## Supreme Court on DNA Testing Rights

Although there isn't a constitutional right to DNA testing, there are a few strong cases to review. In *Ake v. Oklahoma*, 470 U.S. 68 (1985), as I mentioned a few chapters ago, the Supreme Court of the United States cited an overall right for criminal defendants to have expert testimony at their trials to assist the defense.

The Supreme Court also addressed the issue in *DA's Office for the Third Judicial District v. Osborne*, 129 S.Ct. 2308 (2009), where it found a state inmate doesn't have a due process right under the Fourteenth Amendment to obtain post-conviction access to the state's evidence for DNA testing at the inmate's expense.

However, just two years after the *Alaska* case above, a state prisoner filed a §1983 civil rights action under 42 U.S.C. seeking access to biological evidence for DNA testing that allegedly could prove his innocence of murder that led to his death penalty sentence, see *Skinner v. Switzer*, 179 L.Ed.2d 233 (2011). It should be noted that the Supreme Court in the *Skinner* case agreed with his actions and ordered DNA testing and access to the biological evidence. So you may want to take that course of action, if you are up to the fight.

## Locating Evidence for DNA Testing

The hardest part about trying to obtain DNA testing in a post-conviction petition may not be the argument itself. In fact, in may be in trying to find the evidence you want tested. Although the law in most states requires that prosecutors maintain evidence at trial containing DNA for the full duration of the defendant's prison sentence, that sometimes doesn't happen. Sometimes, the evidence is destroyed, lost, or stolen. When you are told that the requested items are missing, you are probably being told that after someone in the prosecutor's office ran a paper search or computer search for the property.

At that point, you need to file a motion or request that a physical search be conducted for the property. You wouldn't believe some of the ridiculous places lost evidence has been located, such as desk drawers, refrigerators, microwave ovens, in an attic, and on one occasion in Iowa, a pair of blood-stained shorts was discovered in the home closet of the prosecutor, who had "accidentally" taken it home in her briefcase after trial.

If you are attempting to seek DNA testing or retesting, I would advise you to look up case law in your state where successful attempts have been granted. Additionally, your law library should have in its holding, a general motion for DNA testing that you can customize to fit your needs.

I promise you, if you go to the law library in your prison or town, you will find a plethora of people willing to assist you.

That being said, and because my intent is to assist you as best as I can, I have taken the liberty of creating a template for you to use and then customize to suit your purposes, as well as your state rules related to DNA testing.

Remember, I am writing the sample motion according to Texas Rule 64, which will not support your cause if you are not in Texas. You will have to do your best in modifying and customizing the motion to fit your needs.

Additionally, I am preparing the motion in consideration that previous DNA testing was performed but failed to yield any probative results. If DNA was never performed in your case, and you are requesting it be done, you can simply amend the motion to reflect that. Preparing a post-conviction petition requires a lot of creativity, so start being creative.

*Notes:*

## FORM NO. 6

Case No._____

| | | |
|---|---|---|
| STATE OF TEXAS | § | IN THE _____DISTRICT COURT |
| VS. | § | _____ COUNTY, TEXAS |
| JOHN DOE | § | |

---

### MOTION FOR FORENSIC DNA TESTING

---

### TO THE HONORABLE JUDGE OF SAID COURT:

**COMES NOW** the petitioner, _____, in the above styled and numbered cause, pro se, and pursuant to Texas Code of Criminal Procedure Article 64.01 and 64.03, files this motion for post-conviction forensic DNA testing. Petitioner respectfully requests that this Court order new Y-Chromosome ("Y-STR") DNA testing, to be performed at an independent and private laboratory, non utilized by the county attorney's office. The petitioner would show in support of this motion the following:

### Brief statement of facts

In _____, a jury convicted Petitioner of _____. The trial court judge assessed punishment at _____years.

On _____, [LIST THE FACTS OF YOUR CASE HERE]

### Argument

**I. DNA KNOWN AS "Y-STR" COULD YIELD A GENETIC PROFILE IF SUBJECTED TO TESTING.**

Evidence collected in this case is in the possession of the state, where

61

it has been since my trial and prior arrest. The evidence was not tested for Y-STR DNA at that time, which could have eliminated the Plaintiff as a contributor, therefore proving his innocence in this case.

**II. AS REQUIRED BY ART.64.01(B)(2) OF THE TEXAS CODE OF CRIMINAL PROCEDURE THE EVIDENCE COLLECTED IN THIS CASE CAN BE SUBJECTED TO A NEWER METHOD OF DNA TESTING (Y-STR) THAT PROVIDES A REASONABLE LIKLIHOOD OF RESULTS THAT ARE MORE ACCURATE AND PROBATIVE THAN THE RESULTS OF PREVIOUS DNA TESTING.**

Autosomal testing of the evidence in this case has already been attempted and failed to produce interpretable results. Y-STR testing has the potential to obtain a male profile from the biological evidence available, and can be used to conclusively exclude Petitioner as a contributor of the biological material in this case. Recent forensic studies validate the usefulness of Y-STR testing in situations such as the Petitioner's, where no male DNA profile was obtained. In one study analyzing 45 samples where standard DNA testing failed to produce results, 87% of the samples produced usable DNA data when subjected to Y-STR testing. **See "Analysis of Samples Lacking Identifiable DNA Using a Y-STR-10-Plex, 50 J. of Forensic Sci. 1116, 1117 (2015).** This proves that Y-STR testing can produce DNA results where the traditional DNA testing done in this case could not.

**III. PETITIONER MEETS ALL OF THE REQUIREMENTS FOR DNA TESTING AS REQUIRED BY ARTICLE 64.03 OF THE CODE OF CRIMINAL PROCEDURE.**

At Petitioner's trial, the state used DNA testing in an attempt to prove guilt. Since that trial, the requirements of Article 64.03 remain the same and the facts of Petitioner's case still meet the statuatory requirements for DNA testing:

**A. Evidence is still available for testing, and is in the custody of the state.**

Following the completion of DNA testing, the crime laboratory returned the evidence to the police department. Texas Code of Criminal Procedure Art. 38.43 requires the county and investigating agency to preserve all evidence in its custody that may contain biological materials for DNA testing through the term of a convicted person'e sentence. The testing evidence is in a condition that makes DNA testing possible and has been subject to a chain of custody sufficient to establish that it has not been substituted, tampered with, replaced, or altered in any material respect.

**B. The Identity of the Perpetratorwas and still remains an issue in this case.**

At trial, Petitioner's conviction rested on the victim's eyewitness in-court identification. In the absence of forensic evidence, the jury's determination turned on the accuracy of the victim's identification alone. The Petitioner denied having committed the offense at trial, and continues to deny it today. Identity still remains in question.

**C. PETITIONER IS PREPARED TO ESTABLISH BY A PREPONDERANCE OF THE EVIDENCE (1) THAT HE WOULD NOT HAVE BEEN CONVICTED IF EXCULPATORY RESULTS HAD BEEN OBTAINED THROUGH DNA TESTING AND (2) THIS REQUEST IS NOT MADE TO DELAY THE EXECUTION OF SENTENCE OR ADMINISTRATION OF JUSTICE.**

In support of this motion, Petitioner has sworn under oath that DNA testing would exclude him as a contributor of the biological material in this case. The current standard governing Article 64.03(a)(2)(A) only requires the petitioner to show there is a 51% chance that he would not have been convicted had exculpatory results been available at trial. If exculpatory results had been available at trial under these facts, even the most of compelling eyewitness identification would have yielded to the power of DNA exclusion.

## III. PETITIONER MEETS ALL REQUIREMENTS FOR DNA TESTING.

Having met all of the requirements of Article 64 of the Texas Code of Criminal Procedure, Petitioner respectfully requests that his motion be granted and DNA testing ordered. As the Texas Department of Public Safety is unable to perform Y-STR testing, Petitioner requests the court grant funding for the DNA testing.


Respecfully submitted,


    [SIGN NAME HERE]
_____
[PRINT NAME HERE]
[ADDRESS]




## CERTIFICATE OF SERVICE

I, _____, under the penalty of perjury, hereby attest that a true and correct copy of the foregoing Motion For DNA Testing, was mailed to _____, at _____, on this _____day of_____, 2019.


                                        [SIGN HERE]

                               _____
                               [NAME AND ADDRESS HERE]

[CAPTION]

## ORDER

Upon consideration of the Petitioner, _____, motion for forensic DNA testing in the above captioned and numbered cause, the Court finds that the motion should be **GRANTED / DENIED** in the interest of justice.

**IT IS HEREBY ORDERED** that the District Attorney immediately produce the requested evidence in relation to the above cause number, so that DNA testing can be performed as Y-STR testing.

**IT IS FURTHER ORDERED** that DNA testing be conducted within (20) days of the signing of this order.

Done on this _____ day of _____, 2019.


_____
PRESIDING JUDGE

*Notes:*

# Chapter Seven:
# Additional Post-Conviction Issues

## Quick Denials

The following issues will result in a fairly quick denial of relief or dismissal of the writ, so it is usually best not to raise them. I will provide Texas case law for my TDCJ and Texas readers. Be sure to do a thorough research on your own case law in your state.

### 4th Amendment Violations

Courts usually will hold that the failure to raise the question of sufficiency of an affidavit for search warrant, evidence, or any other type of sufficiency challenge on direct appeals, is tantamount to an abandonment of that issue, and will not be considered for the first time in a post-conviction writ; see *Ex parte Kirby*, 492 S.W.2d 579 (Tex. Crim. App. 1973). (This is still the seminal case in Texas.)

### Insufficiency of the Evidence

A claim of insufficiency of the evidence does not state a claim for relief in a post-conviction application/petition. But, a claim of no evidence is cognizable in a post-conviction challenge, see *Ex parte Perales*, 215 S.W.3a-418 (Tex. Crim. App. 2007).

### Defective Indictment

This is the most denied issue on post- conviction challenge in the state of Texas, likely in your state also.

Failure to raise objection to the form or substance of an indictment before the day of trial is a waiver of that complaint. The presentation of an indictment charging a person with committing an offense invokes the jurisdiction of the trial court; jurisdiction is no longer contingent on whether the indictment contains defects of form or substance, as in *Teal v. State*, 230 S.W.3d 172, 177 (Tex. Crim. App. 2007).

### Issues Already Raised and Rejected on Direct Appeal

Issues raised and rejected on direct appeal may not be reconsidered on a post-conviction writ; see *Ex parte Schuessler*, 846 S.W.2d 850 (Tex. Crim. App. 1993). Most state post-conviction Courts have also held that post-conviction relief is not available to one who has already litigated his claim at trial, in a post-trial motion or on direct appeal; see *Ex parte Brown*, 205 S.W.3d 538 (Tex. Crim. App. 2006). However, there is a limited exception for some ineffective assistance of counsel issues raised on direct appeal and denied relief at that level, as in *Ex parte Nailor*, 149 S.W.3d 125 (Tex. Crim. App. 2004) and *Ex parte Torres*, 943 S.W.2d 469 (Tex. Crim. App. 1997).

## Issues that *Should* Have Been Raised on Direct Appeal

In Texas, and almost every state I have been able to research, a post- conviction writ should not be used as a substitute for an appeal. Courts are very quick to "kill" these claims, see *Ex parte Clore*, 690 S.W.2d 899 (Tex. Crim. App. 1985). Post-conviction petitions should never be used to litigate matters that should have been raised on direct appeal, such as improperly cumulated (stacked) sentences and improper finding of a weapon. Both be raised on direct appeal, consult *Ex parte Banks*, 769 S.W.2d 539 (Tex. Crim. App. 1989), *Ex parte Townsend*, 137 S.W.3d 79 (Tex. Crim. App. 2004), and Ex parte Carter, 521 S.W.3d 344 (Tex. Crim. App. 2017).

## Miranda Violations

Courts have held that a defendant waived objections to the admission of portions of his confession or statement without proof of proper Miranda warnings because the defendant failed to timely raise the objection at trial, see *Ranson v. State*, 707 S.W.2d 96 (Tex. Crim. App. 1986).

In this situation, you would raise an ineffective assistance of trial counsel claim for failing to raise objection related to Miranda, prior to the confession or statement given to authorities.

## Issues that Have Been Forfeited Under the Objection Rule

This issue is analogous to the previous category. In general, any error that could have been objected to at trial, but was not, is waived for post-conviction purposes. For example, any complaints regarding a ruling made by a trial court will not result in relief on post-conviction attack. Again, this is where you would bring a claim of ineffective assistance of counsel for failing to object.

## Statutory Violations Only

As I mentioned previously, generally any error that could have been raised of a facially valid mandatory statute is not cognizable on post-conviction challenge where no violation of federal constitutional rights has occurred, see *Ex parte Graves*, 70 S.W.3d 103 (Tex. Crim. App.2002).

## Alleging Prior Convictions for Enhancement Violated Double Jeopardy

Enhanced punishment, though extremely unfair and prejudicial for repeat offenders, does not violate the Double Jeopardy Clause of the U.S. Constitution, as in *Witte v. United States*, 515 U.S. 389 (1995). In general, remoteness of a prior conviction does not affect its use for purposes of enhancement, see *Loud v. State*, 499 S.W.2d 295 (Tex. Crim. App. 1973).

## Complaints about Unauthorized Fines

Though such an issue may be raised and found "inaccurate" by courts, it is almost never found to be "void" nor "illegal." Unless you cite a claim of jurisdictional defect, a violation of a constitutional right, or a fundamental error, you will not receive relief on this issue.

### Speedy Trial

Simply stated, these claims are not cognizable. Speedy trial claims based on the federal constitution are "technically" cognizable but will probably not result in relief. If the applicant did not file a motion for speedy trial that was denied by the trial court, error will have been then waived. And, if the applicant did file a motion for speedy trial violation on direct appeal that was rejected, the courts will not reconsider the issue on post-conviction challenge. The best way to raise a federal speedy trial violation is through ineffective assistance of counsel.

### Oath of Office and Anti-Bribery

Though numerous inmates across the country flood the courts with the ridiculous claims that their judges and prosecutors did not have "valid" Oath of Office and Anti-Bribery documents at the time of their trial, it is a non-issue and will not result in a reversal.

The right of a judge or prosecutor to the office in which they then functioned may not be attacked collaterally. When a judge specifically is holding office under color of title by appointment and discharging the duties of the office, his acts are conclusive as to all persons and cannot be attacked in a collateral proceeding, even if the person acting as judge lacks the necessary qualifications and may be incapable of legal holding of the office, as in *Snow v. State*, 114 S.W.2d 898, 900 (Tex. Crim. App. 1937). (This case remains as seminal in Texas.)

## Quick Dismissals

### Misdemeanor Convictions

There is no jurisdiction on post-conviction challenge for misdemeanor convictions. I see numerous people attempt to raise this issue without success. That being said, courts have held that relief is available where applicant's felony conviction was actually a misdemeanor. And post-conviction courts have jurisdiction if the case involves a state jailor lesser-valued felony where the applicant received a misdemeanor sentence pursuant to certain penal codes and state statutes. In Texas, see Article 11.07, §§ 1, 3(a)-(b); *Ex parte Johnson*, 561 S.w.2d 841 (Tex. Crim. App. 1978); *Ex parte Sparks*, 206 S.W.3d 680 (Tex. Crim. App.2006); and Section 12.44 of the Texas Penal Code.

### If Direct Appeal is Still Pending

There is no jurisdiction at this point, as in Art. 11.07, §§1,3(a)-(b); and *Ex parte Johnson*, 12 S.W.3d 472 (Tex. Crim. App. 2000). An appeal is to be considered pending until mandate is issued by the intermediate appellate court. Courts across the country, and specifically here in Texas, have clarified the definition of when mandate is issued. Courts have held an appellant's conviction becomes final for purposes of post-conviction purposes when an appellate court issues a mandate affirming the conviction, even though the court subsequently granted an out-of-time petition for review (PDR in Texas), a petition for review was refused, and the original mandate was never withdrawn. In essence, the original mandate is held dormant until such time as the court can dispose of the out-of-time petition for review. Courts have also held that, absent contrary evidence, a mandate is presumed to issue at 9:00 a.m. on the day the court of appeal issues it, thereby making any writ application filed later in the day as timely, see *Ex parte Webb*, 270 S.W.3d 108 (Tex. Crim. App. 2008); and *Ex parte Hastings*, 366 S.W.3d 199 (Tex. Crim. App. 2012).

## Non-Compliance with the Filing Requirements

Though I am going to address this issue as it is found in most states, I will include specific guidelines for the Texas Court of Criminal Appeals. I have found in my research that the same requirements are common to most state Supreme Courts and Court of Criminal Appeals.

The Court of Criminal Appeals of Texas has held that TRAP requires an applicant to state the grounds for relief, and a concise recitation of the facts in support of the grounds, on the prescribed form, as in *Ex parte Blacklock*, 191 S.W.3d 718 (Tex. Crim. App. 2006). A separate memorandum attached to the form is allowed, but it cannot be a substitute for the form itself. (I have warned numerous inmates not to ignore the form by only sending the memorandum, without success).

The Court set out further guidance for applicants, and their counsel, regarding the filing requirements of TRAP 73.1 and the Code of Criminal Procedure in *Ex parte Rendon*, 326 S.W.3d 221 (Tex. Crim. App. 2010). This application was filed and set for submission to determine: (1) whether Article 11.14 requires an applicant to sign an application for post-conviction relief presented on his behalf, especially if, as is the case, the personal knowledge regarding the allegations in the application lies only with an applicant, and (2) whether an application requires an applicant to sign the application in order to be compliant with Rule 73.1 (d) of the TRAP. The Court ordered the application dismissed because it was not properly verified due to a defect in the prescribed form. Specifically, the Court of Criminal Appeals of Texas held:

"The inmate/applicant may sign the "Oath Before a Notary" (and actually do so before a notary public if you state it) to verify the writ application according to his belief. Alternatively, he may sign the inmate declaration attesting to his belief as to the truth of the allegations *without* a notary public – again, according to his belief."

Any further confusion in this area should have been alleviated by the revised forms here in Texas, which took effect after the issuance of the court's opinion in *Rendon*. The latest version took effect on January 1, 2014, in combination with significant new additions to the TRAP. You should keep in mind the TRAP dictates that applications will be found to be non-compliant for the following reasons:

- Not on the prescribed form
- Grounds not set out on the prescribed form
- Facts not set out on the prescribed form
- Multiple convictions may not be challenged on one form (This does not apply to multiple convictions under the same indictment or cause number.)
- Pages or questions from the form are missing or deleted.

- Applicant has improperly modified the prescribed form (Multiple grounds raised on a single page.)
- Applicant has not completed a proper verification of the form
- Applicant has exceeded the two pages allowed for each ground of relief and supporting facts
- Applicant has filed a computer-generated memorandum that exceeds the 15,000-word limit and the trial court has not granted leave to exceed the limit
- Applicant has filed a non-computer-generated memorandum that exceeds 50 pages in length and the trial court has not granted leave to exceed the limit
- Applicant has filed a computer-generated memorandum that is not printed in standard 10-character-per-inch (cpi) monospaced typeface
- Applicant has filed a computer-generated memorandum that does not include a certificate stating the number of words in the document

It should be noted that the failure to comply with the TRAP rules, or the rules in your state, does not mean the courts do not have jurisdiction to consider an application. In Texas, see *Ex parte Golden*, 991 S.W.2d 859 (Tex. Crim. App. 1999). In 2011, in a case that involved actual innocence, the Texas Court of Criminal Appeals, citing *Golden*, granted relief under its "inherent" jurisdiction because it was apparent from the face of the record the applicant was entitled to relief, the state had not moved to dismiss the application for non-compliance: and the state agreed with the recommendation to grant relief, as in *Ex parte Morton*, 2011.

### Complaints about DNA Hearings per Chapter 64 or Other State DNA Codes

Proceedings under Chapter 64 and most other codes do not challenge an applicant's conviction or sentence, and are thus not applicable on a post-conviction challenge. In this case, you will need to file a motion in the trial court you were convicted in requesting DNA testing to either be performed or retested. If the trial court denies your motion, you are then able to challenge that ruling in the intermediate court of appeals. (*See* Form No. 6.)

### Subsequent Applications

If a subsequent application for a writ of *habeas corpus* is filed after final disposition of an initial application challenging the same conviction, a court may not consider the merits of or grant relief based on the subsequent application unless the application contains sufficient specific facts establishing that:

(1) the current claims and issues have not been and could not have been presented previously in an original application or in a previously considered application filed under this article because the factual or legal basis for the claim was unavailable on the date the applicant filed his previous application; or
(2) by a preponderance of the evidence, but for a violation of the United States Constitution no rational juror could have found the applicant guilty beyond a reasonable doubt.

One helpful case is, *Ex parte Brooks*, 219 S.W.3d 396 (Tex. Crim. App. 2007). A successful claim of Double Jeopardy in a subsequent writ can make a *prima facie* showing of actual innocence, see *Ex parte Knipp*, 236 S.W. 3d 214 (Tex. Crim. App. 2007); and *Ex parte Milner*, 394 S.W.3d 502 (Tex. Crim. App. 2013). However, relief will not be granted if the double jeopardy violation alleged involves multiple punishments, see *Ex parte Aubin*, 2017 Tex. Crim. App. LEXIS 885 (Tex. Crim. App. September 20, 2017).

### Applicant Waived the Right to File a Writ of *Habeas* (Plea)

In most all states, including Texas, as part of a plea agreement a defendant may validly waive claims that reasonably should have been known to him at the time, he waived his right to *habeas corpus* relief, as in *Ex parte Reedy*, 282 S.W.3d 492 (Tex. Crim. App. 2009). However, any waiver would be of limited effect. The courts have held that a waiver of *habeas corpus* relief is not enforceable in order to prohibit an applicant from claiming that his guilty plea was a product of constitutionally ineffective assistance of counsel.

Essentially, if your plea agreement was due to the ineffectiveness of your trial attorney in his lack of adversarial challenge, failure to address mental incapacity, or for any other failures, you can bring an application for post-conviction *habeas corpus* in those regards.

## Post-Conviction Time Credit

This is an incredibly arcane area of *habeas corpus* jurisprudence that is a subject unto itself. However, here are some common issues you must keep in mind when dealing in this area:

### Administrative Remedies

In time credit cases, an applicant must first attempt to have the matter resolved through the time credit resolution system in their State Department of Correction. Here in Texas, it would be the Texas Department of Criminal Justice (TDCJ), see Texas Gov't Code § 501.0081. Both the State Correctional Institutional Division and the State Jail Division have their own time credit resolution systems here in Texas.

The exception to the exhaustion requirement under the statute are, at the time of filing with the district clerk:

- The applicant is on parole or mandatory supervision, see *Ex parte Russell*, 60 S.W.3d 875 (Tex. Crim. App. 2001).
- The applicant has not received a written response to his claim by the Time Office within 180 days.
- The applicant is within 180 days of his presumptive parole date, date of release on mandatory supervision, or date of discharge.

It should be noted that it is *not* an exception to the filing requirement if an applicant is in a county jail. Courts everywhere have held that an individual in this situation is an "inmate" for purposes of exhausting remedies. In Texas, see *Ex. parte Dunlap*, 166. S.W.3d 268 (Tex. Crim. App. 2005).

## If You Are Being Improperly Denied Parole (Texas)

If I had a dollar for every time a fellow inmate asked me about this issue, I would be a billionaire. The state of Texas has a parole system, but, they don't like to use it. Hence it boasts the largest number of incarcerated individuals in the entire world, per capita. Roughly 200,000 men and women are either already in a Texas prison or sitting in county jail waiting for the "chain" to bring them there. Over half – about 53% of them – have sentencing in excess of 50 years to serve. So, for all of you that are subject to this issue, here you go:

While the release of a prisoner to parole is discretionary on the part of the parole board, release to mandatory supervision can be either mandatory or discretionary, as in *Ex parte Geiken*, 28 S.W.3d 553, 558 (Tex. Crim. App. 2000). Prior to September 1, 1996, inmates eligible for mandatory supervision were entitled to release to mandatory supervision when their calendar time in prison, plus their accrued good conduct time, equaled 100% of their sentence.

For offenses committed between August 29, 1977 and August 31, 1987, *all* crimes were eligible for mandatory supervision except for convictions where the sentence was for life or where the offender received the death penalty. For offenses committed on September 1, 1987, and onward, only limited offenses were eligible for release to mandatory supervision. For offenses committed on or after September 1, 1996, all of the mandatory supervision candidates became subject to a discretionary release pursuant to Government Code § 508.149(b). A life sentence will *always* render an inmate ineligible for mandatory supervision, according to *Ex parte Franks*, 71 S.W.3d 327 (Tex. Crim. App. 2001).

The Court has held that inmates have certain due process rights when they are being reviewed for release. In *Ex parte Retzlaff*, 135 S.W.3d 45 (Tex. Crim. App. 2004), the court held that in the normal case, an inmate is entitled to notice of the specific month and year in which he will be reviewed for release to mandatory supervision. The Court also held that the inmate must be given at least thirty days advance notice that he will be reviewed in the specified month so that he has a sufficient time frame to submit materials on his behalf. And the reviewing body can't ever "jump the gun," and hold the hearing on a date earlier than the one that was provided to the inmate, see *Ex parte Shook*, 59 S.W.3d 174 (Tex. Crim. App. 2001).

Government Code § 508.149(a), states that a person is ineligible for release to mandatory supervision if he is serving a sentence for or "has been previously convicted of" one of the enumerated offenses listed in the statute. When interpreting whether a past offense, which is not now specifically listed in § 508.149(a), would render an offender ineligible for release, the court will give effect to the collective intent or the purpose of the Legislature. In *Ex parte Ervin*, 187 S.W.3d 386 (Tex. Crim. App. 2005), the court held that an applicant's previous conviction for sexual abuse, though not specifically listed under § 508.149(a), rendered him ineligible for release. In a case that resulted in relief for the applicant, the court held that an applicant's first degree burglary conviction which, at first look, appeared to be an enumerated offense, was not an offense covered by § 508.149(a), see *Ex parte Mabry*, 197 S.W.3d 58 (Tex. Crim. App. 2004).

## Life Without Parole for Offenders Under Age 18

In *Miller v. Alabama*, 132 S.Ct. 2455 (2012), the Supreme Court held that a mandatory "life without parole" sentence for a defendant who was under the age of 18 at the time of his crime violates the Eighth Amendment prohibition on cruel and unusual punishment. In *Ex parte Maxwell*, 424 S.W.3d 66 (Tex. Crim. App. 2014), the court found that *Miller* announced a new rule under the first *Teague* exception, and held it applies retroactively, see *Teague v. Lane*, 489 U.S. 288 (1989). The court's reasoning in *Maxwell* was subsequently vindicated by the Supreme Court's decision in *Montgomery v. Louisiana*, 577 U.S., 136 S.Ct. 718, 193 L.Ed.2d 599 (2016).

*Notes:*

# Chapter Eight:
# Actual Innocence

Actual innocence claims, also known as "Bare Innocence," are referred to as *Herrera* claims based on the Supreme Court's decision in *Herrera v. Collins*, 506 U.S. 390 (1993). *Herrera* claims involve "a substantive claim in which applicant asserts his bare claim of innocence based solely on newly discovered evidence."

Regarding *Herrera* claims, the courts throughout the country have held that federal due process is violated when an innocent person is incarcerated, and the courts have also held that this applies whether the defendant has pled guilty or not guilty. In Texas, the Criminal Court of Appeals extended the access of actual innocence claims to guilty plea situations in *Ex parte Tuley*, 109 S.W.3d 388 (Tex. Crim. App. 2002). This opinion expanded that court's actual innocence jurisprudence as set out in *Ex parte Elizondo*, 947 S.W.2d 202 (Tex. Crim. App. 1996).

The court also held in *Tuley*:

- A bare innocence claim raises a constitutional challenge to the conviction;
- To be granted relief on a bare innocence claim, the applicant must show that the new evidence unquestionably establishes his innocence; and,
- The burden is on the *habeas* applicant claiming actual innocence to show that no reasonable juror could have found him guilty in light of the new evidence because it is presumed that the conviction is valid.

In cases involving recantation by a complainant or witness, counsel should request a live hearing because credibility is always a key issue. Remember, before you are entitled to a hearing, you must make a claim that, if true, establishes "affirmative evidence of Applicant's innocence," see *Ex parte Franklin*, 72 S.W.3d 671, 678 (Tex. Crim. App. 2002). The importance of a trial court's findings on credibility is amply demonstrated by the court's brief opinion granting relief in *Ex parte Harmon*, 116 S.W.3d 778 (Tex. Crim. App. 2002). In *Harmon*, the applicant alleged that he was in fact actually innocent, as demonstrated by the complainant's affidavit in which she stated that her trial testimony was false, it was prompted by her natural father's sister, and that applicant never sexually assaulted her. The trial court conducted a hearing and entered findings of fact that the complainant's recantation was credible and recommended that relief be granted.

Another example of the importance of establishing a good record in actual innocence claims based upon recantation is found in *Ex parte Calderon*, 309 S.W.3d 64 (Tex. Crim. App. 2010). In that decision, the court ordered the application be filed and set for submission to determine whether the applicant had established that he was actually innocent and whether the State violated *Brady*. The court held that, based on the facts in the record, the applicant was actually innocent based upon evidence (a recantation affidavit from the complainant and testimony from the *habeas* evidentiary hearing) that was "newly discovered" and "newly available," in *Ex parte Brown*, 205 S.W.3d 538, 545 (Tex. Crim. App. 2006). And in *Ex parte Miles*, 359 S.W.3d 647 (Tex. Crim. App. 2012), the court granted relief on both the *Brady* and actual innocence in a subsequent application.

That being said, it's certainly not a "guaranteed" win simply because there is a recantation in your case or a change of testimony. In *Ex parte Mosley*, 2013 Tex. Crim. App. Unpub. LEXIS (Tex. Crim. App. September 11, 2013), the court considered the granting of relief due to the recantation of the complaining witness in a sexual assault case. The trial court made recommendation granting relief after holding a hearing and putting the recanting witness on the stand.

The impact of this unpublished case was felt less than a year later when the court handed down its opinion in *Ex parte Harleston*, 431 S.W.3d 67 (Tex. Crim. App. 2014). In denying the applicant's claim of actual innocence based upon a recantation, the court rejected the *habeas* court's findings that the victim's recantation was credible because those findings were not supported by the record, and held that applicant failed to present clear and convincing evidence that left no question as to his innocence. Specifically, the court said:

"The sheer number of 'back and forth,' inconsistent stories lead us to conclude that Applicant cannot meet the minimum quantum of proof necessary to satisfy Applicant's 'Herculean' burden to establish his actual innocence by clear and convincing evidence. Newly discovered evidence that merely 'muddies the water' and only casts doubt upon an applicant's conviction, such as the multiple recantations and repudiations in this case, is insufficient to prevail in a free-standing actual innocence claim because that evidence does not affirmatively establish an applicant's factual innocence by clear and convincing evidence ..."

Another case that further illustrates the difficulties of obtaining relief on recantation claims is *Ex parte Navarijo*, 433 S.W.3d 558 (Tex. Crim. App. 2014). Here, the complainant recanted her testimony that the applicant was guilty of the offense. In denying relief, the court held the following, in pertinent part:

"Although [applicant] has provided some new evidence in support of his claim that he is actually innocent of the offense, we conclude that he has failed to meet this standard because his new exculpatory evidence, which comes in the form of a recantation from the complainant some thirteen years after his conviction, does not unquestionably establish his innocence when that evidence is considered in light of other incriminating evidence in the record ..."

For a brief while, actual innocence claims appeared to be in play in situations where the court vacates a conviction on the basis that the underlying statute in a conviction is unconstitutional, as in *Ex parte Chance*, 439 S.W.3d 918 (Tex. Crim. App. 2014). In *Chance*, the court, in a brief *per curium* opinion, granted relief on the basis of the court's holding in *Ex parte Lo*, 424 S.W.3d 10 (Tex. Crim. App. 2013, which held unconstitutional the online solicitation of a minor statute. The notable aspect of this case is the dueling three-judge concurrence versus three-judge dissent. The concurrence opined that the court properly granted relief on the claim that the conviction was void *ab initio* (from the beginning) because it had held that the "sexually explicit communications" statute was on its face unconstitutional. In layman's terms, this means that if you were convicted of a statute or law that was later determined to be unconstitutional, you are determined to be actually innocent.

A quasi-actual innocence claim may be raised as a basis for relief in DWI convictions. The courts in numerous states have granted relief because an applicant had not committed a felony DWI offense (only a class A misdemeanor), see *Ex parte Sparks*, 206 S.W.3d 680 (Tex. Crim. App. 2006).

In cases where an actual innocence claim hinges on the evaluation of newly discovered scientific evidence, the court clearly set out the legal standards in *Ex parte Spenser*, 337 S.W.3d 869 (Tex. Crim. App. 2011). The case in *Spenser* involved a claim based on forensic visual science and the court held:

"We agree with the state that not all scientific advances can be treated equally. While we have considered advances in science when we determine whether certain evidence, such as DNA, is newly discovered or newly available, the evidence presented by Applicant is not the sort of evidence that is capable of being preserved and tested at a later date. Forensic visual science may be new, but there is no way for the forensic visual expert to test the conditions as they existed at the time of the offense because there is no way to replicate the lighting conditions.

"We will consider advances in science and technology when we determine whether evidence is newly discovered or newly available, but only if the evidence being tested is the same as it was at the time of the offense. Thus, the science or the method of testing can be new, but the evidence must be able to be tested in the same state as it was at the time of the offense."

When it comes to DNA tests, the result should be looked at in the context of the evidence in the case. In *Ex parte Holloway*, 413 S.W.3d 95 (Tex. Crim. App. 2013), the court held that the results of Chapter 64 DNA testing in the case did not show by clear and convincing evidence that no reasonable juror would have convicted him in light of the new evidence. In essence the court held that, even if evidence had been presented that the victim's blood was not on the knife discovered in the applicant's car, it was unlikely that such evidence would have overcome the testimony of eyewitnesses who saw him with the knife, saw him use the knife, or were themselves injured by the knife-wielding applicant, whether or not it was the same knife found in his car afterwards.

Unfortunately, and strangely, the greatest number of the court's opinions granting relief based upon "new science" are unpublished. However, even though the following opinions have no precedential value, I want to show you how the Court of Criminal Appeals of Texas handles such cases:

- Relief granted on the basis that new DNA test results eliminated applicant as the contributor of the sperm fraction, in *Ex parte Evans*, 2009 (Tex. Crim. App. Unpub. LEXIS 696 (Tex. Crim. App. October 21, 2009).

- Relief granted on the basis that new DNA evidence showed applicant did not commit the underlying sexual assault, and the DNA matched an individual that had now confessed, in *Ex parte Waller*, 2008 Tex. Crim. App. Unpub. LEXIS 656 (Tex. Crim. App. September 24, 2008).
- Relief granted on the basis that new testing revealed that the applicant did not possess a controlled substance, in *Ex parte Cantu*, 2005 Tex. Crim. App. Unpub. LEXIS 319 (Tex. Crim. App. July 27, 2005).

An applicant may also claim that he is "procedurally innocent." These claims are referred to as *Schlup* claims based on the Supreme Court's decision in *Schlup v. Delo*, 513 U.S. 298 (1995). In this situation, the claim of innocence itself does not provide the basis for relief but is tied to a showing of constitutional error at trial. The basis for this type of error/claim is codified in Texas by Article 11.07, § 4(a)(2) and Article 11.071 § 5(a)(2) – "by a preponderance of the evidence, but for a violation of the United States Constitution no rational juror could have found the applicant guilty beyond a reasonable doubt." And, as mentioned earlier in this paper, the foundational case for analysis is *Ex parte Brooks*, 219 S.W.3d 396 (Tex. Crim. App. 2007). Such claims are not proper if raised in an initial *habeas* application, see *Ex parte Villegas*, 415 S.W.3d 885 (Tex. Crim. App. 2013).

A great case to review if you are in Texas, where the court granted relief on the basis of procedural innocence is *Ex parte Milner*, 394 S.W. 3d 502 (Tex. Crim. App. 2013). In *Milner*, the Applicant was convicted of murder and two counts of attempted capital murder and received multiple life sentences. He committed the offenses "during different criminal transactions but the murders [were] committed pursuant to the same scheme or course of conduct," per Tex. Pen. Code § 19.03(a)(7)(B). The Fifth Circuit set aside his murder conviction on double jeopardy grounds. Applicant alleged that his punishments for the same offenses of attempted capital murder violated the double jeopardy prohibition on multiple punishments for the same offense.

In granting relief, the court held that the applicant proved that he was actually innocent of the second conviction for attempted capital murder, and that, but for a violation of the United States Constitution, no rational juror could have found him guilty beyond a reasonable doubt.

## Getting a New Trial

In *Wallace v. State*, 106 S.W.3d 103, 108 (Tex. Crim. App. 2003) the court established that in order for a defendant to be entitled to a new trial on the basis of newly discovered or newly available evidence, he must satisfy the four-pronged test:

1. the newly discovered evidence was unknown or unavailable to the defendant at the time of trial;
2. the defendant's failure to discover or obtain the new evidence was not due to the defendant's lack of due diligence;
3. the new evidence is admissible and not merely cumulative, collateral, corroborative, or impeaching;

4. the new evidence is probably true and will probably bring about a different result in a new trial.

Where the applicant requests a new trial based on newly discovered evidence, he has the burden of establishing by clear and convincing evidence that the new facts unquestionably establish his innocence. A plea of guilt, again, does not preclude an actual innocence claim in a *habeas* post-conviction petition.

One thing to remember, if the newly discovered evidence alone, which should have been discovered in time for trial, can't get you relief, you can always file a claim of ineffective assistance of trial counsel for failing to adequately investigate and discover the evidence.

Also, when you raise the newly discovered evidence claim, be sure to cite a due process claim under the Fourteenth Amendment of the United States Constitution, in order to preserve the issue for a §2254 Federal Habeas Corpus Review.

*Notes:*

# Chapter Nine:
# Ineffective Assistance of Counsel 2.0

If you thought I was joking in Chapter Five about the importance and success rate of raising claims of ineffective assistance of counsel in your post-conviction application, you were wrong.

I was so serious that I decided to write another chapter about the subject, so that you will be better informed of the obligations your trial attorney had in representing you. You will also find here further case law and explanation of those obligations. It's really as simple as this: where you can't raise certain issues on post-conviction for the first time, or at all, you should always raise them as a sub-claim of ineffective assistance of counsel. That is how you get them in the front door, so to speak. This is what we are taught at our prestigious and accredited law schools, paralegal schools, and in every Law Journal detailing the issue of ineffective assistance of counsel. And now, I will teach it to you:

The standards relating to ineffective assistance of counsel in every state constitution arrives by way of the United States Supreme Court ruling in *Strickland*, which establishes that a defendant in a criminal case is entitled to effective assistance of trial counsel, see *Ex parte Duffy*, 607 S.W.2d 507 (Tex. Crim. App. 1980). To obtain *habeas corpus* relief for ineffective assistance of counsel under *Strickland* an applicant must show that his trial counsel's performance was deficient and that there is a "reasonable probability," one sufficient to undermine confidence in the result, that the outcome would have been different but for his counsel's deficient performance, as in *Ex parte Scott*, 190 S.W.3d 672 (Tex. Crim. App. 2006).

Whether a defendant has received effective assistance is to be then judged by "the totality" of the representation, rather than isolated acts or omissions of trial counsel, see *Ex parte Raborn*, 658 S.W.2d 602 (Tex. Crim. App. 1983). The court has also held that, in determining whether the ineffective assistance of counsel has been shown, the court will presume that trial counsel made all significant decisions in the exercise of a reasonable professional judgment, as in *Delrio v. State*, 840 S.W.2d 443 (Tex. Crim. App. 1992). Counsel will never be considered ineffective simply because a different attorney would have done things differently.

1. The courts should consider the effectiveness of counsel's performance as of the time of trial, and not through hindsight, according to *Hawkins v. State*, 660 S.W.2d 65 (Tex. Crim. App. 1983).
2. The right to counsel is required at every stage of a criminal trial proceeding where the substantial rights of the accused may be affected, as found in *Mempa v. Rhay*, 389 U.S. 128 (1967). This would include the revocation of probation.
3. The right to counsel applies to both the guilt-innocence and the punishment phase of a trial. Counsel should perform effectively at both, according to *Ex parte Hernandez*, 988 S.W.2d 770 (Tex. Crim. App. 1999).

Here are a few more ineffective assistances of counsel claims that have won reversals in certain situations and are commonly raised:

1. *Counsel failed to pass along a plea offer from the state* – In *Ex parte Argent* 393 S.W.3d 781 (Tex. Crim. App. 2013), the court determined that its more liberal *Ex parte Lemke*, 13 S.W.3d 791 (2001) test did not survive the Supreme Court's decision in *Lafler v. Cooper*, 132 S.Ct. 1376 (2012) and *Missouri v. Frye*, 132 S.Ct. 1399 (2012). In order to obtain relief, an applicant must now show a reasonable probability that: (1) he would have accepted the plea if counsel had not given ineffective assistance; (2) the prosecution would not have withdrawn the offer; (3) the trial court would not have refused to accept the plea bargain.

2. *Counsel failed to investigate the status of prior conviction* – The court has held that it is fundamental that an attorney who is representing a defendant must acquaint himself not only with the facts of law, but also the facts of the case before he can render reasonably effective assistance of counsel, and that relying upon the facts of the case as represented by a prosecuting attorney is not sufficient in *Butler v. State*, 716 S.W.2d 48 (Tex. Crim. App. 1987). For example, in *Ex parte Pool*, 738 S.W.2d 285 (Tex. Crim. App. 1987), the court granted relief where counsel submitted an affidavit in which he admitted that he relied upon information presented to him by the prosecutor and conducted no independent investigation regarding the status of applicant's prior convictions, and the prosecutor submitted an affidavit admitting that he unintentionally gave defense counsel erroneous information.

3. *Counsel failed to call a defense witness* – On an uncalled witness claim, an applicant must show that the witnesses were available, and that their testimony would have been of some benefit to the defense, as in *King v. State*, 649 S.W.2d 42 (Tex. Crim. App. 1983).

4. *Counsel failed to visit the crime scene* – In *Wilkerson v. State*, 726 S.W.2d 542 (Tex. Crim. App. 1986), the court found that counsel failing to visit the crime scene did not itself constitute ineffective assistance of counsel. However, there is a plethora of Federal Court rulings to the contrary, such as *Siehl v. Grace*, 561 I~.3d 189, 197-98 (3rd Cir. 2009).

5. *Counsel was ineffective due to failure to prepare* – In *Ex parte Dunham*, 650S.W.2d 825 (Tex. Crim. App. 1983), the applicant contended that he was denied effective assistance of counsel because his trial attorney persuaded him to waive his right to a jury trial so counsel would not need to prepare for *voir dire* of the jury panel. At evidentiary hearing counsel admitted that at the time of trial, he knew that this was bad legal advice and was not fair to applicant. The Court found him ineffective and reversed the conviction. [Wow! Some attorney's actually do tell the truth.]

6. *Counsel failed to request an interpreter* – In *Ex parte Lahood*, 401 S.W.3d 45 (Tex. Crim. App. 2013, the court denied relief when it held that while counsel rendered a deficient, poor and unreasonable decision by not to investigating whether an interpreter was required, it was not ineffective. However, just one year later, in *Ex parte Cockrell*, 424 S.W.3d 543 (Tex. Crim. App. 2014), the court held that counsel was in fact ineffective for failing to request an interpreter for the defendant who was deaf.

[Apparently, being unable to hear at all is far more important to the Court of Criminal Appeals than being unable to speak or understand English at all.]

7. *Counsel failed to investigate sanity at the time of offense and to inform of an insanity defense* – In *Ex parte Imoudu*, 284 S.W.3d 866 (Tex. Crim. App. 2009), when the counsel first met with the applicant, he "stared into space, acted weird, made little sense, and seemed a little off." At the time, the applicant was taking 3 different psychiatric medications that have known side effects of paranoia, delusion, psychosis, etc. Applicant also had a history of mental illness, having been seen by a psychiatrist prior to the crime happening and taking medication. Counsel had the applicant examined for competency but failed to investigate if he was sane at the time of the offense. The court reversed the conviction citing, "Counsel erred in failing to investigate applicant's sanity at the time of the offense, and there was a reasonable probability that, if counsel had informed him of the possibility of pursuing an insanity defense, he would not have pled guilty."

More recently, as I indicated previously in Chapter Five, the Court of Criminal Appeals held that counsel was ineffective for failing to present evidence at punishment for insanity caused by voluntary intoxication. Voluntary intoxication is not a defense as to guilt, however, is a very good mitigating factor as to punishment where defendant can prove a long history of drug or alcohol addiction. Juries are statistically very much inclined to hand down lighter sentences where a defendant has struggled with addictions.

8. *Counsel failed to request an accomplice witness testimony instruction to the jury where accomplice testified* – In *Davis v. State*, 278 S.W.3d 346 (Tex. Crim. App. 2009), the court found that this did not amount to ineffective assistance of counsel, but, found it to be "deficient performance."

Are you thinking what I'm thinking? Deficient performance is the requirement under *Strickland* in order to prove a violation of the Sixth Amendment and Fourteenth Amendment. The above case should have been reversed.

9. *Counsel decided not to investigate as a result of funds and not strategy* – In *Ex parte Briggs*, 187 S.W.3d 458 (Tex. Crim. App. 2005), the applicant's claim stemmed from council's decision not to fully investigate medical records or consult with expert witnesses until he had been paid an additional $2,500-$7,500 in expert fees. There was no suggestion in the record that trial counsel declined to fully investigate the medical records because he made a strategic decision that such an investigation was unnecessary or likely to be fruitless or counterproductive. Counsel made the decision because he had not been paid for experts. The court held:

"We conclude that under these circumstances, the failure by applicant's attorney to take any steps to subpoena the treating doctors, withdraw from the case due to the indigency of the applicant interfering with his ability to provide the effective assistance of counselor to request state-funded experts under *Ake V. Oklahoma*, 470 U.S. 68, 77 (1985), was deficient performance and requires reversal.

10. *Counsel failed to impeach the testimony of an eyewitness* – In *Ex parte Saenz*, 491 S.W.3d 819 (Tex. Crim. App. 2016), the court granted relief in a unanimous opinion to applicant on the basis of trial counsel's failure to impeach an eyewitness named

Gonzalez. The trial court had concluded in its findings of fact and conclusions of law that, even if trial counsel was deficient for not impeaching Gonzalez,' applicant was not prejudiced. The court disagreed because the evidence establishing applicant's identity as the person who committed the drive-by shooting was weak, and it rested heavily on the reliability of Gonzalez's in-court identification, which would have been severely crippled by his prior inconsistent statement denying his ability to identify the shooter.

## Conclusion

I simply cannot say it enough: you must research and establish ineffective assistance of counsel claims where they are reflected in the trial record. You have the best chance of obtaining relief, in any shape it may come in, where you raise it.

And again, please purchase *The Habeas Citebook – Ineffective Assistance of Counsel*, by Brandon Sample. It is filled with hundreds of the best Federal and Supreme Court rulings on all things ineffective assistance of counsel. So much so, that it was required issue at my most recent Advanced Paralegal School, studying the topic.

For those of you in states other than Texas, I apologize for the extensive case citings reflecting "local" ruling and etc. That being said, almost all of the Court of Criminal Appeals cases I cited in this chapter, as well as throughout the entire book, are reflective of rulings in your own state as well. All you need to do is type your issue into the law library computer or ask someone who spends time there, and you will be well on your way to finding what you need.

Last piece of advice on the topic, is to always try to raise all issues under ineffective assistance of counsel as a sub-topic, when you are attempting post-conviction attack to your conviction and sentence. It's a sure-fire way to be certain that the court will actually read it and give you a fair shake.

*Notes:*

# Chapter Ten:
# Plea Agreements and Sentencing Issues

So, there you sit, in your cell, or possibly in your home on some sort of electronic monitoring as part of your felony probation. The overall magnitude of the plea agreement beginning to weigh heavily on your mind, soul, and psyche with tremendous force. On top of that, in the fine print of the plea agreement that you signed, you unknowingly signed away your right to appeal the conviction and sentence. You are realizing the final reality of the plea agreement and all of the years of your life it sucked away from you. You feel like there is no hope, having admitted guilt, and having no chance of appealing the plea agreement.

You aren't alone in this deal. In the United States, 87% of all the criminal proceedings end in a plea bargain. In states like Texas, where they have a "heavy foot" on the pedal of justice, that number climbs to 98%, due to the excessive penalties defendant's face if they don't accept a plea agreement before trial. In most of those cases, as well as the cases overturned in exonerations each year, the defendant was actually innocent of the crimes in which they pled guilty to. When the prosecutor tells you in court, or sends the message through your trial counsel who has a great interest in resolving your case as quickly as possible, that you can either accept the ten (10) year prison sentence or face fifty (50) years at the trial, even the innocent will buckle under that weight.

Nevertheless, and in spite of your plea of guilt and waiving your rights to appeal, in most cases and in every state, exceptions exist that will allow you to successfully challenge your conviction and sentence in a post-conviction petition. In this chapter we will focus on attacking the guilty plea as well as the sentence you received, where applicable.

## Attacking the Guilty Plea

There are five successful challenges that can be made to a plea of guilt:

1. No Factual Basis
2. Failure to Admonish
3. Invalid Plea
4. Failure to Reveal Plea
5. Non-Adversarial

Challenges to your plea and sentence are made under the Fourteenth and Sixth Amendments to the United States Constitution, when doing so in a post-conviction petition. Additionally, you may be entitled to more of those protections under your own state constitution than in the United States Constitution, sadly enough.

# Plea Agreements

First and foremost, because plea agreements are contractual agreement between the state and the defendant, the appellate courts apply general contract-law principles, see *Missouri v. Frye*, 132 S.Ct. 1399 (2012); and *Ex parte Cox*, 482 S.W.3d 112, 116 (Tex. Crim. App. 2016).

Although contractual concepts apply to plea bargains, such would not be directly and strictly enforced to the detriment of due process. The terms of the plea agreement, being contractual in nature, are left to the parties to determine and agree upon, and the courts will rarely disturb the terms of such agreements, as in *Ex parte Cox* at 116. It is well established that after the judge has accepted a plea bargain in open court, a defendant has a right to enforce the state's part of the plea bargain (ibid).

Where a plea bargain fails in whole or in part, the proper remedy is generally to return both parties to their original pre-plea position, see *Cox* at 118. A defendant may knowingly and intelligently waive his right to appeal as part of the plea, even when sentencing is not agreed upon, where consideration is given by the state for that waiver, see *Ex parte Broadway*, 301 S.W.3d 694 (Tex. Crim. App. 2009). (Here the state gave up its right to a jury trial in consideration for the defendant waiving his appeal.)

The charge-bargain rules also apply in Texas and most other states, where the defendant pleads guilty to one charge and the state agrees to plea in bar a second charge, see *Shankle v. State*, 119 S.W.3d 808 (Tex. Crim. App. 2003).

## Guilty Plea Admonishments

Admonishment compliance in every state is required. There are no exceptions to be found. In Texas, see *Hughes v. State*, 833 S.W.2d 137 (Tex. Crim. App. 1992). All state trial courts are required to admonish (advise) the defendant of the direct consequences of the guilty plea before accepting the plea. As established in *Bassey v. State*, 239 S.W.3d 809 (Tex. Crim. App. 2007), the proper and mandatory admonishments are as follows:

- The punishment range;
- The fact that the state's recommendation is not binding on the court;
- The possibility of deportation for non-citizens of the United States;
- The limited right to appeal.

The admonishments can be accomplished orally or in writing.

In the State of Texas, after September 1, 2007, courts are required to fully admonish all defendants of the fact that it is unlawful for the defendant to possess or transfer a firearm or ammunition if the defendant is convicted of a misdemeanor involving family violence, as defined by Family Code Art. 26.13(a)(6) § 71.004.

## Admonishments Not Required

The trial court is not required to admonish a defendant of all the consequences of a guilty plea; only those direct consequences of a plea of guilt. Collateral consequences of a guilty plea, such as losing your job, are those which are not definite consequences, as in *Ex parte Morrow*, 952 S.W.2d 530 (Tex. Crim. App. 1997).

The Code of Criminal Procedure does not require the trial court to admonish the defendant of the consequences of deferred probation before he enters an open plea of guilty or *nolo contendere* (no contest), see *Ray v. State*, 919 S.W.2d 125 (Tex. Crim. App. 1996).

## Failure to Properly Admonish

Cases tried before CCP Art. 26.13 in Texas specifically did require admonishment on the sex offender registration requirement. The failure to admonish the defendant is not reversible because the duty to register, although a direct consequence, is not a punitive one, see *Mitschke v. State*, 129 S.W.3d 130 (Tex. Crim. App. 2004).

Because admonishments are a waivable-only right, a defendant can raise the issue for the first time on appeal without having made an objection or raising the issue at trial. However, such an error is subject to a harm analysis, consult *Bessey v. State*, 239 S.W.3d 809 (Tex. Crim. App. 2007); and *Davison V. State*, 405 S.W.3d 682, 687-8 (Tex. Crim. App. 2013).

Thus, a trial court commits non-constitutional error when it fails to properly admonish a defendant on one of the statutorily required plea admonishments, see *Carrazana v. State*, 980 S.W.2d 653 (Tex. Crim. App. 1998). The defendant has the burden of proof to show he was unaware of the consequences of his plea and that he was misled or harmed by the given admonishment of the trial court (ibid). Generally, what most states will surmise is that, a defendant is fully responsible where he was then fully advised of the direct consequences of his plea, and his ignorance of the collateral consequences does not render the plea involuntary, see *State v. Jimenez*, 987 S.W.2d 886 (Tex. Crim. App. 1999).

## Voluntariness of the Plea

Generally, in most all states I have been able to research a guilty plea constitutes a waiver of three constitutional rights: (1) the right to a jury trial, (2) the right to confront one's accusers, (3) the right to not incriminate oneself, see *Boykin v. Alabama*, 395 U.S. 238, 89 S.Ct. 1709, 23 L.Ed.2d 274 (1969); and *Kniatt v. State*, 206 S.W.3d 657 (Tex. Crim. App. 2006).

Accordingly, a guilty plea, to be consistent with due process of law, must be entered knowingly, intelligently, and voluntarily. To be voluntary, a guilty plea must be the expression of the defendant's own free will and must not be induced by threats, misrepresentations, or improper promise, as delineated in *Brady v. United States*, 397 U.S. 742, 90 S.Ct. 1463, 25 L.Ed.2d 747 (1970). A defendant may legitimately waive his right to appeal as part of a plea bargain agreement. This is true even where the sentence is not agreed upon, but where consideration is given by the state for the waiver.

Where the state and defendant agree that the state will not be bound by its recommendation if the defendant commits an offense between the date of his guilty plea and the sentencing hearing, and this agreement is approved by the trial court, it is an enforceable plea bargain agreement. When the defendant breaches this clause of the agreement, he is placed in the position of an open plea at his sentencing hearing, see *Moore v. State*, 240 S.W.3d 248 (Tex. Crim. App. 2007). A defendant must contemporaneously object to preserve error where the trial court intrudes into the plea-bargaining process (ibid).

Because prosecutors have no federal constitutional duty to reveal impeaching or affirmative defense information prior to a defendant's guilty plea, a plea is not rendered involuntary where information is not revealed, as in *U.S. v. Ruiz*, 536 U.S. 622, 122 S.Ct. 2450, 153 L.Ed.2d 586 (2002).

## Challenging Voluntariness of Plea

A defendant's sworn representation that his guilty plea is voluntary constitutes a formidable obstacle in any post-conviction attack, see *Blackledge v. Allison*, 431 U.S. 63, 97 S.Ct. 1621, 52 L.Ed.2d 136 (1977).

The voluntariness of a plea cannot be raised on direct appeal but must be raised on a motion for new trial or on post-conviction *habeas corpus* petition. Where the record reflects that the trial court properly gave all required admonishments to the defendant, there is a *prima facie* showing that the plea was knowingly and voluntarily entered. The burden then goes to the defendant to establish that he did not understand the consequences of his plea. An applicant seeking *habeas corpus* relief on the basis of an involuntary plea must prove his claims by a preponderance of the evidence, as in *Ex parte Morrow*, 952 S.W.2d 530 (Tex. Crim. App. 1997).

An applicant's delay in seeking *habeas corpus* relief may prejudice the credibility of his claim. Simply put, the longer you wait to mount a challenge to the plea, the more it looks like you meant to accept guilt, see *Ex parte Young*, 479 S.W.2d 45 (Tex. Crim. App. 1972).

A defendant's plea may be found involuntary where defense counsel did not advise him of the possibility of removal from the United States, as removal is nearly an automatic result for a broad class of noncitizen offenders, as in *Padilla v. Kentucky*, 559 U.S. 356, 130 S.Ct. 1473, 176 L.Ed. 2d 284 (2010). Therefore, if you are not a U.S. citizen and the record does not reflect that you were admonished about the chances of your then being deported prior to accepting the plea agreement, you have reversible error.

## Involuntary Pleas

Misrepresentations that may cause a plea to be involuntary can come from a variety of sources. While many claims challenge erroneous advice or misinformation by defense counsel, misrepresentations can also come from the trial court or the state, see *Ex parte Barnaby*, 475 S.W.3d 316, 322 (Tex. Crim. App. 2015). A complete failure to admonish a defendant as to the range of punishment he faces renders a plea involuntary without the defendant having to show harm. Improper admonishments do not render a plea involuntary unless the defendant carries his burden to plead and prove that he was harmed.

Where the statute in your state under which you were charged is in violation of the United States Constitution and an improper admonishment resulted, the plea of guilty is not voluntary or knowingly entered if the defendant shows harm, as in *Ex parte Ward*, 716 S.W.2d 529 (Tex. Crim. App. 1986).

Where trial counsel relates incorrect advice to the defendant in regard to eligibility for parole, the defendant's resulting plea of guilt will be involuntary because parole eligibility is easily determined based on the offense charged and the offense date, consult *Ex parte Moussazadeh*, 361 S.W.3d 684 (Tex. Crim. App. 2012). (In Texas, this is where the court disavowed the prior test requiring that the defendant show that advice regarding parole eligibility formed an affirmative part or essential part of the plea agreement).

Where the defendant pleads guilty to a crime without having been informed of the elements of the crime, his plea is involuntary, as in *Bradshaw v. Stumpf*, 545 U.S. 175, 125 S.Ct. 2389, 162 L.Ed.2d 143 (2005).

False evidence used by the state can also cause a defendant to be misinformed. The key factor is whether a defendant has sufficient awareness of the relevant circumstances and likely consequences such that his plea is knowing and intelligent. If a defendant's knowledge of the elements is lacking because of false evidence, his awareness is not sufficient for his plea to be voluntary. But a plea is not voluntarily weak simply because a defendant does not correctly assess every relative factor before entering into his or her decision; see *Ex parte Barnaby*, 475 S.W.3d at 322-3.

The materiality of false evidence is measured by what impact the false evidence had on the defendant's decision to plead guilty. In *Barnaby*, the court found that the value to the defendant of accepting his plea bargain in a drug case outweighed the value of knowing before his plea whether his laboratory report was false.

## Sufficiency of Guilty Pleas

Every state requires substantiation of a guilty plea. Evidence of the guilt is required in addition to, and independent of, the plea itself to establish the defendant's guilt. A judicial confession is generally said to be sufficient to support a plea of guilt, as in *Dinnery v. State*, 592 S.W. 2d 343 (Tex. Crim. App. 1979). In Texas, because a plea of guilt has to be supported by evidence under Article 1.15, a valid plea of guilty or *nolo contendere* waives or forfeits the right to appeal a claim of error only when the judgment was rendered independent of, and not supported by, the error, see *Young v. State*, 8 S.W.3d 656 (Tex. Crim. App. 2000).

A defendant's assertion that the allegations in the indictment are true and correct is a judicial confession. However, a defendant's sworn affirmation reaffirming his guilty plea to the charges in the indictment does not constitute a judicial confession and does not otherwise supply evidence, in whole or in part, sufficient to support the plea.

Also, in Texas, where a guilty plea is entered in open court, it does not have to be orally made by the defendant in order to be voluntary and valid, as in *Costilla v. State*, 146 S.W.3d 213 (Tex. Crim. App. 2004).

## Conditional Guilty Pleas

In most states (and in Texas under Tex. R. App. Proc. 25.2), a defendant may plead guilty pursuant to a plea bargain and reserve for appeal the merits of the denial of written motions or issues on which the trial court had granted permission to file an appeal. A defendant who had entered a plea of guilt pursuant to a plea bargain may appeal all written pretrial motions on the grounds stated in the motions, regardless of the manner of proof at the guilty plea hearing, see Ellis v. State, 705 S.W.2d 261 (1986).

Additionally, a defendant may appeal the denial of a suppression motion despite the fact that he plead guilty and received a sentence of deferred probation, as in *Dillehey v. State*, 815 S.W.2d 623 (Tex. Crim. App. 1991).

## Open Pleas of Guilt

"I've known this judge for years. I think it's best if you do an open plea of guilt, where you should get a good sentence."

Does that statement sound familiar? I bet it does, if you took an open plea. It's the most common statement of trial counsel wanting to quickly disperse of a case he isn't making much money on. Never, I repeat, *never* is it in a defendant's best interest to go in front of a judge in an open plea, who is an elected official and has to show a "tough on crime" approach to those who will have to consider re-electing him, in lieu of a compassionate jury of twelve fair-minded individuals as to his punishment. That is the definition of insanity.

When a defendant pleads guilty to a jury, the trial becomes unitary and the jury will always be called upon to assess punishment. A defendant cannot plead guilty to a jury and then be sentenced by a judge, see *In re The State of Texas ex rel. Jennifer Tharp*, 393 S.W.3d 751, 755 (Tex. Crim. App. 2012). When a defendant enters an open plea of guilty to an offense, he waives the right to appeal any non-jurisdiction defects, other than the voluntariness of his plea, which occurred before entry of the plea, as in *Flowers v. State*, 935 S.W.2d 131,(Tex. Crim. App. 1996).

However, a defendant who enters a plea of guilty to a jury without the benefit of a plea bargain, waives or forfeits the right to appeal a claim of error only when the judgment was rendered independent of, and not supported by, the error, see *Young v. State*, 8 S.W.3d 656 (Tex. Crim. App. 2000) (overruling *Helms v. State*, 484 S.W.2d 924 (1972).

Where a defendant pleads guilty without a punishment recommendation but the state agrees to plea in bar another offense, the sentence is then considered to be a punishment recommended by the state and the defendant has no right to appeal, in *Shankle v. State*, 119 S.W.3d 808 (Tex. Crim. App. 2003).

If you accepted guilt in an open plea without a plea agreement, you are allowed to raise claims of error occurring at or after the entry of the guilty plea. Also, keep in mind that waivers of guilt requiring the defendant to be properly admonished apply only to the guilt stage and do not constitute a waiver of the right to confrontation and cross-examination at the punishment phase, see *Stringer v. State*, 241 S.W.3d 52 (Tex. Crim. App. 2007).

### No-contest (*Nolo Contendere*) Pleas

A plea of *nolo contendere* (no contest) has the same legal effect as a plea of guilty in a criminal case. I have not been able to find any law or case law that reflects differently in any other state. That being said, a *nolo contendere* plea may not be used against the defendant as any such admission in any civil suit based upon or growing out of the act upon which the criminal prosecution is based. In Texas, see Art. 27.02(5).

### Relief Expected

The general answer is that an applicant is sent back to face the charges set out in the indictment. However, this is more complicated if an applicant's guilty plea is part of a "package deal" involving other case numbers or counts. In an attempt to address the situation, the Court of Criminal Appeals of Texas, issued its opinion in *Ex parte Cox*, 482 S.W.3d 112 Tex. Crim. App. 2016). In *Cox*, the court held that because the applicant's plea bargain was a "package deal" and part of this plea bargain cannot be fulfilled, the entire plea bargain is unenforceable, thus all parties must be rendered returned to their original positions.

The short answer is, if you are able to prove any violation related to your plea agreement, you will be awarded relief in some manner.

## Sentencing Errors

In a post-conviction petition you may challenge the sentence itself, without challenging the facts of the conviction in whole. If these issues were available on direct appeal but were not raised, you have essentially waived those for review on post-conviction. And so, what is the golden rule? … Raise it in your post-conviction petition under a sub-claim of ineffective assistance of appeal counsel.

Good, you're learning. That is the sole purpose of this book.

If you are attempting to raise a claim of the appropriateness of the sentence as to proportionality, you will lose. In order to get that in the front door of the court on a post-conviction petition, you must raise the issue of ineffective assistance of trial counsel for failing to object to the disproportionality of the sentence.

That being said, all post-conviction claims of ineffective assistance of counsel will have to meet the *Strickland* standards, where you will be required to prove the deficient performance and the prejudice is caused, see also *Lafler v. Cooper*, 132 S.Ct. 1376, 1385 (2012).

There are many different reasons you may challenge your sentence in a post-conviction petition such as:

- Invalid aggravators
- Re-sentencing issues
- Mitigators were not used
- Improper stacking of sentences
- Single criminal episode (subsumed)
- Double jeopardy violation
- Cruel and unusual punishment (Eighth Amendment)
- Apprendi issues
- Erroneous presentence investigation reports

At this time, I will address some of these issues in no particular order, as well as additional issues not presented in the list above.

### Enhancements/Aggravators

In most every state, especially here in Texas, it is quite common for the state to use a plethora of prior bad acts or convictions in order to enhance the punishment a defendant is facing. Often this is done to entice a quick resolution to the case, and other times it's pure vindictiveness.

You must raise the issue of invalid enhancements as ineffective assistance of counsel for failing to mount an objection to them as the time of trial and punishment purposes. The burden of proving the enhancement allegations are false lies directly on the defendant.

Trial courts are reviewed under an abuse of discretion standard where it makes affirmative rulings as to enhancement material. This standard is an impossibility in determining just how much weight a judge has in these regards. This means, on its own, it's not available in a post-conviction challenge. Again, what is the "golden rule?" That's absolutely right; you must raise it as ineffective assistance of counsel for trial counsel's failure to object to the erroneous enhancement evidence.

### Stacked Sentences (Consecutive)

The stacking of sentences at trial is governed by your state statute, or Code of Criminal Procedure. To preserve the issue for appeal, your trial counsel must have objected to the "stacking" of the sentences at the time it was ordered.

Cumulative or consecutive sentences are those that are served one after the other. Unless the trial court expressly cumulates (stacks) sentences, they must run concurrently (at the same time), as in *Ex parte Applewhite*, 729 S.W.2d 706 (Tex. Crim. App. 1987). A trial court does not have the implied authority to partially cumulate sentences, consult *Morris v. State*, 301 S.W.3d 281 (Tex. Crim. App. 2009).

Where the trial court did not have the authority to order the cumulative of sentences, the remedy on appeal is to delete the cumulation order, see *Morris,* Id. Texas, unlike most every other state, can stack sentences on top of sentences from other states. Texas sentences can be stacked on top of federal sentences as well.

A second sentence in every state I've researched in writing this book can be stacked on top of a sentence that is still on appeal. Where the sentence is reversed on the first sentence on appeal, the second sentence will begin running and thereafter cannot be cumulated on top of the first sentence, reference *Ex parte Nickerson*, 893 S.W.2d 546 (Tex. Crim. App. 1995). The granting of a new punishment hearing removes a sentence from the stacking order. Where the trial judge does not issue a new order stacking the new sentence in the re-sentenced case onto the sentence for an existing conviction, the sentences will run concurrently, as in *Ex parte Vela*, 460 S.W.3d at 611.

The phrase "cease to operate" as used in most states, as well as here in Texas concerning stacked sentences, means the date the prisoner has served the sentence day-for-day in prison, or the date a parole panel has approved the inmate for parole and he would have been released but for the second stacked sentence, see *Ex parte Kuester*, 21 S.W.3d 264 (Tex. Crim. App. 2.000).

## Stacked Sentences of Cases Tried Together

Unless authorized by your states Penal Code, sentences cannot be stacked (cumulated) where the offenses arose out of the same criminal transaction and were tried in a single criminal action. Where the facts of the case do not show the proceedings to be a single criminal action, then stacked sentences are possible, as in *La Porte v. State*, 840 S.W.2d 412 (Tex. Crim. App. 1992).

Where offenses arose out of the same criminal transaction are tied together under Penal Code, any fines for those offenses must also run concurrently, see *State v. Crook*, 248 S.W.3d 172 (Tex. Crim. App. 2007). Any offenses of "attempt" are never permitted to be stacked in any criminal proceeding.

Where a severance hasn't been requested and defendant accepts the imposition of stacked sentences in a single criminal episode for two offenses arising out of the same criminal action, he has waived his right to concurrent sentences. If your trial counsel failed to request severance, and did not object to the stacked sentences, you can raise a claim of his failing to object to stacked sentencing and severance on post-conviction petition.

## Mandatory Stacking

In every state, where a defendant commits an offense while an inmate of the Department of Corrections, any sentence he receives must be stacked with the sentence he is currently serving at the commission of the new offense.

## Timing of Order to Stack

The cumulation order must be entered at the time the sentence is then pronounced. Otherwise, it is void. This is true in every state court, see *Ex parte Vasquez*, 712 S.W.2d 754 (Tex. Crim. App. 1986).

## Preservation of Error

If the defendant does not object to the cumulation order when entered, he has waived appellate review of the order. Here, you may have a claim of ineffective assistance if your trial counsel did not object. Where the objection did occur at trial, it cannot be raised for the first time on a writ of *habeas corpus* post-conviction challenge, because the cumulation error should have been raised on direct appeal, as noted in *Ex parte Townsend*, 137 S.W.3d 79 (Tex. Crim. App. 2004).

In a situation where your appeal counsel failed to raise it on direct appeal, you know the drill – raise a claim of ineffective assistance of appeal counsel for failing to raise the issue.

## Cruel and Unusual Punishment

Most inmates often confuse what constitutes "cruel and unusual," versus "disproportionate" punishment. As a general rule, punishment assessed and within the statutory limits is not cruel, unusual, or excessive under the Eighth Amendment of the U.S. Constitution (though it should be).

Punishments that fall within the statutory limits are not cruel and unusual within the meaning of the Texas Constitution, either. In any case, the defendant is required to make a specific trial objection to preserve a claim of cruel and unusual punishment under the Eighth Amendment; consult *Curry v. State*, 910 S.W.2d 490(Tex. Crim. App. 1995). The defendant must object on grounds of cruel and unusual punishment at the time sentence is imposed to preserve a claim that the sentence violates the Texas Constitution.

The only exception to the above is *Miller v. Alabama*, 567 U.S. ____, 132 S.Ct. 2455, 183 L.Ed.2d 407 (2012), where a claim is not forfeited by a failure to object or to urge the claim in the trial court, where a sentence of mandatory life without parole was given to a person under age 18.

## Disproportionate Sentencing

Punishment assessed within the statutory limits is not cruel and unusual punishment, as you learned above. However, a narrow exception exists where the sentence is grossly disproportionate to the severity of the offense, as in *Solem v. Helm*, 463 U.S. 277, 103 S.Ct. 3001, 77 L.Ed.2d 637 (1983). A narrow rule exception that punishment assessed within the limit of state statute isn't excessive, cruel, or unusual, is recognized where the sentence is grossly disproportionate to the offense exists in Texas, under *Moore v. State*, 54 S.W.3d 529 (Tex. App.- Fort Worth 2001).

In a disproportionality analysis, the courts initially make a showing comparison of the gravity of the offense against the severity of the given sentence. Upon a determination that the sentence is grossly disproportionate to the offense the courts will consider the remaining factors in *Solem*. Those factors are: (1) the sentence imposed on other criminals in the same jurisdiction, and (2) the sentences imposed for the same offense in the surrounding jurisdictions.

Per usual, the defendant must make a timely objection on cruel and unusual punishment grounds in order to preserve a disproportionate sentence claim for appeal. Yep, you guessed it again, if your trial lawyer didn't object to your ridiculous sentence, you can raise it on your post- conviction petition under ineffective assistance of trial counsel.

## Double Jeopardy

Double jeopardy was defined in the United States Supreme Court's decision in *Blockburger v. United States*, 284 U.S. 299, 304, 76 L. Ed 306, 52 S.Ct. 180 (1932). There it was determined that "[t]wo offenses are different, for purposes of double jeopardy, whenever each contains an element that the other does not. That test can be easily and mechanically applied and has the virtue of producing consistent and predictable results," see also *Lewis v. U.S.*, 523 U.S. 155 (1998).

When applying the *Blockburger* test, one must apply the test twice, one for each offense. If either offense contains the same elements that are exactly the same as the other offense, then double jeopardy exists. For example, if your first offense has three elements to the offense, and they are the same as the elements in your second offense, then double jeopardy applies.

## Modification of Sentence

More prisoners seek a modification of their sentences than any other action in a post-conviction petition. It is the most used, and at the same time, the most denied motion there is. Why? Because judges rarely, if ever, change their minds about the punishments they have doled out. It has happened – don't get me wrong – but very rarely. And in the instances that the attempt was granted, I cannot find any that were done by a *pro se* inmate.

Sentence modifications are not a right under the United States Constitution. Any chance you may have of obtaining a modification of your prison sentence depends solely on your trial judge, as well as state statute. All states vary in these regards from what I have been able to uncover.

There is a 365-day period where the trial court may solely grant a modification of the sentence, from the date a defendant was sentenced. This time does not count after a re-sentence from a successful appeal. The court does not have to conduct any hearings before ruling on a motion to modify your sentence, and rarely will. Be prepared to simply have your motion denied without any hearing. Some motions are denied in silence, but sometimes the denial comes quickly with a written response.

If you seriously still want to pursue a motion for modifying your sentence, I recommend you do the following:

- Hire an attorney
- Pray (If you believe)
- Pray some more.

Good luck, my friend. In your motion for sentence modification, you should cite the following reasons for your desire to have your sentence modified:

- You have completed an education program
- You have completed a vocational trade school
- You have maintained a clean prison record
- You have completed treatment for addiction
- You have successfully completed psychological counseling
- Your children are without a parent

Again, good luck.

*Notes:*

# Chapter Eleven:
# Intro to Post-Conviction Habeas Corpus

At this stage, you have conducted your investigation, studied every aspect of your case, researched case law, decided upon your issue to be raised in your post-conviction challenge, and have gathered all of the required forms, etc.

One of the more interesting aspects of *habeas corpus* proceedings here in Texas, is that anyone can play. You don't have to have a lawyer to file a petition seeking relief, nor must you be incarcerated. Any person may file a petition seeking relief for anyone else. There are no fees to pay, and all you must do is follow the rules.

The extent of this ability to seek relief on behalf of another person (an ability usually reserved to attorneys) has not been fleshed out by litigation. While the statute allows the filing of a petition for *habeas corpus* relief, it goes no further. Because of the statutory allowance of filings by non-lawyers, initial requirements are lax. You do not have to attach the judgment, which will be done by the District Clerk. Similarly, you do not have to serve opposing counsel, which will also be done by the clerk. But, this liberality as to access of the court is not extended to matters of proof, unfortunately.

## The History of Habeas Corpus

*Habeas corpus* is a vehicle in which to attack the illegal restraint of a person who, pursuant to the rules, has been convicted in finality of a felony without any remaining appellate possibilities. *Habeas corpus* is truly the "court of last resort" at the state level.

A "writ of *habeas corpus*" is not a mythical item. The word "writ" means nothing more than "order," in this context. Thus, one is applying for an order, or writ, of *habeas corpus*. A writ of *habeas corpus* that is issued by a court pursuant to such an application simply imposes the given requirement on the custodian of a prisoner (the person holding you) to give explanation and justification for doing so. It is then up to the petitioner to show that the justification is incomplete or flawed such as to require a new trial with the mistakes not repeated.

## Up Hill Both Ways

Obtaining relief pursuant to *habeas corpus* is *not* easy! It is not the procedure that is difficult. Only a form is required, making it fairly easy for just about anyone to file an application. But identifying the mistakes or errors that may result in relief is extremely hard, and that is only the first step. There are books such as this one, which can assist you in the process, that are available on the internet or from the publisher of this book at FreebirdPublishers.com. I will also be writing and publishing additional books in the near future to assist you in the appeal and post-conviction process.

Once you have identified those allegations of error which you intend to bring to the court's attention you must face the next, and perhaps harder, obstacle – proving your allegation. Merely having the affected party swear to the factual allegations is not enough proof to obtain relief. In fact, that probably won't even get you a response from the court.

Simply put, you must be prepared to prove, by affidavit attached to the application and, later, by actual live testimony, the truth of the factual allegations demonstrating the error that is so egregious as to entitle you to relief. There is no presumption that will help you out, no lowering of the bar: The person affected in your case is a prisoner.

The courts do, however, tend to investigate some areas in which availability of the proof to a prisoner is somewhat restricted; in lieu of requiring prisoners to try obtaining the records themselves. Though the information in your case is easily obtained by trial officials, don't count on that happening to you in your case. As I mentioned earlier, the courts are very liberal in their attitude towards access to the courts with the allegations raised in an application for relief.

This does not mean that there is any liberality in proof issues, and, in fact, there is not. Any presumption will be against you and in favor of continued incarceration of the affected person.

## One Swing at the Ball

One of the biggest reasons you should not count on anything that resembles luck or official intervention into your situation is that you only get one chance! There are certain exceptions and an inmate might be entitled to multiple applications depending on the availability of one of those exceptions, but my best advice is to recognize and accept that you will probably only get this one chance.

Build your case completely and as fully as you possibly can. If you cannot prove something right now, which if proven, could result in relief, consider holding off from filing anything until such a time as you can prove your issues. Don't hope for luck, despite the disadvantages of waiting. No matter what you do, or how long you wait, be completely aware that you will likely only get one chance to attack the substance of the conviction … *Do not waste it.*

## Time Limitations

There are no time limitations set out within most *habeas corpus* applications, not even in Texas. That does not mean, however, that there are not considerations involving the timing of the filing from other sources that must be considered.

There is, first, a time limit imposed by the federal statutes on the length of time in which a federal § 2254 *habeas* petition attacking a state conviction must be filed. Generally, one year from the date your direct appeal was denied, with the exception of the "clock" being stopped for any other filings or motions pertaining to the same, such as a Petition for Discretionary Review (PDR), or Writ of *Certiorari* in the United States Supreme Court. Since an application for federal relief must show first that the issues were presented to the state courts. This acts directly against the time limitation on when you file your state *habeas corpus*.

The decision as to whether to take an incomplete application to state court so that the federal *habeas* route is not lost, is one of the hardest decisions facing inmates, as well as lawyers, and you should consider it very carefully prior to deciding what to do if the time limitation is a problem in your case. Once you are time barred (tolled) in the federal courts, you will not be allowed back in unless there were provable issues that prevented you from filing on time, such as psychological or physical impairments. But, again, that won't be easy to get around.

Secondly, there is the equitable concept of laches, which punishes an applicant who waits too long to attack the conviction. This doctrine is in effect in both the state and federal courts. This limitation is in effect less precise than that set up by the federal government in its statutes as it depends on the state claiming and showing an inability to respond to the application due to passage of time. Thus, if you think that you can wait, you should reconsider.

## Required Form

All persons filing an application for *habeas corpus* relief must use the appropriate form for their state. In Texas, you must use the form required by the Court of Criminal Appeals, which is obtainable in the prison law library, or by written request to your District Clerk in the county you were convicted in, for no charge. If you attempt to file an application seeking relief under a different form, it will be quickly and effectively rejected by the District Clerk. No exceptions.

Fill out the form as completely as possible. Some questions may not even apply to you and you may indicate it, but do not leave it blank. Do not lie on the form – the courts will quickly catch it. The courts do keep a very detailed record on each application filed and will cross-examine it to see if you have filed any other previous applications. If you have, they will reject it and can impose a severe financial penalty on you to be deducted from your prison account.

It is far better to argue for an exception to the question you are seeking to avoid than simply not answering it. As to lying, if you are caught even a little bit, you will be denied.

## Follow Instructions

One particular pitfall that is not explained very clearly in the form or its instructions is found in question #18. It calls for two parts: the first an allegation and the second a statement of facts that support the allegation. No legal arguments are allowed, which must be made in a separate memorandum attached to the application.

That being said, many applicants set out their issues within the memorandum and then in the first part of question 18, refer to that separate document instead of setting out the allegation as required on the form. This will get the application rejected. The form instructions are clear in that additional pages may only be attached for two reasons: (1) additional factual averments or development (2) for a memorandum of law. The rule does not allow additional pages set out in description of your issues, and thus, they must be on the form in writing.

It might sound like nitpicking or even silly to some, but not doing as the form requests or instructs will keep your application from being seen by the reviewing court, which is a high price to pay. So, put the issue you are raising on the form itself, and in the correct place.

## Filing the Application

Now that you have done your research and painstakingly filled out the form, you are ready to file the application correctly. You must file the application with the District Clerk in the county you were convicted in. This is true notwithstanding your belief that the mistake of which the conviction arose did not happen in the county you were convicted in. The application must, without exception, be filed in the county you were then convicted in. From there, the District Clerk will process it accordingly.

## Processing the Application

The District Clerk of each county will process the application in the same fashion, as required by state law. The application will be transferred to the District Attorney (prosecutor) for reply, which may or may not be forthcoming. It then goes to the District Court of conviction, acting as the *habeas* court for fact-finding and recommendations and for final action to the court deciding the petition. In Texas, that is the Court of Criminal Appeals.

There are time limits in which each stage of the process is supposed to be completed. For the most part, those officials in the counties do not need to be forced to do anything in the area of moving the application as they are usually more than willing to rid themselves of the application. Moving it to the high court is the easiest way to do that.

## The Answer

The District Attorney of the county of conviction is that official who will file an answer to the application for *habeas* relief – maybe. The law seems to require such an answer but there is no penalty for failing to do it. In fact, the law sets up an answer in the form of a general denial which, in the absence of further and specific action, will become the very finding of fact by statutory default. Thus, you cannot win by default or the failure of the state's representative to answer. In fact, many of the State's District Attorneys ignore *habeas* petitions, having safety in the denials created by the statute and secure in the knowledge that no relief will be forthcoming without their being given another chance to rebut the assertions, either through a hearing following remand, or a brief in the high court if the case is set for decision.

## The Trial Court's Role

The trial court is the key to post-conviction *habeas* success. There are other ways to succeed, of course, but the trial court acting as the *habeas* court has a great deal of influence in its power to make specific findings of fact and conclusions of law in regards to your factual allegations, along with recommendations for the disposition based on those findings and conclusions. Simply put, if the *habeas* court comes down on your side, your odds of winning relief just got a whole lot better. Thus, you must make every effort to convince that court of the correctness of your position.

It is generally easier to convince one person than a majority of nine. You should extend every effort to prove your case to the trial court for this reason. Do not make the mistake of thinking that the court deciding your petition in the end will overrule the lower acting court. If the *habeas* court's findings are supported in any way by the record, they will be upheld.

## Processing in the Court of Criminal Appeals

The application will be received by the Clerk of the Court of Criminal Appeals or wherever you file with in your state. From there, it is then delivered to the Central Staff, who will make legal analysis and recommend actions, if applicable. Upon completion, the clerk ensures delivery of the application along with the Central Staff's memorandum to an individual member of the court who has the responsibility of reporting the case to the entire court, known as the Conference. In most cases the individual member of the court is empowered to act on the court's behalf, but, internal rules dictate that some of those cases must be decided by the entire court acting as a collective. The decisions of the court are announced on Wednesday mornings and include applications decided that week.

## Summary

The laws regarding post-conviction applications for *habeas* relief are designed to process inmate complaints quickly and efficiently and, in most instances, succeed. For the most part persons involved in the system are willing to assist in the researching of correct results although in just about every case those people will be defensive and unwilling early on. The law requires them to act, however, and they will do so to process your application, especially if they are treated with the respect they deserve. The law is to be truly admired as it allows a freedom unheard of in other lands. The prisoner has the right to demand justification for his detention and the law will help facilitate that right. The percentages for success are not very high, nor should they be. There will have been several chances for the mistakes to have been rectified prior to the prisoner's petition. But if those mistakes have persisted, we have a system is in place that does result in relief, which cannot be said in many other parts of the world.

*Notes:*

# Chapter Twelve:
# The Evidentiary Hearing

If the court reviewing your application for post-conviction relief granted you the opportunity to present evidence in support of your claims, you are in a good place. Additionally, you will now need to immediately file a motion requesting an attorney to assist you at the hearing. In Chapter Nineteen, I will provide a copy of a motion that you can modify to suit your situation, and file with the same court you filed your *habeas* application with (the court you were convicted in).

## Preparing for the Hearing

The rules of the evidentiary hearing are governed by your state's own Rules of Civil Procedure or Rules of Appellate Procedure. Either way, there are a number of things you need to obtain, and a number of manners in which to obtain them.

In the following list are things you are going to want to consider the value of at your hearing:

- Affidavits
- Expert Reports
- Prosecutor's File
- Police Reports
- Subpoenas
- Depositions
- Interrogatories

You may not need all of these items, and you may already have them.

## Additional Hearings

Because of the scheduling conflicts related to witnesses and the court that will be holding the hearing, additional hearings may be necessary in order to address all of the issues related to your *habeas* petition. It is vital that you let the court know that you require additional hearings in order to adequately establish your claims; otherwise they will consider it to be unnecessary and move to final conclusion.

During this time, and for as long as it takes, you will be held in the county jail where you were convicted. More than likely, the same place you were prior to going to prison. After the initial hearing, you must tell the judge that you require additional hearings to take more evidence in proof of your application for post-conviction relief.

You should anticipate the first hearing being scheduled between 3-5 months after you have filed the application for *habeas corpus* relief.

## Obtaining Evidence

Since you already completed the initial investigation into preparing for a post-conviction challenge, you most likely already have the things you will need to prove your claims – at least most of it. There are three places you need to look for evidence that wasn't used at your trial:

1. Your Client File (Attorney's file)
2. The Prosecutor's File
3. New Evidence

### Client File

Here, you already located most of your discovery from your trial. This is what the prosecution provided to your attorney prior to trial and used to obtain your conviction. You will likely be very surprised with what you discover in the client file, that could have helped you at your trial.

### Prosecutor's File

On rare occasion, the prosecutor will allow you to review their case file. You have the right to know all of the evidence against you, and this includes the prosecution's file. More often than not, it will provide *Brady* evidence that the prosecutor failed to turn over prior to trial that could have changed the outcome of the trial. This is the exact reason they hid the exculpatory evidence in the first place.

If you are able to uncover *Brady* evidence, you are well on your way to obtaining a new trial and relief. Under *Brady v. Maryland*, prosecutors must disclose exculpatory evidence when it is material to guilt or to the punishment. Additionally, a prosecutor must turn over evidence that "creates a reasonable doubt that did not otherwise exist," see *United States v. Agurs*, 427 U.S. 97, 112, 49 L.Ed.2d 342, 96 S.Ct. 2392 (1976).

In Texas, the new standard of exculpatory evidence, and the requirement of prosecutors to turn it over, provides additional requirements that *Brady* does not. Here prosecutors must turn over all exculpatory evidence whether it is material or not, see *William Allen Schultz v. Commission for Lawyer Discipline of the State Bar of Texas*, Case No. 55649.

In truth, getting access to prosecution file is nearly impossible.

What you may be able to do instead is get the court to do a review of the prosecutor's files to see if any potentially exculpatory evidence has been withheld. Trial counsel usually does this before trial, when he feels the prosecution is withholding evidence. Ask the court to do an in-camera review of the prosecutor's file and report to the defense attorney whatever exculpatory information may be there.

In most states, like Texas, prosecutor's boast an open-file policy. Upon asking the court for permission to review the prosecutor's file in the courtroom, request that counsel be appointed to assist with the review.

## Police Reports

Most of the police reports relevant to your case have already been provided to your trial counsel and are likely in your client file. Like the prosecutor's file, it will take an act of congress to obtain it from the prosecutor directly.

However, you are in fact entitled to witness statements given to the police in your case. You can make a meritorious request for these witness statements as an exception to the "work product" doctrine of the state.

If, you are able to obtain copies of police reports that were never introduced at trial and you want to introduce them at the hearing, you will need to subpoena the officer who wrote the report in order to get the report into evidence. This is called "laying foundation."

*Notes:*

# Chapter Thirteen:
# How to Conduct the Hearing

If you were able to convince the court to appoint counsel to assist you with the evidentiary hearing, you are in good shape. If, however, you are forced to proceed on your own, there are a few things you are going to need to know.

## Purpose of the Evidentiary Hearing

This isn't rocket science, though it will require a little thought process on your behalf. The purpose of holding an evidentiary hearing is to get evidence and testimony into the appellate record. This is first and foremost the most important part of the proceeding.

The hearing itself is a platform for you to present evidence, exhibits, testimony and all other forms of evidence in support of your request for relief. The state will be opposing your every step with basically the same things they presented at your trial, which provides you a sneak peek at what you will be up against, with some limitations.

Once the hearing is concluded, you may request the court to hear oral argument to establish a verbal record of the facts that will become part of the court's "Findings of Fact" and "Conclusions of Law." This conclusion by the evidentiary court will be weighed highly by the higher reviewing court and will determined the course of action and any relief you may in line for, if any. If the court agrees to allow oral arguments, it will most likely come at the end of the hearing and will only allow each side about 20 minutes to argue their supporting facts. You may not have much time to prepare in the courtroom, so make sure you are prepared *before* you get there. I promise you; the state will be ready.

The hearing is not intended to reweigh the trial evidence or any of the trial testimony. This is not a new trial to determine guilt or innocence, so to speak. The sole purpose of this hearing is for you to prove the ineffectiveness of your trial counsel, where they failed to admit the new evidence and failed to do a certain thing that prejudiced you at your trial. And, you had better be prepared to *prove* it if you claim it. Any issues that you brought on direct appeal are considered "dead" to the court and will not be reconsidered at this hearing. Here you will be able to put your trial attorney on the stand and question them as to their failed efforts and actions at your trial. At times this may get to be very heated. Keep your composure and put the weight onto your trial counsel. This is where the evidence of his ineffectiveness will prevail, if you in fact have it to present.

You will not be allowed to simply stand in the hearing and recite the plethora of case law you have been reading that supports your position. You will have the opportunity to cite all of that later when you prepare your legal submissions or in the submissions you provided prior to having the hearing, if appropriate. At this point, at the hearing, you only have one single mission: *establish the evidence that supports your issues*.

On the other side of the courtroom there will be the prosecutor and the other people they will be calling in opposition. Their primary goal is getting the entire application dismissed, and to uphold the conviction and sentence. Where you fail to prove your issues, state a claim that entitles you to relief, or fail to offer any evidence to the contrary of the state, dismissal is exactly what will happen. You *must* be prepared, because if you were lucky enough to get this hearing in the first place, you will certainly never get another one.

That being said, don't panic just yet. The state only possesses the authority to move for dismissal if they have provided their equitable defense in the answer to your *habeas* application after you filed it. If the judge grants the dismissal, it is an appealable ruling. Again, a motion for dismissal at an evidentiary hearing is a very rare occurrence, because the court wants to rule on the application as soon as possible and without delay.

## Getting to the Hearing

Once you have filed the application for post-conviction relief (*habeas corpus*), and after a couple of weeks have passed without your being given a notice of a hearing date, you can submit a Motion to Set Hearing and Transport Order as a subtle "nudge" to create action from the court. (I have provided a sample of both Motions in the Forms section numbered, F.7 and F.8). Where your case has been sitting inactive, it will compel the court to take action.

At this point, it is quite common for the state to file a motion that requests the entire hearing be done through written affidavits, instead of a live in-court hearing. This is done usually where the state believes that you don't have issues that entitle you to relief. Having an evidentiary hearing through affidavit is not as powerful and persuasive as live in-court testimony and cross-examination. This is why you should immediately file an opposition response to the state's request.

However, if you are a poor public speaker and tend to get nervous, you may be better off handling the hearing through affidavit. If you find the idea more comforting to you, you can file a Motion to Proceed by Affidavit prior to the state requesting it. In this event, I have provided a sample Motion to Proceed by Affidavit in the Forms section, numbered F.9.

Having the evidentiary hearing live in court, nonetheless, is always your best option.

## At the Hearing

This is where you need to shine and show the court that you are not the "monster" they believe you to be. If nothing else, this should be of the utmost importance to you on general practice. In doing so, you should always do the following:

- Address the judge as "Your Honor."

- Stand confidently, without swinging your arms, swaying, fidgeting, or playing with things in front of you.
- Look directly at the judge when you are speaking.
- Speak properly, never use slang or "street talk."
- Always refer to the prosecution as "the state," and never as "her" or "him."

## When Examining Witnesses

Any witnesses provided by either you or the state at the evidentiary hearing will be subject to both direct and cross examination. The Rules of Evidence in your state will determine the rules the judge will enforce in such examinations. Direct examination is where you will call your witnesses to the stand. Cross examination is where the state gets to question those witnesses after you are done. You may not "lead" your witnesses on direct examination, however, you may "lead" them to their answers when you are cross-examining those same witnesses, once the state has had a turn in questioning. This can go back and forth as many times as necessary until there is no more information to be gotten from the witness.

## Improper Questioning

As you are probably aware and remember from your trial, there are two types of objections that are typically related to testimony. Those are in objecting to form and in objecting to substance. Objections that relate to form are those regarding the structure of the question asked. And the objections relating to substance, are those regarding questions that are seeking testimony and are likely inadmissible.

Many questions are inherently improper regardless of the information you are intending to obtain from the witness. Objections to form include but are not limited to:

- Leading (most commonly used)
- Vague (requires more information)
- Argumentative
- Assumes Facts Not In the Evidence
- Misrepresentation
- Asked and Answered
- Irrelevance

Confused? Allow me to provide a few short examples:

1. Argumentative:

Q: "How could you say that you saw me, when you weren't even there?"

This is a common question when examining an alleged co-defendant. Any question that asks someone to admit any alleged guilt or innocence is taken as argumentative.

2. Assumes Facts Not In the Evidence:

Q: "How many times have you killed prior to killing this victim?"

This would require the witness to admit that he had killed others, which was never in the record.

3. Misrepresentation:

Q:     "Officer Bradley, you saw the witness shoot the victim?"

In this situation, the victim was stabbed to death, not shot.

4. Asked and Answered:

Q:     "Let me ask again, you saw the suspect running?"

In this situation, the question was already asked twice.

5. Irrelevance:

Q: "Officer Bradley, were you aware the appellant has a juvenile conviction for shoplifting?"

In this situation, the juvenile shoplifting conviction has nothing to do with the current conviction, or the purposes of the hearing.

The above would be considered objections as to form. Now, let's quickly talk a little bit about objections to substance. Substance objections are best described as:

- Incompetence of the Witness
- Prejudicial
- Hearsay
- Lacking Foundation
- Privileged Information
- Improper Impeachment of Witness
- Nonresponsive Answer
- Lacking good faith

1. *Incompetent Witness* – The two-part test incorporated and used by almost every court in the country consists of (1) sufficiently competent to understand the oath, and (2) the witness is capable of testifying. Any witness must have a firsthand knowledge of the information testifying about, or it will be considered as hearsay and quickly objected to by the state at your hearing.

2. *Prejudicial* – Any testimony that is intended to prejudice the case and interfere with the jury's ability to reach a fair and impartial decision, will be considered as prejudicial. In reality, the sole purpose of admitting any evidence at a hearing or at trial is specifically for the purposes of it obtaining a prejudice towards the opposing party. That's how you win.

That being said, any testimony at your hearing that tends to hit the emotional strings of the jury, should be immediately objected to.

3. *Hearsay* – This is probably the most objected to and confusing issue you will encounter at your hearing. Hearsay is any statement made outside of the courtroom by someone that is offered to prove the matter of something. It should be known that hearsay is normally

inadmissible, with the exception of a few instances. You should familiarize yourself with your State Rules of Evidence prior to your hearing so that you know which hearsay is and is not admissible in your court.

3. *Lacking Foundation* – Almost all evidence is admitted only after preliminary and foundation is established by the court. If the foundation isn't proven, then an objection will prevent it being admitted. This usually enters the scene when trying to enter an exhibit. Before doing so, you must lay a foundation in order to establish its reliability. You do this by asking questions of the witness presenting the exhibit.

Here are a few objections as to a Lack of Foundation:

- The identities are not established as to the conversation
- The conversation or evidence has no relevancy
- The time or place of the conversation are not established

As to telephone conversations, you should object where the voices are not familiar or recognized by the witness. Where photographs and video is concerned, you should object where the witness is not familiar with those items, or they contain inaccuracies, etc.

4. *Privileged Information* – There are laws in every state that make certain items confidential. Under the proper circumstances however, you may be able to establish an objection as to the right to that evidence. There is however certain privileged information that is absolutely protected, such as:

- Attorney-Client Conversations
- Husband-Wife Conversations
- Physician-Patient Information
- Priest-Penitent Conversations
- Contractual Information

A full list of privileged information will exist in your state statute guidelines, as well as you Rules of Evidence.

5. *Improper Impeachment of Witness* – In some states counsel is not allowed to impeach their own witness, which makes sense. However, in other states an attorney can in fact make all efforts to impeach their own client. The purpose of impeaching any witness for the state at your hearing is to prove to the court that the same false testimony at your trial assisted in your being convicted and therefore is prosecutorial misconduct.

6. *Nonresponsive Answer* – Where any witness provides an answer that is not directly related to the question asked, the person asking the question can object as to "nonresponsive." Upon doing so, you must qualify the objection and request the answer be stricken from the record. This is a good technique to mark the record as to the attempt by state witnesses to "hide" evidence.

7. *Lacking Good Faith* – The person asking the questions of the witness must have a good faith reason for doing so. You may not confront an opposing party's witnesses with negative,

hostile, or statements intended to create a false impression. If the prosecutor does this to your witnesses at your hearing, make a very strong objection in order to "mark the record" to show the higher reviewing court of the prosecutorial vindictiveness.

## Conclusion

At this point, I have attempted to adequately describe the evidentiary hearing and to provide you with information that will assist you. The most important thing to remember is to remain calm. The worst has already happened to you. Nothing additional will matter and nothing worse is going to happen: Be strong, be focused, and go do what needs to be done.

*Get your evidence into the record at all costs!*

*Notes:*

# Chapter Fourteen:
# Findings of Facts and Conclusions of Law

After the evidentiary hearing has concluded, the parties will likely be asked to submit findings to the court to consider when making its decision as to whether relief should be granted. This will be your only opportunity to detail exactly the reasoning why you feel you are truly entitled to relief on your post-conviction challenge. This will be in the form of writing.

## Submitting Findings

First, there are several ways in which the court may determine the findings of facts and conclusions of law. The court has the authority to do one of the following:

1. Request the parties to submit their proposed findings along with a brief in support.

2. The court will simply hand down its judgment and request the parties to prepare their findings for signing by the judge.

3. The court will write its own Findings of Fact and Conclusions of Law.

Keep in mind when writing your findings, that you have to write it *as if you are the court*. You must write it as if you are the judge, and you are writing it from *his* view of the evidence.

## Writing the Findings, Facts and Conclusions of Law

Nope, there aren't any forms you can copy. You will actually have to sit down and write it. If you have a copy of your direct appeal brief, you can use that as an outline since the two are purely identical in substance. The good thing is that there are only two things to cover: (1) facts of the issues, and (2) conclusions of law associated with those facts. A typical Proposed Findings of Fact and Conclusion of Law will have the following included:

- Table of Contents
- Table of Authorities
- Procedural History (statement of facts)
- Statement of the Issues
- Findings of Fact
- Opinion
- Conclusions of Law
- Relief
- Certificate of Service

There truly is no "right" way to write it, so don't be too hard on yourself.

## Advice

Keep it short, be focused, and write in order. Forget about the facts that aren't important to your case as to not distract the judge from the facts that are important. Don't be a "drama queen," sounding like the whole world is against you. Even though you are angry, upset, or any other type of way, be professional and respectful.

Keep it under 30 pages or 15,000 words. Simply put, the judge will not read anything even close to that, so why bother writing it?

Attach a Certificate of Service, send the original to the court, and a copy to the prosecutor. You may want to keep a copy for your records as well.

*Notes:*

# Chapter Fifteen:
# State Habeas Corpus in Texas (11.07)

There is simply no way that I could write this book without including a whole chapter dedicated to my fellow Texas prisoners, related to the Texas *Habeas Corpus* process. Of all the questions I am asked daily, they consist mostly of this topic. And so, without further comment, let's get right to it:

*Habeas Corpus* – This remedy is applied for in the convicting court here in Texas. The remedy is neither an independent civil action nor a post-sentencing phase of the original criminal case, as so many choose to believe. Instead, it is a criminal proceeding separate from the case that resulted in the conviction. The remedy is authorized by statute. There is a custody requirement applicable to the remedy. In short, you must be incarcerated or restricted in your movement and freedoms. There is also an avenue where newly discovered evidence of innocence is a ground for relief in Texas post-conviction *habeas corpus* litigation.

## Statute of Limitations

There is a statute of limitations in Texas post-conviction *habeas corpus* proceedings in death sentence cases, but not in noncapital sentences. In a death sentence case, the petition for a writ of *habeas corpus* must be filed in the convicting court no later than the 180th day after the date the convicting court appoints post-conviction counsel, or no later than the 45th day after the date the state's original brief is filed on the direct appeal – whichever date is later. The convicting court, before the applicable filing date, may for good cause and after notice and opportunity to be heard by the attorney representing the state, grant one 90-day extension that begins on the filing date applicable to the petitioner.

## Secondary Post-Conviction Remedies

- Texas has a post-conviction DNA testing statute, enacted in 2001, and amended in 2007.
- Texas has an erroneous convictions act, originally enacted in 1965, and amended twice in 2003.

## The staff at the Court of Criminal Appeals

The staff at the court is divided into three sections:

1. Petitions for Discretionary Review;
2. Capital Appeals and Death Penalty Habeas;
3. Post-Conviction Writs (non-death penalty)

While the staff in the post-conviction writs section works mainly on *habeas* applications filed pursuant to article 11.07, they also have a significant docket consisting of original writs of *habeas corpus*, mandamus, and other writs under common law. The most voluminous of those are of course the mandamus docket, believe it or not.

When fully staffed, the section consists of seven (7) lawyers who include former prosecutors, defense lawyers, and appellate court staff attorneys. The current staff as of 2018 in the writ section has several decades of combined legal experience in the area of criminal law, as is indicated on the court's registry of counsel.

## Numbers

Post-conviction writs compromise the most significant amount of cases ruled on by the Court of Criminal Appeals of Texas. Here are the numbers representing Fiscal Year 2018:

- 11.07, New Filings – 4,009 applications;
- 11.07, Disposed – 3,970 applications;
- 11.07. Back from Remand – 377 applications;
- Cert. Petitions, New Filings – 7 applications;
- Original *Habeas*, New Filings – 80 applications;
- Original *Habeas*, Back from Remand – 1 application;
- Mandamus, New Filings – 503 applications;
- Mandamus, Back from Remand – 113 applications;
- Prohibited, New Filings – 11 applications
- Prohibition, Back from Remand – 0 applications.

As you can see, there is a lot of paper being dealt with. That is why the wait can sometimes be excessive. So have patience.

## 11.07 The Statute

*Habeas corpus* applications in non-capital felony cases fall under Chapter 11 of the Texas Code of Criminal Procedure. Article 11.01 defines the writ as follows:

"The writ of *habeas corpus* is a remedy to be used when any person is restrained in his liberty. It is an order issued by a Court or judge of competent jurisdiction, directed to anyone having a person in his custody, or under his arrest or restraint, commanding him to produce such a person, at a time and place named in the writ, and show why he is held in custody or under restraint."

There are several different kinds of habeas writs provided for in Chapter 11, such as:

- Article 11.071 applications. This section pertains to final felony convictions that resulted in a death sentence.
- Article 11.072 applications. This section pertains to final felony convictions, or misdemeanor cases in which applicants seek relief from a judgment ordering community supervision (probation).

- Article 11.08 applications. This section pertains to applicants who are confined, after indictment, but before trial, on a felony.
- Article 11.09 applications. This section pertains to applicants who are confined on misdemeanor charges.

And the article that is the main subject of most all writs of *habeas corpus* by inmates:

- Article 11.07 applications. This section pertains to applicants who seek relief from a felony judgment imposing a penalty other than death. For those intending to pursue a writ of *habeas corpus*, the most important things to remember are:

*Where to file the application* – Section 3(b) of article 11.07 states that an application must be filed with the clerk of the court in which the conviction being challenged was obtained, and that the clerk shall assign the application to that court. In *Campbell v. State*, 320 S.W.3d 338 (Tex. Crim. App. 2010), the court held that the pleadings of "*pro se*" inmates shall be deemed filed at any time they are delivered to prison authorities for forwarding to the court clerk.

*Time frames and duties* – After the writ has been filed, the clerk is required to forward a copy of the application by certified mail, return receipt requested, or by personal service to the prosecutor, who shall answer the application not later than the 15th day after the date of the copy of the application is received. Matters alleged in the application, but not admitted by the state, are deemed denied.

Within 20 days of the expiration of the time in which the state is allowed to answer, it is the duty of the convicting court to decide if there are controverted, previously unresolved facts, material to the legal justification of the applicant's confinement. If the court decides that no such issues exist, then the clerk is required to immediately forward the application to the Court of Criminal Appeals. Along with the application, the clerk is required to include a copy of any answers filed and a certificate reciting the date on which the trial court's finding is made.

If the convicting court decides there *are* controverted facts, it is required to enter an order designating issues (ODI) setting out the facts to be resolved. It is important to be aware that the newly enacted Rule 73.5 of the Texas Rules of Appellate Procedure now imposes a 180-day deadline for the trial court to resolve the issues designated in its order. And, that any motion for extension of time must be filed with the court *before* the expiration of the 180-day period.

If the convicting court decides there are controverted facts, it is required to enter an order designating issues setting out the facts to be resolved, as I stated previously. In order to resolve the issues, set out in that ODI, the trial court may:

- Order affidavits from the parties;
- Order depositions;
- Order interrogatories;
- Order hearings;
- Order additional forensic testing; and,
- Use its personal recollection of the specific cause in question.

Article 11.07(d) provides that the trial court may also appoint an attorney or magistrate to hold a hearing and make findings of fact. It should be noted that if a hearing is held, it is the duty of the court reporter to prepare a transcript within 15 days of its conclusion.

Additionally, the state shall pay for the cost of any additional DNA or forensic testing ordered by the trial court, unless the applicant is being represented by retained counsel. In that case, the applicant shall bear the costs for additional testing.

## Frequently Asked Questions

*What if your attorney or the prosecutor believes that you should not remain incarcerated while the court deliberates?* – Article 11.65 provides that bond may be granted for certain *habeas* applicants seeking relief from a judgment imposing a penalty other than death. The conditions set out under subsection (b) of the statute is that the proposed findings of fact and conclusions of law, made either by the trial or an appointed attorney or magistrate, must be stipulated to by *both* the applicant and the state. Once that condition is met, the trial court may order release of the applicant on bond, subject to the conditions imposed by the trial court, until the applicant is denied relief, remanded to custody, or ordered released by the court.

*What if I believe that my trial judge should be recused for bias and shouldn't get to consider the application?* – This is a question that was posed to me not long ago, and one that I hear often. Here is my short answer to that question: In *Ex parte Sinegar*, 324 S.W.3d 578 (Tex. Crim. App. 2010), the court held that Texas Rule of Civil Procedure 18(a), regarding the recusal of judges, applies to *habeas* proceedings. Therefore, in these situations, *habeas* counsel should file a motion to recuse. You can also file it *pro se*, if you feel strongly about it. Just be prepared to prove the bias.

*Can I amend my application once I file it?* – Yep, you certainly can. An applicant is not prohibited from amending or supplementing the application even after it is forwarded to the Court of Criminal Appeals from the trial court, as long as the materials are filed in the trial court. As I said in a previous chapter, in *Ex parte Saenz*, 491 S.W.3d 819 (Tex. Crim. App. 2016), the court rejected the state's argument that it should not consider an amended application as part of an initial application that was properly filed under Art. 11.07. The state suggested that the court should consider an amended or a supplemental claim under those circumstances in a separate proceeding. In rejecting the state's arguments, the court held:

"Because the plain language in Article 11.07 permits the very consideration of amended or supplemental claims filed by an applicant, we hold that we may consider Applicant's amended application under these circumstances."

The state followed with the argument that laches barred applicants from filing an amended application, reflecting the typical attitude of a prosecutor. However, the court replied with the following:

"While we recognize the demands that Article 11.07 might place on the State, we decline to hold that the meaning of prejudice is so broad that it will, as a general rule, encompass the type of hardship incurred by the State in responding to amended and supplemental claims in Article 11.07 applications ..."

Chalk one up for the Court of Criminal Appeals!

One thing to remember about amending your application is that it must be done before the Court of Criminal Appeals rules on your application for *habeas* relief.

*What if I want to file additional evidence in my habeas?* – In *Ex parte Pena*, 484 S.W.3d 428 (Tex. Crim. App. 2016), the court sets out the procedure for filing additional evidence relating to a *habeas corpus* application after it has been filed and set for submission by the court, while the application is pending at the court after being forwarded from the county of conviction, and while the application is still pending at the trial court level. The holding in *Pena* was subsequently codified as Rule 73.7 of the Texas Rules of Appellate Procedure. This rule became effective on February 1, 2017.

## 11.07 Main Issues Handled

The following is a general listing of the types of issues that are considered by the Court of Criminal Appeals when analyzing Article 11.07 applications for writ of *habeas corpus*. This list is not meant to be all inclusive. However, the following issues will most likely cover ninety percent of the claims I have been able to uncover, that *pro se* or hired counsel has raised. (See Chapter Seven for the list.)

### Applicant's Burden

The burden is 100% on you, the applicant. Period.

- An applicant must plead and prove facts within which he believes entitles him to relief, and he must prove his claim by a preponderance of the evidence; see *Ex parte Rains*, 555 S.W.2d 478 (Tex. Crim. App. 1976).

- An applicant must show, or at least allege, the detailed facts that give rise to, and compel each legal conclusion that entitles him to relief; see *Ex parte Hogan*, 556 S.W.2d 352 (Tex. Crim. App. 1977).

- Texas courts have confined the scope of post-conviction writs of *habeas corpus* to jurisdictional or fundamental defects and constitutional claims. Violations of statutes, rules, and other non-constitutional doctrines are not recognized; see *Ex parte Graves*, 70 S.W.3d 103 (Tex. Crim. App. 2002).

- The Court has recognized that delay on the applicant's part will affect his credibility; see *Ex parte Young*, 479 S.W.2d 45 (Tex. Crim. App. 1972).

## What if the State Claims Laches?

Claiming laches is an old trick often argued by the state in response to an application for writ of *habeas corpus* in Texas. I've discovered it in numerous cases I've reviewed for other inmates. Here's the deal:

The Court of Criminal Appeals initially held that the state must make a particular showing of prejudice in its ability to respond to the claims that are caused by applicant's unreasonable delay in filing the writ. But delay alone does not demonstrate such particularized prejudice, see *Ex parte Carrio*, 992 S.W.2d 486 (Tex. Crim. App. 1999). However, in a subsequent opinion, the court reversed its decision in *Carrio* and expanded the definition of prejudice under the existing laches standard to incorporate all forma of prejudice so that a court may consider the totality of the circumstances in deciding whether to hold an applicant barred by laches, as in *Ex parte Perez*, 398 S.W.3d 206 (Tex. Crim. App. 2013). The court does however have the authority to consider laches *sua sponte* (on its own), and whether it should bar an applicant's claim.

## Forfeiture Provisions

You must be very careful not to raise claims in your *habeas* application that the court may find to be frivolous. The provisions of Government Code § 498.0045, allow for the forfeiture of good time credit if an order is entered by the court dismissing a *habeas* application as frivolous. Section 498.0045 states:

"(a) In this section, "final order" means a certified copy of a final order of a state or federal courts that dismisses as frivolous or malicious a lawsuit, including a proceeding arising from an application for a writ of *habeas corpus*, brought by an inmate who is in custody in a prison, or jail, or awaiting transfer to either."

Of course, those of us who are G3, have no give-a-damn about good time.

## Petitions for Writ of Certiorari

The authority of the court to grant and issue original writs of *certiorari* is set out in the Texas Constitution Article 5, § 5(c). This authority is also set out in article 4.04(1) of the Code of Criminal Procedure.

An original petition for a writ of *certiorari* is another available avenue for relief at the court. The writ is issued in order that the court may inspect the proceedings of a lower court and determine whether any irregularities occurred during a proceeding. But its usefulness is very limited. In any case where direct appeal is an option, a writ of *certiorari* shall not be issued; see *Ex parte Brand*, 822 S.W.2d 636 (Tex. Crim. App. 1992).

So, all of you that waived your right to a direct appeal in a plea agreement, you have a way back in! (You are welcome for the information.)

## Motions for Rehearing

The Texas Rules of Appellate Procedure (TRAP) have two pertinent sections relating to motions for rehearing:

1. Rule 79.2(d) pertains to writs filed under art. 11.07 or art. 11.071, of the Code of Criminal Procedure. It states: "A motion for rehearing an order that denies *habeas corpus* relief or dismisses a habeas corpus application under Code of Criminal Procedure, articles 11.07 or 11.071 may not be filed."

2. Rule 72.2 pertains to extraordinary matters such as mandamus petitions, original habeas petitions, etc. This rule states: "If the motion for leave to file is denied, no motion for rehearing or reconsideration will be entertained."

The Texas Rules of Appellate Procedure (TRAP) rules make it clear that motions for rehearing or reconsideration are not allowed and will not be entertained. However, the TRAP rules *do* provide the court the authority to reconsider its rulings denying relief or dismissing a *habeas corpus* application, *sua sponte* (on its own).

## Motions to Dismiss

You can request a late-stage dismissal of your application without prejudice if you show good cause, including an explanation about your reasons for believing why another course of action, such as amending or supplementing the application, would be inadequate; see *Ex parte Speckman*, 2017 Tex. Crim. App. LEXIS 889 (Tex. Crim. App.3September 20, 2017).

## Top Secret Information

I've elected to bury this bit of information deep inside of this chapter, so that only those willing to dig for it should obtain it. Ready?

For those of you who may not be entitled to *habeas corpus* relief under Art. 11.07, you can obtain similar relief by pursing a Constitutional Writ under Texas Constitution Art. V § 8; see *In re Torres*, 476 S.W.2d 883 (Tex. civ. App.-El Paso, 1972, no writ). (Again, you are welcome.)

# Conclusion

The 11.07 writ of *habeas corpus*, though extremely difficult to obtain relief on, is well worth the attempt. But you shouldn't wait years to file one, because the longer you wait, the more guilty you look to the courts. I know that sounds crazy, but it's very true.

Also, be very apprehensive about filing subsequent (additional) *habeas* applications. Being allowed to submit a successive application for *habeas corpus* relief in Texas is extremely rare, as it is any other state. You will never be allowed to submit issues that should have been raised in your first application, and the courts will quickly catch you trying.

Your best chance of relief is when there is compelling, newly found evidence supporting a successive application for *habeas* relief, discovered after you filed your first application for habeas relief, that will then support a claim of actual innocence. To obtain a definition of what the courts consider "actual innocence," you should read *Ex parte Navarijo*, 433 S.W.3d 558, 567 (Tex. Crim. App. 2014); *Ex parte Elizondo*, 947 S.W. 2d 202, 206 (Tex. Crim. App. 1996); and *Ex parte Holloway*, 413 S.W.3d 95, 97 (Tex. Cim. App. 2013). Additionally, before you can file a successive post-conviction *habeas corpus* application in Texas, you must first have requested permission from the court to do so. If you just go ahead and file it because you "feel like it" the application will be either refused or denied without a written order. You have a high chance of a second or successive application being accepted where you followed the rules and requested permission to file it.

In situations where the courts are skeptical about allowing successive applications, let me give you the "secret" to getting them to allow it. You need to claim one of the following:

1. *Newly Discovered Evidence* – This is the sure fire fastest way to be allowed a successive *habeas corpus* application in any state, especially in Texas.
   - A DNA Test
   - Recanted Testimony
   - Changes in the Law that are Retroactive
   - Change in Scientific Methods

2. *Mental or Physical Incapacitation* – If you were mentally or physically incapacitated during the time you submitted your first application for *habeas* relief, and you can prove you were on psychiatric medications, pain medications, had surgery or any type of other physical disability, most every court will allow you to file a successive writ or application. But, be prepared to prove it.

Claims of actual innocence have also been known to be allowed as successive § 2254 federal *habeas corpus* applications. See the following federal cases in support:

- *House v. Bell*, 547 U.S. 518 (2006)
- *Gomez v. Jaimet*, 350 F.3d 673 (7th Cir. 2003)
- *U.S. V. McDonald*, 641 F.3d 596 (4th Cir. 2011)
- *Rivas v. Fisher*, 687 F.3d 514 (2nd Cir. 2011)

If and when a court approves a successive writ of *habeas corpus*, it must hold a hearing. It cannot be submitted by affidavit, nor can summary judgment be used.

## COURT OF CRIMINAL APPEALS OF TEXAS
## APPLICATION FOR A WRIT OF HABEAS CORPUS
## SEEKING RELIEF FROM FINAL FELONY CONVICTION
## UNDER CODE OF CRIMINAL PROCEDURE, ARTICLE 11.07

### DEFINITIONS

In this application form:

1. "Applicant" means a person seeking relief in an application for a writ of habeas corpus from his or her felony conviction imposing a sentence other than the death penalty or a probated sentence that has not been revoked. An applicant can be an inmate or a non-inmate whose liberty is restrained.

2. "Inmate" means a person who is in custody in a prison or jail.

3. "Petitioner" means a person, **including an attorney or a non-attorney**, presenting an application for a writ of habeas corpus on behalf of another person (the applicant). Any petitioner may present an application on behalf of an applicant for the purpose of obtaining relief from the applicant's felony conviction. However, the petitioner presenting the application form must sign and attest that he or she has consulted with the applicant concerning the application and the applicant has given consent to the filing of this application form.

### INSTRUCTIONS

1. **All applicants and petitioners, including attorneys, must use the complete application form**. You must use this application form, which begins on the page following these instructions, to file an application, or an amended or supplemental application, for a writ of habeas corpus seeking relief **from a final felony conviction under Article 11.07 of the Code of Criminal Procedure**. (This application form is not for death-penalty cases, probated sentences which have not been revoked, misdemeanors, or pretrial habeas applications under Article 11.08 of the Code of Criminal Procedure.)

2. **Failure to follow these instructions may cause your entire application to be dismissed.**

3. The district clerk of the county in which you were convicted will make this application form available to you, on request, without charge. The form can also be obtained from the Court of Criminal Appeals' website.

4. You must **file** the entire application form, including those sections that do not apply to you. If any pages are missing from the form, or if the questions have been renumbered or omitted, your entire application may be dismissed as non-compliant.

5. You must make a separate application on a separate form for each case number from which you seek relief. Even if the judgments were entered in the same court on the same day, you must complete a separate application form for each case number. If a case number has multiple counts, include all the counts on one application form.

6.      You **must** include all grounds for relief on the application form as provided by the instructions under item 18. You **must** also briefly summarize the facts of your ground on the application form as provided by the instructions under item 18. Each ground shall begin on a new page, and the recitation of the facts supporting the ground shall be no longer than the two pages provided for the ground in the form.

7.      Answer every item that applies to you on the application form. Do not attach any additional pages for any ground. However, if you have more than five grounds for relief, you may include additional copies of pages 14 and 15 to add more grounds for relief. Additional grounds must still comply with instruction 6.

8.      Legal citations and arguments may be made in a separate memorandum that complies with Texas Rule of Appellate Procedure 73 and certifies that the document does not exceed 15,000 words if computer-generated or 50 pages if not.

9.      You must verify the application form by signing either the appropriate Unsworn Declaration or the "Oath Before a Notary Public," which are at the end of this form. If you are a petitioner presenting the application on behalf of an applicant, you may sign and verify the application form on behalf of the applicant. **However, any petitioner who signs and verifies the application form may be prosecuted and convicted for aggravated perjury if the application form contains any false statement of a material fact.**

10.     When the application form is fully completed, mail the original and any exhibits and memorandum of law to the district clerk of the county of conviction or electronically file the application form with the district clerk of the county of conviction following the current electronic filing rules for criminal cases. Keep a copy of the application form for your records.

11.     You must notify the district clerk of the county of conviction of any change in your address or email address after you have filed your application form. In addition, after the application form has been received by the Court of Criminal Appeals, you must notify the Clerk of the Court of Criminal Appeals of any change in your address or email address.

12.     **Warning: If the application form does not include all of the grounds for relief, additional grounds brought at a later date may be procedurally barred.** *See* TEX. CODE CRIM. PROC. Art. 11.07 § 4.

**Case No.** _____
(The district clerk of the county of conviction will fill in this blank.)

# IN THE COURT OF CRIMINAL APPEALS OF TEXAS
## APPLICATION FOR A WRIT OF HABEAS CORPUS
## SEEKING RELIEF FROM FINAL FELONY CONVICTION
## UNDER CODE OF CRIMINAL PROCEDURE, ARTICLE 11.07

**NAME:** _____

**DATE OF BIRTH:** _____

**PLACE OF CONFINEMENT:** _____

**WARDEN:** _____

**TDCJ-CID NUMBER:** _____ **SID NUMBER:** _____

**(1)** **This application concerns** (check all that apply):

☐  **a conviction**  ☐  **parole**

☐  **a sentence**  ☐  **mandatory supervision**

☐  **time credit**  ☐  **out-of-time appeal or petition for discretionary review**

**(2)** **What are the court number and county of the district court in which you were convicted?**

_____

**(3)** **What was the case number in the trial court?** (Put only one case number here, even if it includes multiple counts. You must make a separate application on a separate form for other case numbers.)

_____

**(4)** **What was the name of the trial judge?**

_____

(5)    Were you represented by counsel?  If yes, provide the attorney's name:

_____

(6)    What was the date that the judgment was entered?

_____

(7)    For what offense were you convicted and what was the sentence?

_____

(8)    If you were sentenced on more than one count of an indictment in the same court at the same time, what counts were you convicted of and what was the sentence in each count?

_____

_____

(9)    What was the plea you entered? (Check one.)

☐ guilty-open plea          ☐ guilty-plea bargain
☐ not guilty               ☐ *nolo contendere*/no contest

If you entered different pleas to counts in a multi-count indictment, please explain:

_____

_____

(10)   What kind of trial did you have?

☐ no jury                  ☐ jury for guilt and punishment
                           ☐ jury for guilt, judge for punishment

(11)    Did you testify at trial?  If yes, at what phase of the trial did you testify?

_____

(12)    Has your sentence discharged?  ☐ yes    ☐ no

If you answered yes, when did your sentence discharge?  _____

(13)    Did you appeal from the judgment of conviction?

☐ yes                            ☐ no

If you did appeal, answer the following questions:

(A)  Which court of appeals decided the appeal? _____

(B)  What was the case number?  _____

(C)  Were you represented by counsel on appeal? If yes, provide the attorney's
     name: _____

(D)  What was the decision and the date of the decision?_____

_____

(14)    Did you file a petition for discretionary review in the Court of Criminal Appeals?

☐ yes                            ☐ no

If you did file a petition for discretionary review, answer the following questions:

(A)  What was the case number? _____

(B)  What was the decision and the date of the decision? _____

_____

(15)    Have you previously filed an application for a writ of habeas corpus under Article
        11.07 of the Texas Code of Criminal Procedure challenging *the conviction in this
        case number*?

☐ yes                            ☐ no

If you answered yes, answer the following questions:

(A)  What was the Court of Criminal Appeals' writ number? _____

(B)  What was the decision and the date of the decision? _____

_____

(C)  Please briefly explain why the current grounds were not presented and could
     not have been presented in your previous application.

_____

_____

_____

_____

(16)  Do you currently have any petition or appeal pending in any other state or federal
      court?

☐ yes                          ☐ no

If you answered yes, please provide the name of the court and the case number:

_____

(17)  If you are presenting a time credit claim, other than for pre-sentence jail time
      credit, have you exhausted your administrative remedies by presenting the time
      credit claim to the time credit resolution system of the Texas Department of
      Criminal Justice? (This requirement applies to any final felony conviction, including
      state jail felonies.)

☐ yes                          ☐ no

If you answered yes, answer the following questions:

(A)  What date did you present the claim to the time credit resolution system?

_____

(B)  Did you receive a decision and, if yes, what was the date of the decision? _____

_____

If you answered no, please explain why you have not presented your time credit claim to the time credit resolution system of the Texas Department of Criminal Justice:

_____

_____

_____

_____

(18)   Beginning on page 6, state concisely every legal ground for why you think that you are being illegally confined or restrained and then briefly summarize the facts supporting each ground. You must present each ground and a brief summary of the facts on the application form. **If your grounds and a brief summary of the facts have not been presented on the application form, the Court will not consider your grounds. A factual summary that merely references an attached memorandum or another ground for relief will not constitute a sufficient summary of the facts.**

If you have more than four grounds, use pages 14 and 15 of the application form, which you may copy as many times as needed to give you a separate page for each ground, with each ground numbered in sequence. The recitation of the facts supporting each ground must be no longer than the two pages provided for the ground in the form.

You may include with the application form a memorandum of law if you want to present legal authorities or provide greater factual detail, but the Court will *not* consider grounds for relief set out in a memorandum of law that were not raised on the application form. The memorandum of law must comply with Texas Rule of Appellate Procedure 73 and must not exceed 15,000 words if computer-generated or 50 pages if not. If you are challenging the validity of your conviction, please include a summary of the facts pertaining to your offense and trial in your memorandum of law.

**If the application form does not include all of the grounds for relief, additional grounds brought at a later date may be procedurally barred.**

**GROUND ONE:**

_____

_____

**FACTS SUPPORTING GROUND ONE:**

_____

_____

_____

_____

_____

_____

_____

_____

_____

_____

_____

_____

_____

_____

_____

_____

_____

_____

_____

_____

_____

_____

_____

_____

_____

**GROUND TWO:**

_____

_____

**FACTS SUPPORTING GROUND TWO:**

_____

_____

_____

_____

_____

_____

_____

_____

_____

_____

_____

_____

_____

_____

_____

_____

_____

_____

_____

_____

_____

_____

_____

_____

**GROUND THREE:**

_____

_____

**FACTS SUPPORTING GROUND THREE:**

_____

_____

_____

_____

_____

_____

_____

_____

_____

_____

_____

_____

_____

_____

_____

_____

_____

_____

_____

_____

_____

_____

_____

_____

**GROUND FOUR:**

_____

_____

**FACTS SUPPORTING GROUND FOUR:**

_____

_____

_____

_____

_____

_____

_____

_____

_____

_____

_____

_____

_____

_____

_____

_____

_____

_____

_____

_____

_____

_____

_____

_____

_____

**GROUND _____ :**

_____

_____

**FACTS SUPPORTING GROUND:**

_____

_____

_____

_____

_____

_____

_____

_____

_____

_____

_____

_____

_____

_____

_____

_____

_____

_____

_____

_____

_____

_____

_____

_____

_____

_____

_____

_____

**WHEREFORE, I PRAY THAT THE COURT GRANT THE RELIEF TO WHICH APPLICANT MAY BE ENTITLED IN THIS PROCEEDING.**

## VERIFICATION

**This application form *must be verified* in one of the following ways by either an applicant or a petitioner or it may be dismissed for noncompliance.**

*Applicants*

In order to verify this application form, an applicant must sign one of the following:

(1) the "Unsworn Declaration" for inmates (page 16) if applicant is an inmate; or
(2) the "Unsworn Declaration" for non-inmates (page 17) if applicant is not an inmate; or
(3) the "Oath Before a Notary Public" before a notary public (page 18).

*Petitioners*

If a petitioner, including an attorney, presents an application form on behalf of an applicant, the petitioner may verify the application form for the applicant. In order to verify this application form, a petitioner must sign one of the following:

(1) the "Unsworn Declaration" for inmates (page 16) if petitioner is an inmate; or
(2) the "Unsworn Declaration" for non-inmates (page 17) if petitioner is not an inmate; or
(3) the "Oath Before a Notary Public" before a notary public (page 18).

In addition, *all petitioners*, including attorneys, presenting an application on behalf of an applicant must complete "Petitioner's Information" and sign "Petitioner's Statement" (page 19).

## UNSWORN DECLARATION (INMATE)

My name is (First)_____ (Middle)_____ (Last)_____,

my date of birth is _____, and my inmate identifying number, if any, is _____.

I am presently incarcerated in (Corrections unit name)_____ in

(City) _____, (County)_____, (State) _____,

(Zip Code)_____.

I declare under penalty of perjury that the contents of this application for a writ of habeas corpus

and the facts stated in the application form are true and correct.

Executed on the _____ day of (Month)_____ (Year)_____.

Signature of Declarant _____

*Article 11.07 Writ Application Form*       16       *Revised 2018*

## UNSWORN DECLARATION (NON-INMATE)

My name is (First) _____ (Middle) _____ (Last)_____,

my date of birth is _____, and my address is (Street)_____

_____, (City)_____ ,

(State)_____, (Zip Code)_____, and (Country)_____.

I declare under penalty of perjury that the contents of this application for a writ of habeas corpus

and the facts stated in the application form are true and correct.

Executed in _____County, State of _____, on the

_____day of (Month)_____ (Year)_____.

Signature of Declarant_____

Raymond E. Lumsden

## OATH BEFORE A NOTARY PUBLIC

STATE OF TEXAS

COUNTY OF _____

_____, being duly sworn, under oath says: "I am the applicant or petitioner in this action and know the contents of this application for a writ of habeas corpus and, according to my belief, the facts stated in the application form are true."

_____
Signature of Declarant

SUBSCRIBED AND SWORN TO BEFORE ME THIS _____ DAY OF _____, 20_____.

_____
Signature of Notary Public

## PETITIONER'S INFORMATION

*(Contact information for a petitioner presenting this application on behalf of the applicant)*

Petitioner's printed name: _____

State bar number, if applicable: _____

Address: _____

_____

_____

Telephone: _____

Fax: _____

Email Address: _____

## PETITIONER'S STATEMENT

"I am signing and presenting this application form on behalf of the applicant for the purpose of obtaining relief from the applicant's felony conviction. I have consulted with the applicant concerning this application and the applicant has given consent to the filing of this application form."

_____
Signature of Petitioner

Signed on _____, 20_____.

*Notes:*

# Chapter Sixteen:
# United States Supreme Court Writ of Certiorari

At some point, either after your direct appeal has failed or after your federal § 2254 *habeas* application, you will want to consider filing a writ of *certiorari* to the U.S. Supreme Court.

My advice is to do so immediately after your Petition for Discretionary Relief (PDR) is denied, in order to stop the "clock" on the AEDPA rules for time to file your federal *habeas* § 2254. This will also provide you with more time to prepare for your writ of *habeas corpus* in your state court. On average it could buy you another 4-6 months.

The U.S. Supreme Court may grant you *certiorari*, which means that they have decided to "hear" your case, not that they are awarding relief. Not at this point, anyway. The United States Supreme Court is very limited in the cases they choose each year. In fact, since they are only in their Session six months out of the year, they only rule on 100 cases in that time. That amounts to 100 out of over 100,000 they receive in that time frame. Your best chance of success is to cite that your issues are those that affect "society" and require the court's decision on the issue.

## When to File

Per the Supreme Court Rule # 13, you must file your writ within (90) days of the final decision rendered by the state court. If you are then denied your Petition for Discretionary Relief (PDR), or a Petition for Rehearing, the clock starts.

## Where to obtain the Writ Petition

You may request a copy of the *Guide for Prospective Indigent Petitioners for Writ of Certiorari*, by writing directly to the Supreme Court at:

- Office of the Clerk
  United States Supreme Court
  One First Street N.E.
  Washington, D.C. 20543

This guide is an easy-to-follow, bound application booklet that most anyone can handle. Your prison law library should also have a copy, which is likely outdated. I suggest you obtain your own from the Supreme Court.

Included in the guide are the following:

- Petition for Writ of *Certiorari*

- Motion for Leave to Proceed in *Forma Pauperis*
- Affidavit in Support

The guide will also provide you with the Supreme Court Rules. As I said, it's a pretty easy form and will give you all the information you need to complete the process. Just follow the steps and include what it requests as applicable to your case. In order to conserve space, I have elected to not supply an example of a writ of *certiorari* that was filed in the Supreme Court. If you would like to review one that relates to your specific facts, your law library will be able to assist you in finding one.

*Notes:*

# Chapter Seventeen:
# Federal Writ of Habeas Corpus § 2254

After you have completed all of your state appeals and post-conviction processes, and you are not time-barred by the AEDPA one-year time limit, you are then ready to file your federal writ of *habeas corpus* § 2254. There are only two grounds for relief available to you:

1. The state's decision was "objectively unreasonable," and
2. The state's decision was "contrary to clearly established federal law, as cited in a U.S. Supreme Court ruling."

Essentially, what you need to prove in order to be granted relief is that your state court ruling was directly in contradiction to the ruling of the United States Supreme Court or that the state court ruling was such that no rational person would agree with the decision.

## Constitutional Issues

You should always begin your federal writ by addressing the violations of the U.S. Constitution that you raised in your state post-conviction application (*habeas corpus*). If you failed to raise any constitutional issues in your state post-conviction application, you effectively waived the right to raise them on the federal application. Violations of your state constitution are of little value at this stage of the process and will be quickly dismissed by the federal courts. The same holds true for claims of state statute violations.

## Exhaustion Requirement

If you have not presented your issues to the state court for their review, you are procedurally barred from raising them at the federal level. The federal courts simply cannot and will not, review a petition for a writ of *habeas corpus* related to questions of federal law, that have not been presented to the state court first. No exceptions; see *Williams v. Taylor*, 529 U.S. 362, 405, 120 S.Ct. 1495, 146 L.Ed.2d 389 (2000).

## Standards

In order to be granted relief by the federal courts, you must make a showing that the ruling of the state court was "totally beyond reason," and not simply "wrong;" see *Holland v. Jackson*, 542 U.S. 649, 652, 125 S.Ct. 2736, 159 L.Ed.2d 683 (2004).

The "abuse of discretion" standard applies to the United States District Court's finding of facts, as in *Holland*.

## AEDPA Restrictions

Thank you, Bill Clinton, for this wonderfully oppressive, unfair, and unjust means to stifle the poor and vulnerable. It looks like this:

Under the AEDPA (Antiterrorism and Effective Death Penalty Act of 1996) a prisoner in state custody has only a one-year timeframe to petition the United States District Court for a writ of *habeas corpus* § 2254.

Under § 2244(d)(1)(A), the time limit begins to run when the U.S. Supreme Court affirms the conviction, denies a petition for writ of *certiorari*, or when the time for filing a *certiorari* petition expires; see *Clay v. United* States, 537 U.S. 522, 527,123 S.Ct., 1072, 155 L.Ed.2d 88 (2003). If a petitioner chooses not to file a writ of *certiorari* in the United States Supreme Court, he is entitled to add that 90 day period in which he could have filed the petition to determine the final judgment date under § 2244 (d) (1 ) (A).

### Challenging the AEDPA (Equitable Tolling)

Equitable tolling claims related to a § 2254 petition are reviewed in *Holland v. Florida*, 130 S.Ct. 2549, 2562, 177 L.Ed. 2d 130 (2010).

## Denial of Certificate of Appealability (COA)

When a U.S. District Court denies your COA, you cannot usually then proceed to the Court of Appeals Circuit in your jurisdiction. You can do a review of cases related to a denial of a COA at the following:

- *Barefoot v. Estelle*,463 U.S. 880, 893 (1983) (First due to the importance of it)
- *Miller-el v. Cockrell*, 527 U.S. 322, 336 (2003)
- *Lindh v. Murphy*, 521 U.S. 320 (1997)

## 5th Circuit Court Cases

The following are a few important cases from the 5th Circuit, for my fellow Texas inmates to use in preparing their federal §2254 petition. For cases in your own state's respective Circuit Court of Appeals, I suggest you obtain a book specifically dedicated to those cases, such as the book I specified earlier: *The Habeas Citebook*, By Brandon Sample.

- *Thomas v. Thaler*, 2011 U.S. Dist. LEXIS 153658 (W.D. Tex. 2011)
  Multiple claims of ineffective assistance of counsel

- *Banks v. Warden*, 2011 U.S. Dist. LEXIS 124595 (W.D. La. 2011)
  Multiple claims, writ granted for *pro se* inmate

- *Kimble v. Cain*, 2010 U.S. Dist. LEXIS 73353 (W.D. La. 2010)
  Confrontation clause violation, writ granted

- *Bridges v. Thaler*, 2010 U.S. Dist. LEXIS 10523 (N.D. Tex. 2010) Multiple ineffective assistance of counsel claims, writ granted

- *Brooks v. Kelly*, 579 F.3d 521 (5th Cir. 2009)
  Ineffective appellate counsel, writ granted

- *Garcia v. Dretke*, 2005 U.S. Dist. LEXIS 2168 (W.D. Tex. 2005)
  Numerous issues raised, writ granted

- *Martin v. Maxey*, 98 F.3d 844, 848 (5th Cir. 1996)

- *Woodeard v. Collins*, 898 F.2d 1027, 1029 (5th Cir. 1990)

*Notes:*

Raymond E. Lumsden

# Petition for Relief From a Conviction or Sentence
# By a Person in State Custody

### (Petition Under 28 U.S.C. § 2254 for a Writ of Habeas Corpus)

### Instructions

1.     To use this form, you must be a person who is currently serving a sentence under a judgment against you in a state court. You are asking for relief from the conviction or the sentence. This form is your petition for relief.

2.     You may also use this form to challenge a state judgment that imposed a sentence to be served in the future, but you must fill in the name of the state where the judgment was entered. If you want to challenge a federal judgment that imposed a sentence to be served in the future, you should file a motion under 28 U.S.C. § 2255 in the federal court that entered the judgment.

3.     Make sure the form is typed or neatly written.

4.     You must tell the truth and sign the form. If you make a false statement of a material fact, you may be prosecuted for perjury.

5.     Answer all the questions. You do not need to cite law. You may submit additional pages if necessary. If you do not fill out the form properly, you will be asked to submit additional or correct information. If you want to submit any legal arguments, you must submit them in a separate memorandum. Be aware that any such memorandum may be subject to page limits set forth in the local rules of the court where you file this petition.

6.     You must pay a fee of $5. If the fee is paid, your petition will be filed. If you cannot pay the fee, you may ask to proceed in forma pauperis (as a poor person). To do that, you must fill out the last page of this form. Also, you must submit a certificate signed by an officer at the institution where you are confined showing the amount of money that the institution is holding for you. If your account exceeds $         , you must pay the filing fee.

7.     In this petition, you may challenge the judgment entered by only one court. If you want to challenge a judgment entered by a different court (either in the same state or in different states), you must file a separate petition.

8.     When you have completed the form, send the original and       copies to the Clerk of the United States District Court at this address:

**Clerk, United States District Court for**
**Address**
**City, State  Zip Code**

If you want a file-stamped copy of the petition, you must enclose an additional copy of the petition and ask the court to file-stamp it and return it to you.

9.     **CAUTION: You must include in this petition all the grounds for relief from the conviction or sentence that you challenge. And you must state the facts that support each ground. If you fail to set forth all the grounds in this petition, you may be barred from presenting additional grounds at a later date.**

10.     **CAPITAL CASES: If you are under a sentence of death, you are entitled to the assistance of counsel and should request the appointment of counsel.**

AO 241 (Rev. 09/17)

**PETITION UNDER 28 U.S.C. § 2254 FOR WRIT OF**
**HABEAS CORPUS BY A PERSON IN STATE CUSTODY**

| **United States District Court** | District: |
|---|---|

| Name (under which you were convicted): | Docket or Case No.: |
|---|---|

| Place of Confinement : | Prisoner No.: |
|---|---|

| Petitioner (include the name under which you were convicted) | Respondent (authorized person having custody of petitioner) |
|---|---|
| v. | |

| The Attorney General of the State of: |
|---|

**PETITION**

1.    (a) Name and location of court that entered the judgment of conviction you are challenging:

 

      (b) Criminal docket or case number (if you know):

2.    (a) Date of the judgment of conviction (if you know):

      (b) Date of sentencing:

3.    Length of sentence:

4.    In this case, were you convicted on more than one count or of more than one crime?    ❐ Yes    ❐ No

5.    Identify all crimes of which you were convicted and sentenced in this case:

 

6.    (a) What was your plea? (Check one)

          ❐ (1)    Not guilty        ❐ (3)    Nolo contendere (no contest)

          ❐ (2)    Guilty            ❐ (4)    Insanity plea

AO 241 (Rev. 09/17)

(b) If you entered a guilty plea to one count or charge and a not guilty plea to another count or charge, what did you plead guilty to and what did you plead not guilty to?

(c) If you went to trial, what kind of trial did you have? (Check one)

       ❒ Jury     ❒ Judge only

7.    Did you testify at a pretrial hearing, trial, or a post-trial hearing?

       ❒ Yes     ❒ No

8.    Did you appeal from the judgment of conviction?

       ❒ Yes     ❒ No

9.    If you did appeal, answer the following:

(a) Name of court:

(b) Docket or case number (if you know):

(c) Result:

(d) Date of result (if you know):

(e) Citation to the case (if you know):

(f) Grounds raised:

(g) Did you seek further review by a higher state court?    ❒ Yes    ❒ No

    If yes, answer the following:

    (1) Name of court:

    (2) Docket or case number (if you know):

    (3) Result:

(4) Date of result (if you know):

(5) Citation to the case (if you know):

(6) Grounds raised:

(h) Did you file a petition for certiorari in the United States Supreme Court?     ❐ Yes     ❐ No

If yes, answer the following:

(1) Docket or case number (if you know):

(2) Result:

(3) Date of result (if you know):

(4) Citation to the case (if you know):

10.   Other than the direct appeals listed above, have you previously filed any other petitions, applications, or motions

concerning this judgment of conviction in any state court?     ❐ Yes     ❐ No

11.   If your answer to Question 10 was "Yes," give the following information:

(a)     (1) Name of court:

(2) Docket or case number (if you know):

(3) Date of filing (if you know):

(4) Nature of the proceeding:

(5) Grounds raised:

(6) Did you receive a hearing where evidence was given on your petition, application, or motion?

❐ Yes     ❐ No

(7) Result:

(8) Date of result (if you know):

(b) If you filed any second petition, application, or motion, give the same information:

    (1) Name of court:

    (2) Docket or case number (if you know):

    (3) Date of filing (if you know):

    (4) Nature of the proceeding:

    (5) Grounds raised:

    (6) Did you receive a hearing where evidence was given on your petition, application, or motion?

    ❏ Yes    ❏ No

    (7) Result:

    (8) Date of result (if you know):

(c) If you filed any third petition, application, or motion, give the same information:

    (1) Name of court:

    (2) Docket or case number (if you know):

    (3) Date of filing (if you know):

    (4) Nature of the proceeding:

    (5) Grounds raised:

AO 241 (Rev. 09/17)

(6) Did you receive a hearing where evidence was given on your petition, application, or motion?

❒ Yes ❒ No

(7) Result:

(8) Date of result (if you know):

(d) Did you appeal to the highest state court having jurisdiction over the action taken on your petition, application, or motion?

(1) First petition: ❒ Yes ❒ No

(2) Second petition: ❒ Yes ❒ No

(3) Third petition: ❒ Yes ❒ No

(e) If you did not appeal to the highest state court having jurisdiction, explain why you did not:

12. For this petition, state every ground on which you claim that you are being held in violation of the Constitution, laws, or treaties of the United States. Attach additional pages if you have more than four grounds. State the facts supporting each ground. Any legal arguments must be submitted in a separate memorandum.

**CAUTION: To proceed in the federal court, you must ordinarily first exhaust (use up) your available state-court remedies on each ground on which you request action by the federal court. Also, if you fail to set forth all the grounds in this petition, you may be barred from presenting additional grounds at a later date.**

**GROUND ONE:**

(a) Supporting facts (Do not argue or cite law. Just state the specific facts that support your claim.):

(b) If you did not exhaust your state remedies on Ground One, explain why:

AO 241 (Rev. 09/17)

(c)     **Direct Appeal of Ground One:**

(1) If you appealed from the judgment of conviction, did you raise this issue?     ❏  Yes     ❏  No

(2) If you did not raise this issue in your direct appeal, explain why:

(d) **Post-Conviction Proceedings:**

(1) Did you raise this issue through a post-conviction motion or petition for habeas corpus in a state trial court?

❏  Yes     ❏  No

(2) If your answer to Question (d)(1) is "Yes," state:

Type of motion or petition:

Name and location of the court where the motion or petition was filed:

Docket or case number (if you know):

Date of the court's decision:

Result (attach a copy of the court's opinion or order, if available):

(3) Did you receive a hearing on your motion or petition?     ❏  Yes     ❏  No

(4) Did you appeal from the denial of your motion or petition?     ❏  Yes     ❏  No

(5) If your answer to Question (d)(4) is "Yes," did you raise this issue in the appeal?     ❏  Yes     ❏  No

(6) If your answer to Question (d)(4) is "Yes," state:

Name and location of the court where the appeal was filed:

Docket or case number (if you know):

Date of the court's decision:

Result (attach a copy of the court's opinion or order, if available):

(7) If your answer to Question (d)(4) or Question (d)(5) is "No," explain why you did not raise this issue:

154

AO 241 (Rev. 09/17)

(e) **Other Remedies:** Describe any other procedures (such as habeas corpus, administrative remedies, etc.) that you have used to exhaust your state remedies on Ground One: _____

**GROUND TWO:** _____

(a) Supporting facts (Do not argue or cite law. Just state the specific facts that support your claim.):

(b) If you did not exhaust your state remedies on Ground Two, explain why: _____

(c)    **Direct Appeal of Ground Two:**

      (1) If you appealed from the judgment of conviction, did you raise this issue?    ❐  Yes    ❐  No

      (2) If you did <u>not</u> raise this issue in your direct appeal, explain why: _____

(d)    **Post-Conviction Proceedings:**

      (1) Did you raise this issue through a post-conviction motion or petition for habeas corpus in a state trial court?

        ❐  Yes    ❐  No

      (2) If your answer to Question (d)(1) is "Yes," state:

      Type of motion or petition: _____

      Name and location of the court where the motion or petition was filed: _____

      Docket or case number (if you know): _____

AO 241 (Rev. 09/17)

Date of the court's decision:

Result (attach a copy of the court's opinion or order, if available):

(3) Did you receive a hearing on your motion or petition? ☐ Yes ☐ No

(4) Did you appeal from the denial of your motion or petition? ☐ Yes ☐ No

(5) If your answer to Question (d)(4) is "Yes," did you raise this issue in the appeal? ☐ Yes ☐ No

(6) If your answer to Question (d)(4) is "Yes," state:

Name and location of the court where the appeal was filed:

Docket or case number (if you know):

Date of the court's decision:

Result (attach a copy of the court's opinion or order, if available):

(7) If your answer to Question (d)(4) or Question (d)(5) is "No," explain why you did not raise this issue:

(e) **Other Remedies:** Describe any other procedures (such as habeas corpus, administrative remedies, etc.) that you have used to exhaust your state remedies on Ground Two :

**GROUND THREE:**

(a) Supporting facts (Do not argue or cite law. Just state the specific facts that support your claim.):

156

AO 241 (Rev. 09/17)

(b) If you did not exhaust your state remedies on Ground Three, explain why:

(c) **Direct Appeal of Ground Three:**

(1) If you appealed from the judgment of conviction, did you raise this issue? ❐ Yes ❐ No

(2) If you did not raise this issue in your direct appeal, explain why:

(d) **Post-Conviction Proceedings:**

(1) Did you raise this issue through a post-conviction motion or petition for habeas corpus in a state trial court?

❐ Yes ❐ No

(2) If your answer to Question (d)(1) is "Yes," state:

Type of motion or petition:

Name and location of the court where the motion or petition was filed:

Docket or case number (if you know):

Date of the court's decision:

Result (attach a copy of the court's opinion or order, if available):

(3) Did you receive a hearing on your motion or petition? ❐ Yes ❐ No

(4) Did you appeal from the denial of your motion or petition? ❐ Yes ❐ No

(5) If your answer to Question (d)(4) is "Yes," did you raise this issue in the appeal? ❐ Yes ❐ No

(6) If your answer to Question (d)(4) is "Yes," state:

Name and location of the court where the appeal was filed:

Docket or case number (if you know):

Date of the court's decision:

Result (attach a copy of the court's opinion or order, if available):

AO 241 (Rev. 09/17)

(7) If your answer to Question (d)(4) or Question (d)(5) is "No," explain why you did not raise this issue:

_____

_____

_____

(e)    **Other Remedies:** Describe any other procedures (such as habeas corpus, administrative remedies, etc.) that you have used to exhaust your state remedies on Ground Three:

_____

_____

## GROUND FOUR:

(a) Supporting facts (Do not argue or cite law. Just state the specific facts that support your claim.):

_____

_____

_____

_____

_____

_____

(b) If you did not exhaust your state remedies on Ground Four, explain why:

_____

_____

_____

(c)    **Direct Appeal of Ground Four:**

(1) If you appealed from the judgment of conviction, did you raise this issue?     ☐ Yes    ☐ No

(2) If you did not raise this issue in your direct appeal, explain why: _____

_____

(d)    **Post-Conviction Proceedings:**

(1) Did you raise this issue through a post-conviction motion or petition for habeas corpus in a state trial court?

    ☐ Yes      ☐ No

(2) If your answer to Question (d)(1) is "Yes," state:

Type of motion or petition: _____

AO 241 (Rev. 09/17)

Name and location of the court where the motion or petition was filed:

Docket or case number (if you know):

Date of the court's decision:

Result (attach a copy of the court's opinion or order, if available):

| | | |
|---|---|---|
| (3) Did you receive a hearing on your motion or petition? | ❏ Yes | ❏ No |
| (4) Did you appeal from the denial of your motion or petition? | ❏ Yes | ❏ No |
| (5) If your answer to Question (d)(4) is "Yes," did you raise this issue in the appeal? | ❏ Yes | ❏ No |

(6) If your answer to Question (d)(4) is "Yes," state:

Name and location of the court where the appeal was filed:

Docket or case number (if you know):

Date of the court's decision:

Result (attach a copy of the court's opinion or order, if available):

(7) If your answer to Question (d)(4) or Question (d)(5) is "No," explain why you did not raise this issue:

(e)     **Other Remedies:** Describe any other procedures (such as habeas corpus, administrative remedies, etc.) that you have used to exhaust your state remedies on Ground Four:

AO 241 (Rev. 09/17)

13.     Please answer these additional questions about the petition you are filing:

    (a)     Have all grounds for relief that you have raised in this petition been presented to the highest state court

            having jurisdiction?     ❐ Yes      ❐ No

            If your answer is "No," state which grounds have not been so presented and give your reason(s) for not

            presenting them:

    (b)     Is there any ground in this petition that has not been presented in some state or federal court?  If so, which

            ground or grounds have not been presented, and state your reasons for not presenting them:

14.     Have you previously filed any type of petition, application, or motion in a federal court regarding the conviction

       that you challenge in this petition?     ❐ Yes     ❐ No

       If "Yes," state the name and  location of the court, the docket or case number, the type of proceeding, the issues

       raised, the date of the court's decision, and the result for each petition, application, or motion filed.  Attach a copy

       of any court opinion or order, if available.

15.     Do you have any petition or appeal now pending (filed and not decided yet) in any court, either state or federal, for

       the judgment you are challenging?     ❐ Yes     ❐ No

       If "Yes," state the name and location of the court, the docket or case number, the type of proceeding, and the issues

       raised.

AO 241 (Rev. 09/17)

16.  Give the name and address, if you know, of each attorney who represented you in the following stages of the judgment you are challenging:

(a) At preliminary hearing:

(b) At arraignment and plea:

(c) At trial:

(d) At sentencing:

(e) On appeal:

(f) In any post-conviction proceeding:

(g) On appeal from any ruling against you in a post-conviction proceeding:

17.  Do you have any future sentence to serve after you complete the sentence for the judgment that you are challenging?  ❐ Yes  ❐ No

(a) If so, give name and location of court that imposed the other sentence you will serve in the future:

(b) Give the date the other sentence was imposed:

(c) Give the length of the other sentence:

(d) Have you filed, or do you plan to file, any petition that challenges the judgment or sentence to be served in the future?  ❐ Yes  ❐ No

18.  TIMELINESS OF PETITION: If your judgment of conviction became final over one year ago, you must explain why the one-year statute of limitations as contained in 28 U.S.C. § 2244(d) does not bar your petition.*

AO 241 (Rev. 09/17)

---

\* The Antiterrorism and Effective Death Penalty Act of 1996 ("AEDPA") as contained in 28 U.S.C. § 2244(d) provides in part that:

(1)     A one-year period of limitation shall apply to an application for a writ of habeas corpus by a person in custody pursuant to the judgment of a State court. The limitation period shall run from the latest of -

      (A)     the date on which the judgment became final by the conclusion of direct review or the expiration of the time for seeking such review;

      (B)     the date on which the impediment to filing an application created by State action in violation of the Constitution or laws of the United States is removed, if the applicant was prevented from filing by such state action;

      (C)     the date on which the constitutional right asserted was initially recognized by the Supreme Court, if the right has been newly recognized by the Supreme Court and made retroactively applicable to cases on collateral review; or

      (D)     the date on which the factual predicate of the claim or claims presented could have been discovered through the exercise of due diligence.

AO 241 (Rev. 09/17)

(2)    The time during which a properly filed application for State post-conviction or other collateral review with respect to the pertinent judgment or claim is pending shall not be counted toward any period of limitation under this subsection.

Therefore, petitioner asks that the Court grant the following relief: _____

_____

or any other relief to which petitioner may be entitled.

_____

Signature of Attorney (if any)

I declare (or certify, verify, or state) under penalty of perjury that the foregoing is true and correct and that this Petition for

Writ of Habeas Corpus was placed in the prison mailing system on _____ (month, date, year).

Executed (signed) on _____ (date).

_____

Signature of Petitioner

If the person signing is not petitioner, state relationship to petitioner and explain why petitioner is not signing this petition.

_____

_____

_____

_____

Page 16 of 16

163

# RULES GOVERNING SECTION 2254 CASES IN THE UNITED STATES DISTRICT COURTS

## (EFFECTIVE FEBRUARY 1, 1977, AS AMENDED TO FEBRUARY 1, 2010)

Rule

## Rule 1.    Scope

1     (a) Cases Involving a Petition under 28 U.S.C. § 2254.

2     These rules govern a petition for a writ of habeas corpus filed

3     in a United States district court under 28 U.S.C. § 2254 by:

4         (1) a person in custody under a state-court

5     judgment who seeks a determination that the custody violates

6     the Constitution, laws, or treaties of the United States; and

2    RULES GOVERNING SECTION 2254 AND 2255 CASES

1    (2) a person in custody under a state-court or

2    federal-court judgment who seeks a determination that future

3    custody under a state-court judgment would violate the

4    Constitution, laws, or treaties of the United States.

5    (b) Other Cases. The district court may apply any or all

6    of these rules to a habeas corpus petition not covered by Rule

7    1(a).

### Rule 2.    The Petition

1    **(a) Current Custody; Naming the Respondent.** If

2    the petitioner is currently in custody under a state-court

3    judgment, the petition must name as respondent the state

4    officer who has custody.

5    **(b) Future Custody; Naming the Respondents and**

6    **Specifying the Judgment.** If the petitioner is not yet in

7    custody - but may be subject to future custody - under the

8    state-court judgment being contested, the petition must

9    name as respondents both the officer who has current

## RULES GOVERNING SECTION 2254 AND 2255 CASES     3

1     custody and the attorney general of the state where the

2     judgment was entered. The petition must ask for relief from

3     the state-court judgment being contested.

4     **(c) Form.** The petition must:

5     (1) specify all the grounds for relief available to

6     the petitioner;

7     (2) state the facts supporting each ground;

8     (3) state the relief requested;

9     (4) be printed, typewritten, or legibly

10     handwritten; and

11     (5) be signed under penalty of perjury by the

12     petitioner or by a person authorized to sign it for the

13     petitioner under 28 U.S.C. § 2242.

14     **(d) Standard Form.** The petition must substantially

15     follow either the form appended to these rules or a form

16     prescribed by a local district-court rule. The clerk must

17     make forms available to petitioners without charge.

4          RULES GOVERNING SECTION 2254 AND 2255 CASES

1          **(e) Separate Petitions for Judgments of Separate**

2          **Courts.** A petitioner who seeks relief from judgments of

3          more than one state court must file a separate petition

4          covering the judgment or judgments of each court.

**Rule 3.    Filing the Petition; Inmate Filing**

1          **(a) Where to File; Copies; Filing Fee.** An original

2          and two copies of the petition must be filed with the clerk

3          and must be accompanied by:

4                    (1) the applicable filing fee, or

5                    (2) a motion for leave to proceed in forma

6          pauperis, the affidavit required by 28 U.S.C. § 1915, and a

7          certificate from the warden or other appropriate officer of

8          the place of confinement showing the amount of money or

9          securities that the petitioner has in any account in the

10         institution.

11         **(b) Filing.** The clerk must file the petition and enter it

12         on the docket.

1    **(c) Time to File.** The time for filing a petition is

2    governed by 28 U.S.C. § 2244(d).

3    **(d) Inmate Filing.** A paper filed by an inmate

4    confined in an institution is timely if deposited in the

5    institution's internal mailing system on or before the last

6    day for filing. If an institution has a system designed for

7    legal mail, the inmate must use that system to receive the

8    benefit of this rule. Timely filing may be shown by a

9    declaration in compliance with 28 U.S.C. § 1746 or by a

10    notarized statement, either of which must set forth the date

11    of deposit and state that first-class postage has been

12    prepaid.

**Rule 4.    Preliminary Review; Serving the Petition and Order**

1    The clerk must promptly forward the petition to a

2    judge under the court's assignment procedure, and the

3    judge must promptly examine it. If it plainly appears from

4    the petition and any attached exhibits that the petitioner is

6    RULES GOVERNING SECTION 2254 AND 2255 CASES

1    not entitled to relief in the district court, the judge must

2    dismiss the petition and direct the clerk to notify the

3    petitioner. If the petition is not dismissed, the judge must

4    order the respondent to file an answer, motion, or other

5    response within a fixed time, or to take other action the

6    judge may order. In every case, the clerk must serve a copy

7    of the petition and any order on the respondent and on the

8    attorney general or other appropriate officer of the state

9    involved.

**Rule 5.    The Answer and the Reply**

1    **(a) When Required.** The respondent is not required

2    to answer the petition unless a judge so orders.

3    **(b) Contents: Addressing the Allegations; Stating a**

4    **Bar.** The answer must address the allegations in the

5    petition. In addition, it must state whether any claim in the

6    petition is barred by a failure to exhaust state remedies, a

1    procedural bar, non- retroactivity, or a statute of

2    limitations.

3        **(c) Contents: Transcripts.** The answer must also

4    indicate what transcripts (of pretrial, trial, sentencing, or

5    post-conviction proceedings) are available, when they can

6    be furnished, and what proceedings have been recorded but

7    not transcribed. The respondent must attach to the answer

8    parts of the transcript that the respondent considers

9    relevant. The judge may order that the respondent furnish

10   other parts of existing transcripts or that parts of

11   untranscribed recordings be transcribed and furnished. If a

12   transcript cannot be obtained, the respondent may submit a

13   narrative summary of the evidence.

14       **(d) Contents: Briefs on Appeal and Opinions.** The

15   respondent must also file with the answer a copy of:

16           (1) any brief that the petitioner submitted in an

17   appellate court contesting the conviction or sentence, or

1    contesting an adverse judgment or order in a post-

2    conviction proceeding;

3        (2) any brief that the prosecution submitted in an

4    appellate court relating to the conviction or sentence; and

5        (3) the opinions and dispositive orders of the

6    appellate court relating to the conviction or the sentence.

7        **(e) Reply.** The petitioner may submit a reply to the

8    respondent's answer or other pleading within a time fixed

9    by the judge.

**Rule 6.    Discovery**

1        **(a) Leave of Court Required.** A judge may, for good

2    cause, authorize a party to conduct discovery under the

3    Federal Rules of Civil Procedure and may limit the extent

4    of discovery. If necessary for effective discovery, the judge

5    must appoint an attorney for a petitioner who qualifies to

6    have counsel appointed under 18 U.S.C. § 3006A.

1   **(b) Requesting Discovery.** A party requesting

2   discovery must provide reasons for the request. The request

3   must also include any proposed interrogatories and requests

4   for admission, and must specify any requested documents.

5   **(c) Deposition Expenses.** If the respondent is granted

6   leave to take a deposition, the judge may require the

7   respondent to pay the travel expenses, subsistence

8   expenses, and fees of the petitioner's attorney to attend the

9   deposition.

10

**Rule 7.    Expanding the Record**

1   **(a) In General.** If the petition is not dismissed, the

2   judge may direct the parties to expand the record by

3   submitting additional materials relating to the petition. The

4   judge may require that these materials be authenticated.

5   **(b) Types of Materials.** The materials that may be

6   required include letters predating the filing of the petition,

10    RULES GOVERNING SECTION 2254 AND 2255 CASES

1    documents, exhibits, and answers under oath to written

2    interrogatories propounded by the judge. Affidavits may

3    also be submitted and considered as part of the record.

4        **(c) Review by the Opposing Party.** The judge must

5    give the party against whom the additional materials are

6    offered an opportunity to admit or deny their correctness.

**Rule 8.    Evidentiary Hearing**

1        **(a) Determining Whether to Hold a Hearing.** If the

2    petition is not dismissed, the judge must review the answer,

3    any transcripts and records of state-court proceedings, and

4    any materials submitted under Rule 7 to determine whether

5    an evidentiary hearing is warranted.

6        **(b) Reference to a Magistrate Judge.** A judge may,

7    under 28 U.S.C. § 636(b), refer the petition to a magistrate

8    judge to conduct hearings and to file proposed findings of

9    fact and recommendations for disposition. When they are

10    filed, the clerk must promptly serve copies of the proposed

1     findings and recommendations on all parties. Within 14

2     days after being served, a party may file objections as

3     provided by local court rule. The judge must determine de

4     novo any proposed finding or recommendation to which

5     objection is made. The judge may accept, reject, or modify

6     any proposed finding or recommendation.

7     **(c) Appointing Counsel; Time of Hearing.** If an

8     evidentiary hearing is warranted, the judge must appoint an

9     attorney to represent a petitioner who qualifies to have

10     counsel appointed under 18 U.S.C. § 3006A. The judge

11     must conduct the hearing as soon as practicable after giving

12     the attorneys adequate time to investigate and prepare.

13     These rules do not limit the appointment of counsel under

14     Sec. 3006A at any stage of the proceeding.

**Rule 9.    Second or Successive Petitions**

1     Before presenting a second or successive petition, the

2     petitioner must obtain an order from the appropriate court

12    RULES GOVERNING SECTION 2254 AND 2255 CASES

1    of appeals authorizing the district court to consider the

2    petition as required by 28 U.S.C. § 2244(b)(3) and (4).

### Rule 10.   Powers of a Magistrate Judge

1    A magistrate judge may perform the duties of a

2    district judge under these rules, as authorized under 28

3    U.S.C. § 636.

### Rule 11.   Certificate of Appealability; Time to Appeal

1    **(a) Certificate of Appealability.** The district court

2    must issue or deny a certificate of appealability when it

3    enters a final order adverse to the applicant. Before

4    entering the final order, the court may direct the parties to

5    submit arguments on whether a certificate should issue. If

6    the court issues a certificate, the court must state the

7    specific issue or issues that satisfy the showing required by

8    28 U.S.C. § 2253(c)(2). If the court denies a certificate, the

9    parties may not appeal the denial but may seek a certificate

10   from the court of appeals under Federal Rule of Appellate

1     Procedure 22. A motion to reconsider a denial does not

2     extend the time to appeal.

3          **(b) Time to Appeal.** Federal Rule of Appellate

4     Procedure 4(a) governs the time to appeal an order entered

5     under these rules. A timely notice of appeal must be filed

6     even if the district court issues a certificate of appealability.

**Rule 12.   Applicability of the Federal Rules of Civil Procedure**

1          The Federal Rules of Civil Procedure, to the extent

2     that they are     not inconsistent with any statutory

3     provisions or these rules, may be applied to a proceeding

4     under these rules.

\* \* \* \* \*

14  RULES GOVERNING SECTION 2254 AND 2255 CASES

## RULES GOVERNING SECTION 2255 PROCEEDINGS FOR THE UNITED STATES DISTRICT COURTS

## (EFFECTIVE FEBRUARY 1, 1977, AS AMENDED TO FEBRUARY 1, 2010)

Rule
1. Scope.
2. The Motion.
3. Filing the Motion; Inmate Filing.
4. Preliminary Review.
5. The Answer and the Reply.
6. Discovery.
7. Expanding the Record.
8. Evidentiary Hearing.
9. Second or Successive Motions.
10. Powers of a Magistrate Judge.
11. Certificate of Appealability; Time to Appeal.
12. Applicability of the Federal Rules of Civil Procedure and the Federal Rules of Criminal Procedure.

**Rule 1.    Scope**

1      These rules govern a motion filed in a United States

2      district court under 28 U.S.C. § 2255 by:

3          (a) a person in custody under a judgment of that court

4      who seeks a determination that:

1          (1) the judgment violates the Constitution or

2    laws of the United States;

3          (2) the court lacked jurisdiction to enter the

4    judgment;

5          (3) the sentence exceeded the maximum allowed

6    by law; or

7          (4) the judgment or sentence is otherwise subject

8    to collateral review; and

9          (b) a person in custody under a judgment of a state

10   court or another federal court, and subject to future custody

11   under a judgment of the district court, who seeks a

12   determination that:

13          (1) future custody under a judgment of the

14   district court would violate the Constitution or laws of the

15   United States;

16          (2) the district court lacked jurisdiction to enter

17   the judgment;

16    RULES GOVERNING SECTION 2254 AND 2255 CASES

1           (3) the district court's sentence exceeded the

2    maximum allowed by law; or

3           (4) the district court's judgment or sentence is

4    otherwise subject to collateral review.

**Rule 2.    The Motion**

1         **(a) Applying for Relief.** The application must be in

2    the form of a motion to vacate, set aside, or correct the

3    sentence.

4         **(b) Form.** The motion must:

5           (1) specify all the grounds for relief available to

6    the moving party;

7           (2) state the facts supporting each ground;

8           (3) state the relief requested;

9           (4) be printed, typewritten, or legibly

10   handwritten; and

11          (5) be signed under penalty of perjury by the

12   movant or by a person authorized to sign it for the movant.

1    **(c) Standard Form.** The motion must substantially

2    follow either the form appended to these rules or a form

3    prescribed by a local district-court rule. The clerk must

4    make forms available to moving parties without charge.

5    **(d) Separate Motions for Separate Judgments.** A

6    moving party who seeks relief from more than one

7    judgment must file a separate motion covering each

8    judgment.

**Rule 3.    Filing the Motion; Inmate Filing**

1    **(a) Where to File; Copies.** An original and two

2    copies of the motion must be filed with the clerk.

3    **(b) Filing and Service.** The clerk must file the motion

4    and enter it on the criminal docket of the case in which the

5    challenged judgment was entered. The clerk must then

6    deliver or serve a copy of the motion on the United States

7    attorney in that district, together with a notice of its filing.

18    RULES GOVERNING SECTION 2254 AND 2255 CASES

1    **(c) Time to File.** The time for filing a motion is

2    governed by 28 U.S.C. § 2255 para. 6.

3    **(d) Inmate Filing.** A paper filed by an inmate

4    confined in an institution is timely if deposited in the

5    institution's internal mailing system on or before the last

6    day for filing. If an institution has a system designed for

7    legal mail, the inmate must use that system to receive the

8    benefit of this rule. Timely filing may be shown by a

9    declaration in compliance with 28 U.S.C. § 1746 or by a

10    notarized statement, either of which must set forth the date

11    of deposit and state that first-class postage has been

12    prepaid.

(As amended Apr. 26, 2004, eff. Dec. 1, 2004.)

**Rule 4.    Preliminary Review**

1    **(a) Referral to a Judge.** The clerk must promptly

2    forward the motion to the judge who conducted the trial

3    and imposed sentence or, if the judge who imposed

1    sentence was not the trial judge, to the judge who

2    conducted the proceedings being challenged. If the

3    appropriate judge is not available, the clerk must forward

4    the motion to a judge under the court's assignment

5    procedure.

6    **(b) Initial Consideration by the Judge.** The judge

7    who receives the motion must promptly examine it. If it

8    plainly appears from the motion, any attached exhibits, and

9    the record of prior proceedings that the moving party is not

10    entitled to relief, the judge must dismiss the motion and

11    direct the clerk to notify the moving party. If the motion is

12    not dismissed, the judge must order the United States

13    attorney to file an answer, motion, or other response within

14    a fixed time, or to take other action the judge may order.

**Rule 5.    The Answer and the Reply**

1    **(a) When Required.** The respondent is not required

2    to answer the motion unless a judge so orders.

20 RULES GOVERNING SECTION 2254 AND 2255 CASES

1 **(b) Contents.** The answer must address the

2 allegations in the motion. In addition, it must state whether

3 the moving party has used any other federal remedies,

4 including any prior post- conviction motions under these

5 rules or any previous rules, and whether the moving party

6 received an evidentiary hearing.

7 **(c) Records of Prior Proceedings.** If the answer

8 refers to briefs or transcripts of the prior proceedings that

9 are not available in the court's records, the judge must order

10 the government to furnish them within a reasonable time

11 that will not unduly delay the proceedings.

12 **(d) Reply.** The moving party may submit a reply to

13 the respondent's answer or other pleading within a time

14 fixed by the judge.

**Rule 6.    Discovery**

1 **(a) Leave of Court Required.** A judge may, for good

2 cause, authorize a party to conduct discovery under the

1    Federal Rules of Criminal Procedure or Civil Procedure, or

2    in accordance with the practices and principles of law. If

3    necessary for effective discovery, the judge must appoint

4    an attorney for a moving party who qualifies to have

5    counsel appointed under 18 U.S.C. § 3006A.

6    **(b) Requesting Discovery.** A party requesting

7    discovery must provide reasons for the request. The request

8    must also include any proposed interrogatories and requests

9    for admission, and must specify any requested documents.

10    (c) Deposition Expenses. If the government is granted

11    leave to take a deposition, the judge may require the

12    government to pay the travel expenses, subsistence

13    expenses, and fees of the moving party's attorney to attend

14    the deposition.

## Rule 7.    Expanding the Record

1    **(a) In General.** If the motion is not dismissed, the

2    judge may direct the parties to expand the record by

22    RULES GOVERNING SECTION 2254 AND 2255 CASES

1    submitting additional materials relating to the motion. The

2    judge may require that these materials be authenticated.

3    **(b) Types of Materials.** The materials that may be

4    required include letters predating the filing of the motion,

5    documents, exhibits, and answers under oath to written

6    interrogatories propounded by the judge. Affidavits also

7    may be submitted and considered as part of the record.

8    **(c) Review by the Opposing Party.** The judge must

9    give the party against whom the additional materials are

10    offered an opportunity to admit or deny their correctness.

**Rule 8.    Evidentiary Hearing**

1    **(a) Determining Whether to Hold a Hearing.** If the

2    motion is not dismissed, the judge must review the answer,

3    any transcripts and records of prior proceedings, and any

4    materials submitted under Rule 7 to determine whether an

5    evidentiary hearing is warranted.

1      **(b) Reference to a Magistrate Judge.** A judge may,

2      under 28 U.S.C. § 636(b), refer the motion to a magistrate

3      judge to conduct hearings and to file proposed findings of

4      fact and recommendations for disposition. When they are

5      filed, the clerk must promptly serve copies of the proposed

6      findings and recommendations on all parties. Within 14

7      days after being served, a party may file objections as

8      provided by local court rule. The judge must determine de

9      novo any proposed finding or recommendation to which

10     objection is made. The judge may accept, reject, or modify

11     any proposed finding or

12      recommendation.

13     **(c) Appointing Counsel; Time of Hearing.** If an

14     evidentiary hearing is warranted, the judge must appoint an

15     attorney to represent a moving party who qualifies to have

16     counsel appointed under 18 U.S.C. § 3006A. The judge

17     must conduct the hearing as soon as practicable after giving

24  RULES GOVERNING SECTION 2254 AND 2255 CASES

1   the attorneys adequate time to investigate and prepare.

2   These rules do not limit the appointment of counsel under

3   Sec. 3006A at any stage of the proceeding.

4       **(d) Producing a Statement.** Federal Rule of Criminal

5   Procedure 26.2(a)-(d) and (f) applies at a hearing under this

6   rule. If a party does not comply with a Rule 26.2(a) order to

7   produce a witness's statement, the court must not consider

8   that witness's testimony.

### Rule 9.  Second or Successive Motions

1       Before presenting a second or successive motion, the

2   moving party must obtain an order from the appropriate

3   court of appeals authorizing the district court to consider

4   the motion, as required by 28 U.S.C. § 2255, para. 8.

### Rule 10.  Powers of a Magistrate Judge

1       A magistrate judge may perform the duties of a

2   district judge under these rules, as authorized by 28 U.S.C.

3   § 636.

## Rule 11.  Certificate of Appealability; Time to Appeal

1    **(a) Certificate of Appealability.** The district court

2    must issue or deny a certificate of appealability when it

3    enters a final order adverse to the applicant. Before

4    entering the final order, the court may direct the parties to

5    submit arguments on whether a certificate should issue. If

6    the court issues a certificate, the court must state the

7    specific issue or issues that satisfy the showing required by

8    28 U.S.C. § 2253(c)(2). If the court denies a certificate, a

9    party may not appeal the denial but may seek a certificate

10   from the court of appeals under Federal Rule of Appellate

11   Procedure 22. A motion to reconsider a denial does not

12   extend the time to appeal.

13   **(b) Time to Appeal.** Federal Rule of Appellate

14   Procedure 4(a) governs the time to appeal an order entered

15   under these rules. A timely notice of appeal must be filed

16   even if the district court issues a certificate of appealability.

26      RULES GOVERNING SECTION 2254 AND 2255 CASES

1      These rules do not extend the time to appeal the original

2      judgment of conviction.

**Rule 12.     Applicability of the Federal Rules of Civil Procedure and the Federal Rules of Criminal Procedure**

1      The Federal Rules of Civil Procedure and the Federal

2      Rules of Criminal Procedure, to the extent that they are not

3      inconsistent with any statutory provisions or these rules,

4      may be applied to a proceeding under these rules.

\* \* \* \* \*

\*\*This posting of the rules governing Section 2254 and 2255 cases excludes all notes to the rules. The rules and applicable notes can be found on the Office of Law Revisions Counsel's website using the following links for Sections 2254 and 2255.

*Notes:*

# Chapter Eighteen:
# Legal Writing and Research

It was once said, "You can teach Algebra to a chimpanzee, if you can find a way to relate the subject matter." This is the exact idea behind legal writing in briefs, memorandums, motions, pleadings, and all other legal matters: getting the ideas (facts) across to your audience so that they can understand them.

Let's say you write a memorandum in support of your post-conviction *habeas corpus* application. In that memorandum, you cite hundreds of case laws and precedents that support your issues. Can the court formulate an opinion at that point? Of course not. They don't have the facts.

However, on the flipside of that argument, if you only provide the facts and not a single piece of case law or precedent, can the court then come to an opinion? Of course, they can, they have all of the facts. The judges can apply the correct case law to support your claim, because they know the law. It's the facts that they don't know and require. Where you can clearly and adequately relay both the facts and the precedent, you have a far greater chance of winning relief in your case.

Let me show you how:

## Memorandums

There are three (3) basic reasons to write a memorandum. The first is to provide a clear record of your legal research. The legal analysis, investigation, and facts are contained in a memorandum. The second reason for writing a memorandum is to compile all of the facts and to analyze the grounds that support your issues. The third reason for a legal memorandum is to cite those precedents that the courts are supposed to follow. This is called *stare decisis* or standing on the decision.

### Tone and Style

You want to be honest, consistent, and fair. You should always include the unfavorable portions of the law without going into detail as to them. This will show the judge that you are fair and can argue both sides. If you aren't prepared to argue both sides, then you aren't prepared to argue either side. Yes, your job is to persuade the court in your favor. This requires subtleness and agreeability.

If you come across as angry, slippery, one-sided, or arrogant, you will lose the court's attention and compassion. As you write, put yourself in the judge's position and ask, "Would you agree with you?" If not, the judge reading your memorandum won't either.

## Word Selection

Selecting the right wording is critical in both convincing and impressing the judge that your argument should win. Present you issues in strong, agreeable, positive format. When you are addressing the state's side of the argument, do so in a way that makes them sound weak, doubtful, and wrong, without insulting them.

You should never attack the opposition in character or make it a personal vendetta. This will immediately cause you harm with the court. I recommend that you remember the case isn't about who the better person is, who is more likeable, or who has done what. It's about the facts and the precedent that supports them – period.

You should never write in a narrative form consistent on first-name basis. Using "I" or "We" unnecessarily injects you as an opposing party in the case. The facts should always take center stage.

## Writing the Memorandum

Writing is simply organizing your thoughts and then relaying them in an organized, coherent manner. If you take too long to reach your point, you will lose the audience very quickly. Nobody likes to read something that goes on, and on, and on, and on … without reaching the point. Plus, the longer you take to arrive at the point, the more likely you will fail to even remember it.

## IRAC Formula

The IRAC formula is the most common legal writing technique taught in paralegal and law schools. Compiling a legal analysis might seem a bit daunting at first glance. Figuring out how to evaluate and to present the facts and the proposed outcome of a cause can be very hard. The IRAC formula will help you to overcome those fears and succeed. The IRAC stands for: Issue, Rule, Analysis, and Conclusion.

1. *I = Issue* – The issue is a reason that the case is being appealed. In the first step, you'll consider the facts of the case and the situations that the issues are about. In short, what the problem is and what happened. You will research the law in order to discover the rule. Additionally, you will need to do this step for every issue you present in your appeal.

2. *R = Rule* – When you apply a rule of law to a case, you are basically explaining which law presides over the issue you are claiming on your appeal. When analyzing a rule, consider all parts of the rule, including its authority and exceptions. Did the state prove all of the elements in your case? You will need to read the rule to know that.

There are types of rules of law:

   a. *Common Law* – Law that is developed over time and is based on judicial precedent rather than on legislative action.
   b. *Statutory Law* – Law that is created by legislative statutes.
   c. *Constitutional Law* – Law that is set forth by the federal and state constitutions.

No matter what type of law you are dealing with, the main goal is to extract the rule from the law. First, you identify the rule within the law. Try describing the rule of the law you are trying to raise in your appeal. If you can't restate the law, then you probably don't understand it yet, and won't be able to argue how it applies to you.

Legal researchers often use an "if-then" model when analyzing the elements that have to be proven. Basically, *if* the situation can be said so that it meets the language of the law, (i.e., *if* the act was committed with "malice"), *then* the circumstances meet one or more of the criteria that must be prove (i.e., *then* the act was a "crime").

Do not attempt to misquote or bend the words of the rule/law to favor your issue. The court will quickly see that and you will lose all of your credibility. Denial is sure come rapidly.

3. *A = Analysis* – In your analysis of the case, you'll apply the rule of law to the facts and describe your analysis in a way a judge will agree with. Does that make sense to you? Basically, you'll take your own idea of the issue and explain it in a way that proves the rule.

You may also want to discuss the weaknesses of your case. Not only will this help you maintain credibility with the courts, but it will also help you see things from the prosecution's eyes, so you can defend against it.

4. *C = Conclusion* – The conclusion of your legal analysis will describe your expected outcome based on the facts and rule of law. Make sure you take a strong stance on your issues, that this stance is mentioned in your conclusion, and that your position is supported by the law.

Show the court what the issue is and how the law supports relief.

## Proper Sentences

The average length of your sentences will determine whether it can be read effectively. However, you don't want every sentence to be the exact same length either. You want a variety of sentence length. That being said, your average sentence should be about 20 words.

There should be some 30-word sentences and some 10-word sentences. I know that sounds crazy, but if you go back and look at how I've written this book, I've tried to follow my own policy. I'm not talking about the paragraph length ... I'm talking about the sentence length.

## Verbosity

Verbosity means using too many words. In order for your readers to be able to read faster, and for you to get your thoughts out faster, you must use fewer words to do so – especially in legal writing. For example:

"In order for prisoners to receive commissary, they must have money."

That sentence is only 11 words. Cut down from a passage in the *Texas Prisoner Orientation Handbook* that read:

"It is necessary that an Offender who wishes to purchase goods from the Unit Commissary have adequate resources in which to accommodate that purchase."

The above sentence has 24 words – totally unnecessary and excessive.

Simple rule, if you can say it with less words, then do so. The judge will reward you for it, trust me.

## Drop the Legal Jargon

Not only will the judge reward you for doing so, it's also the law not to use legal jargon when you write. In simple words, write the way you speak, in proper English, and to the point. Don't use big words they only make you sound like you're trying to be a lawyer. That won't sit well with any judge. Here are some examples:

| Legal Jargon | Plain English |
|---|---|
| in the event that | if |
| not less than | at least |
| thereafter | later |
| therein | in it, inside |
| prior to | before |
| instant case | this case |

I think you get the point. Keep it simple and easy.

## Refer to People by Name

Plaintiff, Defendant, Petitioner, Appellant, Applicant – Never do it. Use real last names when talking about real people. "Johnson rode in the ambulance after the shooting. Anderson stayed at the scene with the police."

When using your true name, it tends to humanize you instead of the court just considering you as an "Appellant" or a case number. You are much better off personalizing your documents by using particular names, whether you're writing a brief, memorandum, or pleading.

## Keep the Emotions in Check

This is huge and cannot be understated. As you write and are forced to re-live the trial or whatever happened to you, anger, animosity, and other feelings will build up. Keep them under control or they will come out in your words – a sure and fast way to lose your argument.

If you won't say it to a judge, then *don't* write it.

## Writing About Things Not in the Record

This is a pretty good trick taught to me in my Advanced Paralegal Studies Class. People are so intent on writing about what did happen that they forget that what didn't happen (but could have) can also be used to argue your issues.

Let's say your police report in your case is very detailed, describing the location, type of house, items stolen from the home, witnesses, etc. Despite such specificity, however, there is no mention of anyone having heard any barking dogs on the night of the burglary, nor anybody being bitten or mauled. You can certainly show the court that those implications support your innocence because, there are two very large German Rott's in the backyard of the home, inside of the fence you were alleged to have climbed, protecting the window you were alleged to have used to steal all of the property … and yet not a single bark, not a single bite.

Get it? Just let the judge know that those facts are not in the record, but that they point out the truth in your arguments.

**The Sixteen Rules of Legal Writing**

1. Never lie, under any circumstances.
2. Don't misquote case law.
3. Always use truth, never euphemisms.
4. If it's not required, don't add it.
5. Always cite accurately.
6. Don't engage in personal attack.
7. Use the cases that don't support your issues also.
8. Don't argue in the facts section.
9. Don't quote case law in the facts section.
10. Show don't tell.
11. Don't misstate your opponent's words.
12. Don't guess. Just say you don't know.
13. Use real names to humanize yourself.
14. Keep it short.
15. Don't use long sentences.
16. Never use more than 3 case citings in a row.

Good luck.


*Notes:*

# Chapter Nineteen:
# Forms

F.1

## CERTIFICATE OF SERVICE

I, the undersigned, hereby certify that on this _____ day of _____,

20_____, I served a true and accurate copy of the foregoing: _____

_____ upon:

_____        _____

_____        _____

_____        _____

_____        _____

by submitting same to a designated prison mailbox for prompt mailing, first class postage prepaid, and it shall be deemed **FILED** as of the above date.

_____
(signature)

_____
(name, printed), pro se

_____
(mailing address)

_____, _____
(city, state)      (zip)

F.2

IN THE _____ COURT OF _____ COUNTY

STATE OF _____

_____ )
        Petitioner,        )        Cause No. _____
                           )
    V.                     )
                           )
_____ )
        Respondent.        )

## AFFIDAVIT OF INDIGENCY

I, the undersigned, who being first duly sworn upon my oath, attests:

1. I am presently incarcerated at _____

and have been since my conviction on _____, _____.

2. I have not worked since _____, _____.

3. I do not have any means to pay filing fees and court costs.

4. I do not own any stocks, bonds, checking or saving accounts, nor do I own any real estate, notes, automobiles or other property.

5. I have attached a copy of my previous twelve (12) months inmate account statement for your review.

6. I please request that you allow me to proceed In forma pauperis in these proceedings.

Attach Copy of Notarization (F.3)

F.3

STATE OF _____ )
                                         SS: **AFFIRMATION**
COUNTY OF _____ )

    I, the undersigned, do hereby swear or affirm under the penalty of perjury, that the foregoing statements are true and correct.

Dated: _____

                                                     _____
                                                     (signature in front of Notary)

                                                    _____, **Affiant**
                                                    (print name)

                                                    DOC# _____

                                                    _____
                                                     (mailing address)

                                                    _____' _____
                                                    (city, state)    (zip)

STATE OF _____ )
                                         ) SS: **NOTARIZATION**
COUNTY OF _____ )

    **SUBSCRIBED AND SWORN TO BEFORE ME**, a Notary Public in and for the above State and County, on this _____day of _____, 20_____.

                                                      _____
                                                    Notary - Signature

                                                    _____
                                                    Notary - Print Name

                                                    _____
                                                    County of Residence

_____
Date My Commission Expires

F.4

CASE NO. _____

EX PARTE                           §      IN THE _____JUDICIAL

                                   §      DISTRICT COURT OF

[Your name here]                   §      _____ COUNTY, TEXAS

## APPLICANT'S MOTION FOR APPOINTMENT OF COUNSEL

**TO THE HONORABLE JUDGE OF SAID COURT:**

COMES NOW _____, Applicant in the above entitled and numbered cause, and requests this court to appoint counsel to represent him in perfecting an Application for a Writ of Habeas Corpus under Code of Criminal Procedure, Article 11.07. In support of this motion, Applicant attests the following:

### JURISDICTION

Applicant seeks appointment of counsel in this Court pursuant to Texas Code of Criminal Procedure, Articles 11.07 and 1.051(d)(3), which provide the Court with limited jurisdiction over the parties and subject matter, whereas Applicant was convicted in this Court in Cause No. F15-1103-211, on September 21, 2016.

### AUTHORITY

An eligible indigent defendant is entitled to have the trial court appoint an attorney to represent him in a habeas corpus proceeding if the court concludes that the interest of justice requires representation. **TEX. CODE. CRIM. PROC. art. 1.051(d)(3).**

(Attach Form F.1)

### INDIGENCE

This Court has twice made the finding of indigency when it appointed both trial counsel, and appeal counsel, to assist the Applicant. Since those findings of indigency, Applicant has remained incarcerated in the Texas Department of Criminal Justice. Applicant has no way of earning any income, does not own any proprty or real estate, and does not have any cash or coin to hire counsel. A certified six month trust fund account statement for the Applicant is hereby attached.

### IN THE INTEREST OF JUSTICE

Applicant attests that he has meritorious claims that entitle him to relief such as; Ineffective assistance of counsel, Brady violations, and newly discovered evidence. In the interest of justice, Applicant should be able to have the assistance of counsel to assist him in developing said evidence.

### EVIDENTIARY HEARING

Applicant is confidant that an evidentiary hearing will establish the constitutional violations that will entitle him to relief, where he may gather evidence, interview witnesses, present new evidence, and prove his innocence, all in the interest of justice.

### PRAYER

**WHEREFORE, PREMISED CONSIDERED**, Applicant hereby prays this Court will grant him an attorney to assist him in preparing a writ of habeas corpus, and also grant him an evidentiary hearing.

Respectfully submitted,

[Sign here]

_____
[Your name]
APPLICANT
Address

F.5

NO. _____

EX PARTE                          §        IN THE _____ JUDICIAL

                                  §        DISTRICT COURT OF

[Your name here]                  §        _____ COUNTY, TEXAS

ORDER ON
APPLICANT'S MOTION FOR APPOINTMENT OF COUNSEL

**CAME ON** this day for consideration, Applicant's Motion for the aapointment of counsel to assist him in an application for habeas corpus under Texas Code of Criminal Procedure, Article 11.07. After having now reviewed the motion, and in the interest of justice, this court finds the Applicant's motion for appointment of counsel is hereby APPROVED / DENIED in the interest of justice.

**IT IS THEREFORE ORDERED**, that attorney _____, is hereby appointed to represent Applicant.

**IT IS FURTHER ORDERED**, that the Clerk of this court is to mail a copy of this order to Applicant and said counsel.

    **SIGNED AND ENTERED** this _____ day of _____ , 20 _____ .

_____
PRESIDING JUDGE

F.6

## UNSWORN DECLARATION

Under both Federal (28 U.S.C § 1746) and State Law (V.T.C.A. Civil Practice & Remedies Code § 132.001- 132.003), offenders in Texas may use an unsworn declaration under penalty of perjury in place of a written declaration, verification, certification, oath, or affidavit sworn before a Notary Public.

"My name is _____, my date of birth is_____,
my TDCJ number is _____, I am presently incarcerated in

_____. I declare under penalty of

perjury that the foregoing is true and correct.

Executed on the _____day of _____, 20_____.

_____
(Offender Signature)

F.7

IN THE _____COURT OF _____COUNTY

STATE OF _____

_____,
      Petitioner,

v.

STATE OF _____,
      Respondent.

§
§
§
§
§
§
§
§
§
§

Cause No. _____

### MOTION TO SET EVIDENTIARY HEARING AND
### AND ISSUE TRANSPORT ORDER

**COMES NOW**, Petitioner, pro se, pursuant to _____ Rule_____, and moves this Court to set a hearing in this case, and to order the Petitioner's presence at the hearing. In support, Petitioner would show the following:

1. Petitioner filed a Petition for Post-Conviction Relief on _____day of _____, 20_____.

2. An Evidentiary Hearing is necessary because: _____

_____

_____

_____

**WHEREFORE**, Petitioner respectfully requests this Court schedule a hearing in this case, and that Petitioner's presence be ordered.

**Respectfully submitted this** _____day of _____, 20\_\_\_\_.

_____
Petitioner, pro se

(include F.1, to:prosecutor)

F.8

IN THE_____COURT OF _____COUNTY

STATE OF _____

|                          |   |                        |
|--------------------------|---|------------------------|
| _____,  | § |                        |
| Petitioner,              | § | Cause No. _____ |
| v.                       | § |                        |
| STATE OF_____,    | § |                        |
| Respondent.              | § |                        |

### TRANSPORT ORDER

It appearing to the Court that the presence of the Petitioner, who is now in the custody of the _____, is now required in the above-named Court, on the _____day of _____, 20_____, at _____:_____A.M. /P.M. for an evidentiary hearing.

It is now **ORDERED** by the Court that the Sheriff of _____ County is required to, and authorized, to bring Petitioner to this Court.

It is further **ORDERED** by the Court that a copy of this Order shall constitute authority for the Sheriff to act accordingly to carry the provisions of this Order into effect.

_____
PRESIDING JUDGE

Note:

(Provide copies to: Sheriff, Dpt of Corrections, Prosecutor)

F.9

IN THE _____ COURT OF _____ COUNTY

STATE OF _____

| | |
|---|---|
| _____, <br> Petitioner, <br><br> v. <br><br> STATE OF _____, <br> Respondent. | §<br>§<br>§   Cause No. _____<br>§<br>§<br>§ |

### MOTION TO ISSUE TRANSPORT ORDER

**COMES NOW**, Petitioner, pro se, pursuant to _____ Rule_____,
TO Order Petitioner's presence at the post-conviction evidentiary
hearing scheduled for the _____day of_____, 20_____.


   **WHEREFORE**, Petitioner respectfully requests that Petitioner's
presence at the hearing be ordered, and the Sheriff of _____
County arrange the transporting of the Petitioner to the hearing.



   Respectfully submitted this_____day of_____,20_____.



                                     _____
                                     Petitioner, pro se

(Include form F.1, and F.8)

F.10

IN THE _____ COURT OF _____ COUNTY

STATE OF _____

| | | |
|---|---|---|
| _____, | § | |
| Petitioner, | § | Cause No. _____ |
| | § | |
| v. | § | |
| | § | |
| STATE OF_____, | § | |
| Respondent. | | |

### MOTION TO PROCEED BY AFFIDAVIT

COMES NOW, Petitioner, pro se, pursuant to _____Rule_____,
to respectfully move this Court to order this cause submitted upon
affidavits. In support of this Motion, Petitioner asserts the following:

1. This is an action for post-conviction relief.

2. Petitioner is proceeding pro se in this matter.

3. Petitioner's presence is not needed at the hearing.

WHEREFORE, Petitioner respectfully requests that this Court issue an
Order directing that this cause be submitted upon affidavit's, and for
all other just and proper relief.

Respectfully submitted this _____day of _____, 20_____.


_____
Petitioner, pro se


(Attach form F.1 to: prosecutor)

# Appendix

1. Checklist for Texas Court of Criminal Appeals (Rules)
2. Durable Power of Attorney
3. Texas Prisoner Innocence Questionnaire
4. Texas Government Code § 552.028 Information
5. Texas Commutation of Sentence (Time Cut) Application
6. List of all State Bar Associations

# Checklist for Texas Court of Criminal Appeals (Rules)

*Please refer to the complete Texas Rules of Appellate Procedure. This document should be used only as a guide.*

The Texas Rules of Appellate Procedure require attorneys to file documents electronically. Rule 9.2(c)(1). **(For this purpose, the original is considered the electronically filed version)**

By <u>miscellaneous order</u>, the Court of Criminal Appeals requires 10 paper copies of PDRs, Briefs, and Motions for Rehearing that are filed electronically.

---

## PETITIONS FOR DISCRETIONARY REVIEW - RULE 68

| | |
|---|---|
| Time to file - Rule 68.2(a) | 30 days after court of appeals judgment or 30 days after rehearing or motion for en banc reconsideration is overruled. |
| Motion for Extension of Time - Rule 68.2(c) | File with Court of Criminal Appeals Original only<br>Due no later than 15 days after the last day for filing the petition |
| Where to file - Rule 68.3 | Court of Criminal Appeals |
| Contents of Petition - Rule 68.4) | |
| Length of Petition - Rule 9.4(i)(2)(D) | 4,500 words or 15 pages |
| Number of copies - Misc. Order | Original + 10 paper copies |
| Reply to Petition - Rule 68.9 | Due 15 days after PDR is filed |
| Amend/Supplement - Rule 68.10 | Upon motion/may be amended any time justice requires |

## BRIEFS ON GRANTED PETITIONS FOR DISCRETIONARY REVIEW
Briefs must comply with the requirements of Rules 9 and 38.

### Initial Brief

| | |
|---|---|
| Number of copies - Misc. Order | Original + 10 paper copies |
| Time to file - Rule 70.1 | Due within 30 days after review is granted |
| Word/page limit 9.4(i)(2)(B) | 15,000 words or 50 pages |

### Respondent's Briefs

| | |
|---|---|
| Number of copies - Misc. Order | Original + 10 paper copies |
| Time to file - Rule 70.2 | 30 days after filing of initial brief |
| Word/page limit 9.4(i)(2)(B) | 15,000 words or 50 pages |

## AMICUS BRIEFS - RULE 11

Comply with briefing rules
Received not filed
Extension of time is not required

## MOTION FOR REHEARING  - RULE 79

| | |
|---|---|
| Due date (Rule 79.1) | 15 days after judgment or order of Court of Criminal Appeals |
| Extension of Time (Rule 79.6) | File with Court of Criminal Appeals Original only |
| Contents (Rule 79.2) | |
| Contents (Rule 79.2(c)) | For Refused PDRs only |
| Amendments (Rule 79.3) | May be amended anytime before period for filing expires or with leave of the court |

## EXTRAORDINARY MATTERS - RULE 72

Number of copies - Misc. Order

Must be accompanied by motion for leave to file
Counsel will be advised if copies are required

## POSTCONVICTION APPLICATIONS FOR WRITS OF HABEAS CORPUS (11.07) - RULE 73

Must be filed with the district clerk of the convicting court on the prescribed form - Art. 11.07, Sec. 2; Rule 73.1(a)

Memorandum - Rule 73.1(d)

Shall not exceed 15,000 words or 50 pages

Summary Sheet - Rule 73.4(b)(3)

Information summary sheet must contain....

Order Designating Issues - Rule 73.4(b)(1)

District Clerk shall immediately transmit to CCA

Resolution of Claims Raised - Rule 73.5

Trial Court shall resolve issue in 180 days - Extension of time must be filed with CCA

District Clerk shall forward record -
Rule 73.4(5)

District clerk shall forward record on 181$^{st}$ day if no extension is granted

## DEATH PENALTY CASES DIRECT APPEALS - RULE 71

### DEATH PENALTY BRIEFS

Briefs should prepared and filed in accordance with Rule 38

Briefs must be in the form as prescribed by Rule 9.4

Appellant's Brief - Rule 38.6(a) and Rule 71.3    Appellant's brief is due 30 days after the reporter's record is filed in this court.

| | |
|---|---|
| State's Brief - Rule 38.6(b), Rule 71.3 | State's brief is due 30 days after the appellant's brief is filed in this court. |
| Reply Brief - Rule 38.6(c) and Rule 71.3 | Due 20 days after appellee's brief was filed |
| Additional Briefs - Rule 71.4 | Upon motion the Court may permit the filing of additional briefs |
| Binding and covers - Rule 9.4(f) | Covers on paper briefs should not be dark blue, red, black or plastic |
| Word/page limit 9.4(i)(2)(A) | 37,500 words or 125 pages |
| Oral argument - Rule 71.3 | Must include a short statement of why oral argument would be helpful |

## CLERK'S RECORD - RULE 34.5

| | |
|---|---|
| Contents - Rule 34.5 | |
| Due Date - Rule 35.2(a) | The clerk's record is due 60 days from the date sentence is imposed if no motion for new trial is filed    .... |
| Due Date - Rule 35.2(b) | ....or 120 days if motion for new trial is filed |

## REPORTER'S RECORD - RULE 34.6

| | |
|---|---|
| Contents - Rule 34.6 (a) | |
| Due Date - Rule 35.2(a) | The reporter's record is due 60 days from the date sentence is imposed if no motion for new trial is filed..... |
| Due Date - Rule 35.2(b) | ....or 120 days if a motion for new trial is filed. |

*(SEE ALSO UNIFORM FORMAT MANUAL FOR COURT REPORTERS)*


## APPEALS FROM TRIAL COURT ORDERS ON DNA CASES
See C.C.P. Chapter 64, Art. 64.01

# Durable Power of Attorney

A power of attorney is basically a written document that gives authorization to someone other than yourself to act on your behalf, as an extension of you. If you issue a power of attorney, you are known as the principal. The person to whom you have extended the power of your attorney is referred to as the attorney in fact or agent.

Your power of attorney can either be general, which authorizes your "agent" to conduct your entire business and affairs. A limited or special power of attorney authorizes your agent to conduct special and specific business or perform a single act on your behalf.

Your power of attorney primarily serves as evidence to others of your principal-agent relationship created by your power of attorney. It also serves as an agreement between you and your agent regarding the business to be transacted under your power of attorney.

A power of attorney can be very useful, especially to someone who is incarcerated and cannot perform certain business or requests that may be part of pursuing your post-conviction challenge. For example, it could be useful if you still own property in the world, have a retirement or bank account, and especially in obtaining documents you will need to establish proof in your post-conviction application. Here in Texas, we are often denied in our written requests to obtain legal documents and records, under Texas Government Code Section § 552.028, which agencies will attempt to hide under. In your state, there are likely the same kinds of rules under a different code. Either way, a power of attorney allows your agent to obtain those documents where your signature may be required. It should be noted, however, Texas Government Code § 552.048 (b) has a specific exception to the rules regarding requests for information from an "Incarcerated Individual," as they call it.

For almost any situation that you can do on your own behalf, you can issue your power of attorney to someone to act on your behalf. This includes the power to contract, buy and sell property, sign checks, make deposits, get loans, credit card transactions, run a business, and just about every other type of activity. They can also file lawsuits and collect debts owed to you by anyone, including the I.R.S.

## Making a Power of Attorney

Power of Attorney contracts are governed by the laws that regulate agents for the state where the power of attorney is made, or the acts will be performed. Generally, any person who has the legal capacity to contract or appoint an agent can give his or her power of attorney to another person, corporation, or entity. The principal should be of legal age and considered mentally competent.

You can make a durable power of attorney, which will remain valid even if you later lose capacity to contract and appoint an agent. Your durable power of attorney must be in writing and must contain language that shows that you intend the power of attorney to remain in effect if you are disabled or incapacitated. It should include your name, address, and that of the agent. You should indicate the status of your agent as an individual, corporation, association, etc.

Your power of attorney should clearly show the scope and extent of the power of attorney and the powers granted. It should indicate whether the power of attorney is a *general* or a *limited* one. It should include the effective date and the time period during that the power of attorney will be in effect. To the extent possible, you should list the specific acts you will be asking your agent to perform.

Property that is subject to the power of attorney should be very clearly described. Indicate the nature, ownership, and location of such property, whether personal property, securities, real estate, and the like. It is recommended that a provision be included that covers the manner by which you can later revoke your power of attorney. Your power of attorney should be signed and dated by both you and your agent. It should also be notarized in states that don't authorize an Inmate Signed Declaration in place of a notary, such as Texas and the Federal Government do.

A sample power of attorney form is provided hereafter and will be useful in the previous situations I described. It should be noted that if you are legally married a power of attorney serves you no real purpose, since your spouse can legally sign your name in most states and can also act as your legal agent without a power of attorney.

## DURABLE POWER OF ATTORNEY

I, _____, my social security number being ___-
_____ - _____, hereby appoint _____, who is
located at _____ in _____
County, in the State of _____, as my agent to act
for me in my absence related to any and all of the following matters:

_____(A) real property transactions;

_____(B) tangible personal property transactions;

_____(C) stock and bond transactions;

_____(D) Commodity and options transactions;

_____(E) banking and all other financial transactions;

_____(F) business related transactions;

_____(G) insurance transactions;

_____(H) estate, trust, and all beneficiary transactions;

_____(I) claims and litigations;

_____(J) social security, medicare, medicaid, military, benefits;

_____(K) 401k, retirement, savings, and all others;

_____(L) tax matters and all other I.R.S. transactions;

_____(M) All of the powers listed in A-L above.

## Special Instructions

_____

_____

_____

_____

\* Unless indicated otherwise, this power of attorney remains in its
effect and is not terminated by my disability or incapacity.\*

In the event that the named agent associated with my power of attorney, then dies, or becomes legally disabled or incapacitated, or resigns and refuses to act as my agent, I name the following to act alone, and in succesion, in the others place: _____

_____, residing at _____,

in the County of _____, State of _____.


**SIGNED THIS** _____ day of _____, _____.


State of _____.

County of _____.

Signed under oath before me on _____,

by _____, Respondent personally

known to me and/or identified by signature.


_____
Notary Public


I, the notary public whose name appears above, certifies that I am not an attorney in this action.


_____
Notary Public


(In Texas, attach Form F.6 in place of Notary)

## Texas Prisoner Innocence Questionnaire

If you  want to make an innocence claim, you should first read Chapter 13 of the Offender Legal Handbook, Eleventh Edition. The Offender Legal Handbook is in your unit law library.

If you think you meet the requirements and criteria for making a claim of innocence, fill out the Texas Prisoner Innocence Questionnaire (TPIQ), along with the Consent for Release of Information, and send them to an innocence clinic. Follow the mailing instructions which you will find near the end of the TPIQ. If you do not know the answer to a question, simply say "I do not know." Whenever you are given a choice for an answer (for example, YES or NO) circle the correct answer.

You should not fill out the TPIQ unless you are innocent of the crime(s) holding you in prison. Courts require new, clear and convincing evidence that proves your innocence. "New evidence" means evidence that was not available at the time of trial and was not considered by the court. If your case does not meet the definition above, no new evidence exists to prove your innocence, or the evidence available does not meet a clear and convincing standard, the law school clinics will not take your case. Use your best hand writing. If they can't read it, they can't help you. If you run out of space, write "see attached." On a clean sheet of paper, write the corresponding number of the question you are finishing and complete your answer. If you need more than one additional page of paper to explain a question you are probably writing too much. Keep it short and to the point!

You may need to fill out more than one TPIQ if you are claiming innocence on more than one conviction. Use the following examples to know whether to fill out more than one TPIQ:

- if you were charged with the kidnapping and aggravated sexual assault in an incident that involved a single victim, fill out only one TPIQ.
- if the conviction involves multiple counts against the same victim (for example, sexual assault of the same child on different days), fill out only one TPIQ.
- if you were convicted in two or more sexual assaults, involving different victims who were attacked at different times, fill out a TPIQ for each conviction.

# TEXAS PRISONER INNOCENCE QUESTIONNAIRE

I.  **APPLICANT CHECKLIST- Check "yes" or "no" for each question below as it relates to the conviction you are claiming innocence for. If you are claiming innocence on more than one conviction, reread the first page to see if you need to fill out a separate TPIQ for each conviction.**

| YES | NO | THE CRIME YOU CLAIM INNOCENCE FOR: |
|---|---|---|
| | | Was it committed in Texas? |
| | | Was it for an offense that occurred while in custody? |
| | | Is it a FELONY? |
| | | Is it a FEDERAL conviction? |
| | | Is it a DEATH PENALTY conviction? |
| | | Is it a drug-related conviction? |
| | | Did you plead GUILTY, NO CONTEST or NOLO CONTENDERE? |
| | | Have you exhausted your direct appeals? |
| | | Do you currently have a state and/or federal writ pending? |
| | | Are you currently represented by an attorney? |
| | | Have you ever been released to parole/probation on the conviction? |
| | | If you were released to parole/probation on the conviction, was that parole/probation ever revoked? |
| | | If your parole/probation was revoked, is the innocence claim on the underlying offense (not on the reason for the revocation)? |
| | | Are you currently incarcerated? |

## I. PERSONAL INFORMATION

A.  Full name (first, middle, last): _____

B.  Date of birth: _____

C.  TDCJ number: _____

D.  Current unit and mailing address:


E.  Email address (if any):


F.  What was your Driver's License Number at the time of conviction (even if now currently invalid)? _____ State of issuance: _____

G. Closest relative or personal friend for contact outside of prison (name, relationship, address, phone #):

H. What is your primary/first language? _____

I. What was the highest grade you completed in school? _____

J. Have you been given an IQ Test?    Yes    No    If yes, what was your score? _____
Who gave the test and what year?

K. Please list the school(s) you have attended:

L. Are you currently represented by an attorney or innocence organization?
Yes    No

If yes, list the name, address, and phone number of the attorney or organization and describe the proceedings in which you are represented:

M. Have you ever been diagnosed with a mental problem (for example, schizophrenia, bipolar, etc.)?    Yes    No
If yes, what was the diagnosis, who made it, and when?

N. What kind of legal help do you want (DNA motion, state writ, clemency, etc)?

## II. CURRENT CONVICTION INFORMATION

A. List all convictions for which you are currently incarcerated. Provide the offense type, date of offense, length of sentence, county of conviction and cause number.

B. For the conviction that you are claiming innocence, fill out the chart below. Reread the instructions on the first page to see whether you need to fill out a separate TPIQ if you have more than one conviction that you are claiming innocence for. If you are filling out more than once TPIQ, be sure to send all the TPIQs to the same clinic at the same time.

| | | | |
|---|---|---|---|
| Offense | | | |
| City, County | | | |
| Trial Cause Number | | | |
| Offense Date | | | |
| Arrest Date | | | |
| Conviction Date | | | |
| Conviction By (circle one) | PLEA | BENCH TRIAL | JURY TRIAL |
| Sentence Length | | | |
| Parole Eligibility Date | | | |
| Sentence Discharge Date | | | |
| Are you claiming self-defense | YES | NO | |
| Are you Innocent? (circle one) | YES | NO | |

### III. INNOCENCE CLAIM (check all that apply to your claim of innocence)

_____ **DNA will prove my innocence**

_____ **An alibi will prove my innocence**

_____ **The victim(s) mistakenly identified me as the criminal actor**

_____ **The victim has recanted**

_____ **The victim lied about the incident**

_____ **There are additional witnesses who never testified**

_____ **Someone else has admitted committing the crime and said I was not involved**

_____ **I gave a false confession**

_____ **Other:** Explain, describing what new evidence exists that would lead to proof of innocence:

A. Describe what the police or prosecutor say you did to commit the crime for which you were convicted but are claiming innocence. If you were charged as an accomplice, or as a party-to-the-crime, describe what role they say you played in the offense.

B. Describe your version of events. Include a detailed description of what you were doing that day, what happened, and any other information you feel is important, including why you think important information was not presented on your behalf.

## IV. LAW ENFORCEMENT INVESTIGATION/EVIDENCE

A. List the law enforcement agency that investigated the crime and the names of the investigating officers if you know them:

B. How did you become a suspect in the investigation?

C. To your knowledge, were there any other suspects the police investigated? If so, whom?

D. To your knowledge, why did the investigation into that person stop?

E.  Why do you think the "victim(s)" made complaints against you?

F.  When was the first time you spoke with your trial lawyer?

G.  Did the police or investigating detective(s) ever interview you, and if so, how many times were you interviewed?

H.  How long were the interviews?

I.  Did you ask to speak to a lawyer during the interview(s)?   Yes     No

    If so, did the interview stop when you requested your lawyer?    Yes    No

J.  Did you sign any papers during the interview, and if so, what did you sign?

K.  Did you sign any papers after the interview, and if so, what did you sign?

L.  Did you give a confession or make statements to investigating officers?   Yes    No

    If yes:

    1.  Please give a detailed description of what you told officers:

    2.  Why did you give the statement?

3.  Was it a written statement?   Yes   No
    If it was written, did you sign it?   Yes   No

4.  Was your lawyer with you when you signed the statement?   Yes   No

5.  Was the statement admitted at trial?   Yes   No

M.  Please list the name(s) of all co-defendants (others who were charged with the same crime) or other suspects investigated for this crime:

N.  Do you know if the co-defendant(s) were offered anything in exchange for their testimony, and if so, what were they offered?

O.  What sentence(s) did the co-defendant(s) receive?  Where are they now?

P.  Please list the name(s) of all alleged victim(s) of the offense for which you were convicted:

Q.  Did any eyewitnesses identify you, and if so, when and where?  (for example, at the scene of the crime, photo line up, in court, other)

R.  Did anyone else identify or implicate you, and if so, who, where, when?

S.  If someone identified you, specify who it was and whether they testified.

## V.  COURT PROCEEDINGS

A.  Pre-Trial:

1.  Were you offered a plea?  Yes    No       What was it?    _____

2.  Did you take the plea agreement?    Yes    No

    Why or why not?

    Circle your final plea:   NOT GUILTY    GUILTY   NOLO CONTENDERE

3.  Name, address and phone number of trial lawyer:



    Circle one:    RETAINED      APPOINTED       PRO BONO

4.  Name, address, and phone number of any investigator (other than police officers) who worked on your case:



5.  Name(s) of the prosecuting District Attorney(s) on your case:



6.  Name of the judge presiding in your case:



B.   Trial Information (skip if you took a plea and go to C., below):

1.  Did you testify?    Yes    No

    If no, why not?

2.  Did the "victims" testify?   Yes    No

3.  Did any surviving family member or friend give a victim impact statement, and if so, who?

4. List the witnesses that testified for the STATE, how they are related to the case, and briefly describe the testimony of each witness:

5. Did any expert(s) testify for the STATE (for example, a doctor, handwriting expert, scientist, etc.)?   Please provide the name of the expert, what kind of expert testified, address, and telephone number.

6. List the witnesses that testified for the DEFENSE, how they are related to the case, and briefly describe the testimony of each witness:

7. Did any expert(s) testify for the DEFENSE (for example, a doctor, handwriting expert, scientist, etc.)?  Please provide the name of the expert, what kind of expert testified, address, and telephone number.

C.  Evidence (answer even if you took a plea):

1.  Physical Evidence/Non-Biological.  Was any physical/non-biological evidence recovered (for example, fingerprints, weapons, fibers, tire tracks, etc.) during the investigation of your case?    Yes    No

If yes, please describe:

Was that evidence used at trial?    Yes    No

2. Biological Evidence. Was any biological evidence (DNA) recovered during the investigation of your case? Yes ___ No ___

If yes:

   a. Were any bodily fluids or hair samples obtained from the victim, and if so, what samples were obtained? (for example, vaginal swabs, anal swabs, blood, hair, fingernail scrapings, saliva, etc.)

   b. Were any bodily fluids or hair samples obtained from you, and if so, what samples were obtained?

   c. Who took the samples from you and where was it done?

   d. Was any biological evidence found at the crime scene, and if so, what was found?

   e. Were bodily fluids or hair(s) found on you, your clothing, in your car, home, etc., and if so, what was found and where?

   f. Was any biological evidence found on the victim or at the crime scene, and if so, what was found and where? (for example, blood or semen stains, hair, etc.)

g.  Was any testing done on the bodily fluids or hair samples, and if so, what kind of testing was performed?

h.  Who arranged to have the testing done, prosecution or defense?

i.  Which lab performed the test(s)?

j.  If applicable, who arranged to have the second test done, prosecution or defense?

k.  Which lab performed the second test?

l.  Was testing done on all of the physical/biological evidence recovered during the investigation of your case?

m.  Were the results of the test(s) used at trial, and if no, why not?

n.  Were the results of the test(s) used on appeal, and if no, why not?

o.  Please list what items(s) of evidence you think can be subjected to a DNA test and state how that test will show you are innocent.

p.  Is there any physical evidence that is still available other than bodily fluids or hair, and if so, what is it, where is it, and who has it?

q. Have you received written noticed that evidence in your case has been destroyed?  If so, when and from whom?

D.  Direct Appeal

1.  Did you/your attorney appeal?     Yes     No

   If yes, what is that appeal cause number?  _____

2.  Is your case still on appeal (waiting for a decision)?     Yes     No

3.  Name, address and phone number of appellate lawyer:

   _____

E.  Petition for Discretionary Review (PDR)

1.  Did you/your attorney file a petition for discretionary review (PDR)?  Yes   No

   If yes, what is the PDR cause number?  _____

2.  Is your case still waiting for a decision on PDR?   Yes     No

3.  Name, address and phone number of PDR lawyer.

   _____

4.  Did you/your attorney file a writ of certiorari to the United States Supreme Court?  Yes    No

F.  Writ of Habeas Corpus

1.  Did you/your attorney file a writ of habeas corpus in STATE court?  Yes   No

   If yes, how many STATE writs have been filed?

2.  Name, address, and phone number of STATE writ lawyer:

3. For each STATE writ filed, list the issues raised. Which issues, if any, did the court decide in your favor?

4. Did you/your attorney file a writ of habeas corpus in FEDERAL court?

   Yes    No     If yes, how many FEDERAL writs have been filed?

5. Please state the name, address and phone number of your FEDERAL writ lawyer.

6. For each FEDERAL writ filed, list the issues raised. Which issues, if any, did the court decide in your favor?

## VI. CASE MATERIALS

Please check the materials that are available to you. DO NOT SEND ANY OF THE MATERIALS until asked to do so.

A. Pretrial transcripts                          _____

B. Trial transcripts                             _____

C. Police offense reports                        _____

D. Police field notes  (Handwritten notes)       _____

E. Affidavits                                    _____

F. Witness Statements                            _____

G.  Laboratory reports                                    _____

H.  Direct appeal brief- State                            _____

I.  Direct appeal  brief – Petitioner (yours)             _____

J.  Any other briefs  (Specify)                           _____

K.  Petition for Discretionary Review                     _____

L.  Habeas Corpus writs                                   _____

M.  DNA motions                                           _____

N.  Other documents or legal materials of any kind        _____
    Please describe:

**VII.  CHILD SEXUAL ABUSE CASES** (skip if you are not convicted of child sexual
abuse)

a.  How many children accused you of molesting them?    _____

b.  For each child, list the child's name, age at time of abuse, how old the child
would be now, gender and the child's relationship to you (for example:
daughter, son, step-child, niece, nephew, neighbor, etc.)

c.  What did the child/children say that you did?

d.  When did the child/children first make the accusation and whom did they tell?

e.  Why do you think the child/children made complaints against you?

f.  Did a doctor examine the child/children?  Yes   No
    If yes, what was the doctor's name?

g.  Describe the results/findings of the exam and any evidence collected:

h.   Has the child/children told anyone that they lied or made up the accusation?
     Yes    No

     If Yes, what did they say and to whom did they say it?

**VIII.  ANY OTHER INFORMATION YOU THINK THE  INNOCENCE CLINIC
SHOULD KNOW ABOUT YOU OR YOUR CASE.**

**IX.**     LIST THE NAME(S) AND CONTACT INFORMATION (address, phone, email)
         OF ANYONE WHO HELPED YOU COMPLETE THIS FORM.

**X.**      Sign the two-page waiver that appears at the end of the packet.  If you do not sign
         the waiver the clinic cannot accept your case.  If you have questions about the
         waiver, write SCFO.

## Mailing Instructions:

When you complete your TPIQ and have signed the "Consent for Release of Information," send the TPIQ and consent form to one of the following innocence clinics. Although you can send the TPIQ to more than one clinic, that may not be helpful because only one clinic at a time will work on your case. The clinics share a database and will know you have sent it to one of them. For more information about the clinics and the type of cases they accept, read Chapter 13 of the Offender Legal Handbook. Your unit law library has a copy.

The Innocence Project of Texas, 1511 Texas Avenue, Lubbock, TX 79401

Texas Center For Actual Innocence, 727 E. Dean Keeton St., Austin, TX 78705

Texas Innocence Network, 100 Law Center, Houston, TX 77204-6060

Thurgood Marshall School of Law Innocence Project, 3100 Cleburne St., Houston, TX 77004

**DO NOT SEND ANY OTHER DOCUMENTS AT THIS TIME.** If the clinic needs additional information it will request it from you. You may attach additional pages to explain your case if necessary.

The clinics you send your TPIQ to do not represent you. However, the information you provide in the TPIQ and send to the clinic is in an effort by you to establish an attorney-client relationship with them. As such, that information is confidential and is protected in law by the attorney-client privilege. That is true whether or not an attorney-client relationship is ever formed between you and the clinic.

You must sign the attached "Consent for Release of Information" so that the clinic may review your case. Place the name of the clinic you will be sending the TPIQ to in the space where it says "Name of Clinic." If there is something about the Release you do not understand, send an I-60 to State Counsel for Offenders.

**Mailing Checklist** (Sender please check off and fill out):

_____ TPIQ enclosed. If more than one, list the number here: _____

_____ **Signed** Consent for Release of Information enclosed

_____ Additional pages enclosed. List the number here: _____

## CONSENT FOR RELEASE OF INFORMATION

By signing below, I authorize _____

*[insert name of clinic]*

(hereinafter "Clinic") its staff or representatives to investigate my case, communicate with my former attorneys, prosecutors, witnesses, the Texas Department of Criminal Justice, Texas Board of Pardons and Paroles, probation and parole officers, and all other persons or governmental agencies that may have information that the Clinic deems necessary in evaluating my case. I specifically waive the attorney-client privilege existing between myself and my former attorneys, paralegals, legal assistants, investigators and other representatives who worked on my behalf and grant them permission to speak to the Clinic's attorneys, staff and representatives investigating my case.

I authorize any and all entities to release to the Clinic or its staff or representatives, any and all records, files, reports and information of any kind related to me or to any criminal case involving me, including police reports, witness statements, post conviction pleadings and correctional records, pre-sentencing reports and other documents in prison social services and legal files, legal papers, court documents, medical records, laboratory analysis, probation reports, attorneys' files and records, and any information necessary to the Clinic to work on my behalf.

I also authorize the release to the Clinic or its staff or representatives any and all records and information in the possession of the Texas Department of Criminal Justice Correctional Institutions Division, Custodian of Medical Records, Unit Classification, or any other state or federal penal institution, including juvenile facilities or mental health or medical facilities, rehabilitation clinics or centers, and any court or probation department, including juvenile. I authorize the release of any documents in the possession of the Federal Bureau of Investigation or any other federal, state, or local law enforcement agency. I also authorize the release of any and all military records.

I further authorize the release of any and all information and records from public or private schools, medical or mental health institutions, or other such institutions, including all prison reports and records, all medical and psychiatric or mental health records, notes, nursing sheets, hospitalization records, physician notes or prescriptions, or any other type of report or record maintained by any of the above institutions, including records concerning substance abuse. I also authorize release of any and all employment records. I also authorize release of any and all records made by or in the possession of any and all attorneys.

I understand that there may be statutes, rules and regulations that protect my confidentiality of some of the records, files, reports and information covered by this release; it is my specific intent to waive the protection of all such statutes, rules and regulations so that confidential information can be shared with the Clinic.

I further authorize the Clinic to disseminate information, other than confidential information, to other persons or entities as may be necessary to fully investigate my case or to assist me with receiving services from such persons. I authorize the Clinic to enter pertinent information into a network database that will be accessed by other clinics pursuing innocence claims.

I understand that by conducting an initial investigation, the Clinic is not agreeing to represent me. I further understand that at any point the Clinic, at its sole discretion, may determine that further investigation is not warranted, and is under no obligation to continue to represent me or investigate my case.

A photocopy of this document shall have the same effect as the original.

By my signature below, I represent that this waiver is voluntary and given without any reservation. This authorization is effective until revoked by the undersigned in writing.

Signature: _____ Date of Birth:_____

Printed Name: _____TDCJ No.:_____

Date: _____

Witness Signature: _____

Witness Printed Name: _____Date: _____

# Texas Government Code § 552.028 Information

Sec. 552.028 – Request for Information from Incarcerated Individual

    (a) A governmental body is not required to accept or comply with a request for information from:

        (1) an individual who is imprisoned or confined in a correctional facility; or

        (2) an agent of that individual, other than that individual's attorney when the attorney is requesting information that is subject to disclosure under this chapter.

    (b) This section does not prohibit a governmental body from disclosing to an individual described by Subsection (a)(1), or that individuals' agent, information held by the governmental body pertaining to that individual.

    (c) In this section, "correctional facility" means:

        (1) a secure correctional facility, as defined by Section 1.07, Penal Code;

        (2) a secure correctional facility and a secure detention facility, as defined by Section 51.02, Family Code; and

        (3) a place designated by the law of this state, another state, or the federal government for the confinement of a person arrested for, charged with, or convicted of a criminal offense.

Sec. 552.029 – Right of Access to Certain Information Relating to Inmate of Department of Criminal Justice

Notwithstanding Section 508.313 or 552.134, the following information about an inmate who is confined in a facility operated by or under a contract with the Texas Department of Criminal Justice is subject to required disclosure under Section 552.021:

    (1) the inmates name, identification number, age, birthplace, department photograph, physical description, or general state of health or the nature of an injury to or critical illness suffered by the inmate;

    (2) the inmates assigned unit or the date on which the unit received the inmate, unless disclosure of the information would violate federal law relating to the confidentiality of substance abuse treatment;

    (3) the offense for which the inmate was convicted or the judgment and sentence for that offense;

    (4) the county and court in which the inmate was convicted;

    (5) the inmates earliest or latest possible release dates;

    (6) the inmates parole date or earliest possible parole date;

    (7) any prior confinement of the inmate by the Texas Department of Criminal Justice or its predecessor; or

    (8) basic information regarding the death of an inmate in custody, an incident involving the use of force, or an alleged crime involving the inmate.

Sec. 552.101 – Exception: Confidential Information

Information is excepted from the requirement of Section 552.021 if it is information considered to be confidential by law, either constitutional, statutory, or by judicial decision.

Sec. 552.107 – Exception: Certain Legal Matters.

Information is excepted from the requirements of Section 552.021 if:

> (1) it is information that the attorney general or an attorney of a political subdivision is prohibited from disclosing because of a duty to the client under the Texas Rules of Evidence or the Texas Disciplinary Rules of Professional Conduct; or
>
> (2) a court by order has prohibited disclosure of the information.

Sec. 552.108 – Exception: Certain Law Enforcement, Corrections, and Prosecutorial Information.

(a) Information held by a law enforcement agency or prosecutor that deals with the detection, investigation, or prosecution of crime is excepted from the requirements of Section 552.021 if:

> (1) release of the information would interfere with the detection, investigation, or prosecution of crime;
>
> (2) it is information that deals with the detection, investigation, or prosecution of crime only in relation to an investigation that did not result in conviction or deferred adjudication;
>
> (3) it is information relating to a threat against a peace officer or detention officer collected or disseminated under Section 411.048; or
>
> (4) it is information that:
>> (A) is prepared by an attorney representing the state in anticipation of or in the course of preparing for criminal litigation; or
>>
>> (B) reflects the mental impressions or legal reasoning of an attorney representing the state.

(b) An internal record or notation of a law enforcement agency or prosecutor that is maintained for internal use in matters relating to law enforcement or prosecution is excepted from the requirements of Section 552.021 if:

> (1) release of the internal record or notation would interfere with law enforcement or prosecution;
>
> (2) the internal record or notation relates to law enforcement only in relation to an investigation that did not result in conviction or deferred adjudication; or
>
> (3) the internal record or notation:
>> (A) is prepared by an attorney representing the state in anticipation of or in the course of preparing for criminal litigation; or
>>
>> (B) reflects the mental impressions or legal reasoning of an attorney representing the state.

(c) This section does not except from the requirements of Section 552.021 information that is basic information about an arrested person, an arrest, or a crime.

Sec. 552.1085 – Confidentiality of Sensitive Crime Scene Image

(a) In this section:

> (1) "Deceased persons next of kin" means:
>> (A) the surviving spouse of the deceased person;
>>
>> (B) if there is no surviving spouse of the deceased, an adult child of the deceased person; or
>>
>> (C) if there is no surviving spouse or adult child of the deceased, a parent of the deceased person.

(2) "Defendant" means a person being prosecuted for the death of the deceased person or a person convicted of an offense in relation to that death and appealing that conviction.

(3) "Expressive work" means:

    (A) a fictional or nonfictional entertainment, dramatic, literary, or musical work that is a play, book, article, musical composition, audiovisual work, radio or television program, work of art, or work of political, educational, or newsworthy value;

    (B) a work the primary function of which is the delivery of news, information, current events, or other matters of public interest or concern; or

    (C) an advertisement or commercial announcement of a work described by Paragraph (A) or (B).

(4) "Local governmental entity" means a county, municipality, school district, charter school, junior college district, or other political subdivision of this state.

(5) "Public or private institution of higher education" means:

    (A) an institution of higher education, as defined by Section 61.003, Education Code; or

    (B) a private or independent institution of higher education, as defined by Section 61.003, Education Code.

(6) "Sensitive crime scene image" means a photograph or video recording taken at a crime scene, contained in or part of a closed criminal case, that depicts a deceased person in a state of dismemberment, decapitation, or similar mutilation or that depicts the deceased persons genitalia.

(7) "State agency" means a department, commission, board, office, or other agency that is a part of state government and that is created by the constitution or a statute of this state. The term includes an institution of higher education as defined by Section 61.003, Education Code.

(b) For purposes of this section, an Internet website, the primary function of which is not the delivery of news, information, current events, or other matters of public interest or concern, is not an expressive work.

(c) A sensitive crime scene image in the custody of a governmental body is confidential and excepted from the requirements of Section 552.021 and a governmental body may not permit a person to view or copy the image except as provided by this section. This section applies to any sensitive crime scene image regardless of the date that the image was taken or recorded.

(d) Notwithstanding Subsection (c) and subject to Subsection (e), the following persons may view or copy information that constitutes a sensitive crime scene image from a governmental body:

    (1) the deceased persons next of kin;

    (2) a person authorized in writing by the deceased persons next of kin;

    (3) a defendant or the defendants attorney;

    (4) a person who establishes to the governmental body an interest in a sensitive crime scene image that is based on, connected with, or in support of the creation, in any medium, of an expressive work;

    (5) a person performing bona fide research sponsored by a public or private institution of higher education with approval of a supervisor of the research or a supervising faculty member;

(6) a state agency;

(7) an agency of the federal government; or

(8) a local governmental entity.

(e) This section does not prohibit a governmental body from asserting an exception to disclosure of a sensitive crime scene image to a person identified in Subsection (d) on the grounds that the image is excepted from the requirements of Section 552.021 under another provision of this chapter or another law.

(f) Not later than the 10th business day after the date a governmental body receives a request for a sensitive crime scene image from a person described by Subsection (d)(4) or (5), the governmental body shall notify the deceased persons next of kin of the request in writing. The notice must be sent to the next of kin last known address.

(g) A governmental body that receives a request for information that constitutes a sensitive crime scene image shall allow a person described in Subsection (d) to view or copy the image not later than the 10th business day after the date the governmental body receives the request unless the governmental body files a request for an attorney general decision under Subchapter G regarding whether an exception to public disclosure applies to the information.

# Freedom of Information Appeals and Litigation

## FOIA Appeals

What do you do when, after all of your best efforts and after you've exhausted all of your administrative options, yet the agency refuses to release the information? You can then go to court. You may also contest the type or amount of fees which you were charged. Moreover, you can appeal any other type of adverse determination, including a rejection of a request for failure to describe adequately the documents being requested or a response indicating that no requested records were located.

You can also appeal because the agency failed to conduct an adequate search for the documents that you requested. The filing of an appeal does not affect or delay the release of documents which the agency ruled should be disclosed in response to your initial FOIA request. In other words, a partial "win" at the first administrative level is not put at risk if you decide to appeal. There is no charge for filing an appeal.

Reviewing courts should undertake their analysis of FOIA requests by "recognizing the enduring beliefs underlying freedom of information laws: that an informed public is desirable, that access to information prevents governmental abuse and helps secure freedom, and that, ultimately, government must answer to its citizens." *Pansy v. Borough of Stroudsburg*, 23 F.3d 772, 792 (3rd Cir. 1994).

## Practice Tips:

A. If the agency rules against you at the administrative level-on either disclosure or fee waiver issues-the agency is bound to adhere to the reasons it provides at that stage; it cannot raise new issues later if litigation is required. "Taken together, these principles lead us to the following conclusion: on judicial review, the agency must stand on whatever reasons for denial it gave in the administrative proceeding." *Friends of the Coast Fork v. U.S. Dept. of the Interior*, 110 F.3d 53, 55 (9th. Cir 1997). The practical impact of this requires you to understand very early in your request process if you have a reasonable chance to get the requested materials at the administrative level, or if you are merely going through the motions to exhaust your administrative remedies in order to get into court. If you are in the former context; go ahead and make your best argument. Try to work with the agency to best inform it of your needs and the correct application of the law to your request. If you are in the latter realm-for some reason you are sure that you are going to get hosed at the administrative level-it is important not to do anything to help the agency, make its best arguments during the administrative phase. In this situation, you want the agency to ignore you, to make unreasonable and unlawful arguments; they will be stuck with them once you are in court. You will win.
B. An administrative appeal may be undertaken upon either, the denial of an initial FOIA request, or an agency's failure to issue a determination within the statutory 20-day time deadline. 5 U.S.C. §§ 552(a)(6)(A)(i), 552(a)(6)(C).
C. An appeal should outline all facts which you think are relevant to your request. Reviewing courts, while not limited to the record before the agency (except for fee waivers, for which they are limited to review on the administrative record), do tend to consider what a

reasonable agency decision-maker would do when confronted with the facts before it. In other words, if you fail to mention an important fact at the administrative level, it will work against you when raising it at the litigation stage. This is a frequent problem we encounter which can severely limit one's options in court.

D. Deadlines for the filing of an appeal are noted in each agency's FOIA regulations located in CFRs. They are often as short as 20 working days, so it is important to act promptly when a denial of your initial request is issued. Although, if you miss your appeal deadline you could always refile your another FOIA request, it would just add to the delay in reaching the ultimate resolution of your information request.

E. Appeals need not include reference to statutory, regulatory, or case law, but it helps. Even if you are not comfortable with legal research, simply citing the agency's rules which have been violated can make the appeal much more effective.

F. An agency is required to make a "determination" on the merits of a FOIA appeal within 20 working days of receipt. 5 U.S.C. § 552(a)(6)(A)(ii). The agency must "immediately notify the person making such request of the provisions for judicial review of that determination." Id.

　　1. An agency may unilaterally extend the response deadline by up to 10 working days in "unusual circumstances," but only upon giving written notice to the requester. 5 U.S.C. § 552(a)(6)(B)(i). This right may not be exercised if the agency has already exceeded its 10-day response deadline for the initial request. Id.

　　2. FOIA requires any denial of a request to list the "names and titles or positions of each person responsible for the denial." 5 U.S.C.§ 552(a)(6)(C).

G. Avoid impassioned prose ("you are killing all of the animals in the ocean, I must know why!"), it may make you feel better, but it will not convince the reviewer that you are right and may cloud the issues.

H. Remember that you are not only trying to convince the agency to release the requested materials, you are also creating a record for a judge to review should legal action be required. If you think of additional issues or arguments which have not been included in either the initial request or the appeal, draft a letter (not a phone call-you want a paper trail) which sets them out. Make a record for review, make a record for review, make a record for review.

"The Freedom of Information Act: 'a federal regulation obliging government agencies to release all information they had to anyone who made application for it, except information they had that they did not want to release.'" Joseph Heller, *Closing Time* (1994).

## FOIA Litigation

What do you do when after all of your best efforts, you have exhausted your administrative options, yet the agency has proven Mr. Heller to be correct? You must seek judicial review. Litigating FOIA cases requires considerable knowledge of the Federal Court Rules of Civil Procedure (FRCP) and other specific Federal Court rules, as well as strong legal research and writing skills. As one appellate court has frankly acknowledged: "Freedom of Information Act cases are peculiarly difficult." Miscavige v. IRS, 2 F.3d 366, 367 (11th Cir. 1993); see also Summers v. Department of Justice, 140 F.3d 1077, 1080 (D.C. Cir. 1998) (noting "peculiar nature of the FOIA"). Moreover, in order to actually file a case or appear in court on behalf of any party (other than as a *pro se* (for yourself) litigant), federal rules generally require admission by the Federal Court as an attorney authorized to practice in the specific federal district where the FOIA case is filed. For these reasons,

FOIA Advocates suggests that anyone interested in filing a FOIA lawsuit should carefully consider the benefits of obtaining legal counsel from an attorney who is familiar with both FOIA litigation and federal civil practice. If a lawsuit is filed on your behalf and you substantially prevail, you may be awarded reasonable attorney fees and litigation costs reasonably incurred.

"The statute is a commitment to the principle that a democracy cannot function unless the people are permitted to know what their government is up to." *Id.* (internal quotations omitted) *Favish v. OIC*, (9th. Cir., July 12, 2000).

This guide to FOIA litigation is designed to provide a very cursory over-view of litigation related issues pertaining to FOIA in order to assist you to best develop your case to ensure that if you are required to seek judicial review, you will have a winning case. However, this information should not be viewed as a substitute for obtaining legal counsel with an attorney qualified to evaluate the specific merits, issues or tactical considerations presented by your specific case.

FOI Advocates provides free initial consultations on all FOIA and public record matters, and our staff attorneys have considerable experience litigating FOIA cases and appeals. We are available to provide you legal counsel and representation in all manner of FOIA litigation before both trial and appellate courts.

What follows is a very brief overview of what you should expect if you retain an attorney to litigate a FOIA claim - and some of the pitfalls to avoid. Remember; the issue of whether you will win or lose your FOIA litigation will have been largely determined by the time you have exhausted the administrative phase of your case by the documentation which has been submitted to the agency's administrative record. This is particularly true regarding fee waiver issues because the court's review, while de novo, is limited to the administrative record. 5 U.S.C. § 552(a)(4)(vii).

A. Remember the golden rule of FOIA: "An agency seeking to withhold information under an exemption to FOIA has the burden of proving that the information falls under the claimed exemption." GC Micro Corp. v. Defense Logistics Agency, 33 F.3d 1109, 1113 (9th Cir. 1994); see also Lewis v. IRS, 823 F.2d 375, 378 (9th Cir.1987). This favorable burden of proof provides rarefied air indeed for a plaintiff's attorney to breathe.

B. Federal courts have jurisdiction to "enjoin the agency from withholding agency records" 5 U.S.C. § 552(a)(4)(B). But before going to court, a FOIA requester must "exhaust" their administrative remedies, that is, they must use every option available at the agency level if they expect the court to review their case. 5 U.S.C. § 552(a)(6)(B). This can occur when the agency takes too long to respond to a request or appeal, or if the agency denies an appeal. If you file your suit before one of these things occurs, your case will be dismissed.

C. The action may be filed in the federal district court in the district where the complainant resides, has a principal place of business, in which the agency records are located, or in the District of Columbia. 5 U.S.C. § 552(a)(4)(B).

D. The court may review the case de novo, that is, the court may create its own record of events without depending on the agency's administrative record. 5 U.S.C. § 552(a)(4)(B). Thus, courts reviewing FOIA cases may grant somewhat less deference to an agency interpretation of the case than would normally be the case when a court reviews and administrative action.

E. In almost all circumstances, a FOIA complaint should also plead an APA claim as a violation of the terms of FOIA can also usually be framed as either "arbitrary and capricious" or an "abuse of discretion."

F. The complaint, in addition to demanding the release of the records at issue, and/or the granting of a fee waiver, could further seek:
   1. A request for an order enjoining the agency from relying on an invalid regulation or practice in all future FOIA undertakings. Cf. McGehee v. CIA, 697 F.2d 1095 (D.C. Cir. 1983).
   2. An order declaring the agency's actions to be violative of FOIA.
   3. An award of attorney's fees and costs pursuant to 5 U.S.C. § 552(a)(4)(E). Attorney fees may be awarded when the plaintiff has "substantially prevailed." Id.
   4. If the actions of the agency were so flagrant to be arbitrary and capricious, ask that the court make a specific finding of that fact and refer the matter to the Merit System Protection Board for investigation. 5 U.S.C. § 552(a)(4)(F).

G. Consider the active use of requests for admission (RFA's) as a discovery tool. Outline the elements of your claim in your RFA's. If not admitted or denied by the government within 30 days from service of the RFA's, they will be deemed admitted pursuant to the Federal Rules of Civil Procedure. FRCP 36(a).

H. Generally, FOIA cases are well suited for resolution by summary judgment pursuant to Federal Rule of Civil Procedure 56. There are usually few material facts in dispute and the conflict is often based on divergent interpretations of the relevant law. Thus FOIA cases may often be litigated relatively cheaply (in comparison to other types of federal litigation).

## Texas Commutation of Sentence (Time Cut) Application

# NOTICE TO APPLICANT

Please read the application instructions carefully, and complete the application accordingly.

Submission of incomplete applications or applications that do not comply with instructions may result in the Board's Clemency Section soliciting you in writing for the correct documentation.

Failure to comply with instructions will delay processing.

\*\*\*\*\*\*\*\*\*\*\*\*\*\*\*\*\*\*\*\*\*\*\*\*\*\*\*\*\*\*\*\*\*\*\*\*\*\*\*\*

**For your records, make <u>copies</u> of all documentation that you submit to the Board's Clemency Section.**

Due to the inability to retain records for extended time periods for incomplete applications, we are advising you NOT to <u>provide originals</u> of personal items, including but not exclusive to photos, transcripts, birth and other certificates, achievement awards, licenses, literature, social security and other identification cards or items, notebooks or binders, and clemency proclamations. You may in lieu of originals provide copies of these documents with your submitted application.

\*\*\*\*\*\*\*\*\*\*\*\*\*\*\*\*\*\*\*\*\*\*\*\*\*\*\*\*\*\*\*\*\*\*\*\*\*\*\*\*

COS-10 (R-01/11/2010)

# COMMUTATION OF SENTENCE
## INSTRUCTIONS & CHECKLIST

Mail completed applications to:

TEXAS BOARD OF PARDONS AND PAROLES
ATTN: CLEMENCY SECTION
8610 SHOAL CREEK BLVD.
AUSTIN, TX  78757

1.  Submit a completed application form. Please respond to **all** items. If necessary, use "N/A," "Unknown," "None," or "Do not remember."

2.  Applications must be typed or printed legibly in **black or blue** ink.

3.  Certified court documentation (indictment, judgment and sentence) for each adult conviction for which you are requesting a Commutation of Sentence. For complete instructions, refer to Page 2 of 2.

4.  Offense (arrest) reports for each adult conviction for which you are requesting a Commutation of Sentence. Obtain these documents from the arresting agency. The documents do not need to be certified. For complete instructions, refer to Page 2 of 2.

5.  **A written recommendation of a majority of the current trial officials** (the present prosecuting attorney, judge, and sheriff/chief of police of the arresting agency from the county and court of offense, conviction and release) and compliance with board rules governing Commutation of Sentence.

6.  Complete the attached application form as presented. You may submit attached documents as instructed in the application. Do not alter the presentation of this application either through reformatting or rewriting. Do not bind or staple the application with any other submitted material.

7.  The application must be signed and dated by the applicant.

   *  If the Board recommends a Commutation of Sentence, the Governor makes the final decision. The applicant will be notified in writing upon final action.

   *  Please let us know of any change of address or telephone number.

   *  On the Application Page 1 of 6, A. Demographic Information, where asked to provide the applicant's current name, input the full name as it might appear on a Governor's proclamation.

## GENERAL INFORMATION

**Definition** - A Commutation of Sentence results in a reduction of the sentence to a lesser time period. A commutation can be granted for time served. Commutations of sentence will be granted only upon the written recommendation of a majority of the applicant's trial officials in the county of conviction, stating that the penalty now appears to be excessive, recommending a definite term, based on new information not before the judge or jury at trial, or a statutory change in the penalty.

# PROCEDURES FOR OBTAINING COURT DOCUMENTATION

All court documents must be **CERTIFIED**, whether they originate from the office of the District, County, or Municipal Clerk. Acquire the proper documentation, accordingly:

**IF** convicted and the judgment included a court ordered **fine** and or **restitution**, furnish a statement from the appropriate clerk confirming the amount paid.

**IF** convicted and the sentence is probated or deferred, furnish the Complaint/Indictment or Information, Judgment and Sentence.

**IF** convicted of a misdemeanor resulting in a fine and/or jail time, furnish the Complaint, Judgment and Sentence.

**IF** convicted of a felony probation and revoked to the Texas Department of Criminal Justice – Correctional Institutions Division (TDCJ-CID), furnish the Indictment, Judgment and Sentence granting probation and the revocation document(s).

**IF** convicted of a felony, sentenced to TDCJ-CID and currently on parole or mandatory supervision or on annual report status, or have discharged the sentence, furnish the Indictment, Judgment and Sentence and a copy of the TDCJ parole certificate. Contact the following office(s) to obtain the appropriate certificate:

TDCJ-CID RECORDS OFFICE
P. O. BOX 99
HUNTSVILLE, TEXAS 77342

or

TDCJ PAROLE SUPERVISION
8610 SHOAL CREEK BLVD.
AUSTIN, TEXAS 78758

# PROCEDURES FOR OBTAINING ARREST/OFFENSE REPORTS

For **each** criminal offense, acquire from the appropriate law enforcement arresting agency copies of the arrest/offense reports. These copies of reports do not have to be certified. For offenses involving drugs, please provide copies of laboratory reports.

_____

# APPLICATION FOR COMMUTATION OF SENTENCE TO THE TEXAS BOARD OF PARDONS & PAROLES

## *TO THE BOARD OF PARDONS AND PAROLES OF TEXAS:*

I hereby request the Board of Pardons and Paroles or its designated agent to file this application for Clemency, to investigate the statements herein made under oath and, if the facts so justify, make a favorable recommendation to the Governor of the State of Texas that a Commutation of Sentence, to which I may be entitled under the laws of the State of Texas, be granted.

## A. DEMOGRAPHIC INFORMATION

| | | | | |
|---|---|---|---|---|
| Current full name | Last Name | ☐ Jr. ☐ III ☐ Sr. ☐ IV | First Name | Full Middle Name |
| Name(s) convicted under | | | | |
| Race and sex | Race _____ Sex _____ | | | |
| Date and place of birth | Date of birth _____ Place of birth _____ | | | |
| Driver's license | State _____ License Number _____ | | | |
| Alias names (including maiden name, name by former marriage and nicknames), birth dates, social security #'s, etc. | | | | |
| Current marital status | ☐ Married – Spouse's Name: ☐ Divorced ☐ Separated ☐ Single | | | |
| Children / support / alimony | I have _____ children under the age of 18 years. I am supporting the following named children under the age of 18 years: _____ I currently pay $ _____ / month in child support. I currently pay $ _____ / month in alimony. | | | |

## B.    ADDRESSES

| Current Mailing Address | Current Physical Address |
|---|---|
| *Indicate your current mailing address.* | *Provide information even if the physical and mailing addresses are the same.* |
| Number and street                    Apartment | Number and street                    Apartment |
| City                    State    Zip Code | City                    State    Zip Code |
| Home phone number  [          ]  _____ | County of residence  _____ |
| Work phone number  [          ]  _____ | Years resided at physical residence  _____ |
| Email Address  _____ | |

## Previous Addresses

List **all** previous physical addresses since age 18. Do not use post office boxes. If you lived in an apartment complex, list your apartment number. *All time periods must be accounted for.* Include complete dates (months and years of residence), addresses, city, state and zip codes.  Complete this page before attaching any additional page(s). Place attachments behind this page.

| From (month/year): | Number and street | | Apartment |
|---|---|---|---|
| To (month/year): | City | State | Zip Code |

| From (month/year): | Number and street | | Apartment |
|---|---|---|---|
| To (month/year): | City | State | Zip Code |

| From (month/year): | Number and street | | Apartment |
|---|---|---|---|
| To (month/year): | City | State | Zip Code |

| From (month/year): | Number and street | | Apartment |
|---|---|---|---|
| To (month/year): | City | State | Zip Code |

248

## C. EMPLOYMENT

Please give a comprehensive adult (since age 18) employment history, beginning with your present employment and working backwards. Include employer's name, address, your job position working title, description of job duties, salary, dates employed, and reason for leaving. Complete this page before attaching any additional page(s). Place attachments behind this page.

| From (month/year): | Employer name |
|---|---|
| To (month/year): | Employer address |
| Job position (working title) | Description of your work duties |
| Average monthly salary | Reason for leaving |

| From (month/year): | Employer name |
|---|---|
| To (month/year): | Employer address |
| Job position (working title) | Description of your work duties |
| Average monthly salary | Reason for leaving |

| From (month/year): | Employer name |
|---|---|
| To (month/year): | Employer address |
| Job position (working title) | Description of your work duties |
| Average monthly salary | Reason for leaving |

| From (month/year): | Employer name |
|---|---|
| To (month/year): | Employer address |
| Job position (working title) | Description of your work duties |
| Average monthly salary | Reason for leaving |

Raymond E. Lumsden

_____

## D.    STATUS

| | |
|---|---|
| Are you currently incarcerated in a Texas penal institution?<br><br>*If "yes," list your (TDCJ-CID) identification number.* | ☐ Yes   ☐ No<br><br>ID number: _____ |
| Were you ever incarcerated in a Texas penal institution?<br><br>*If "yes," list all (TDCJ-CID) identification numbers.* | ☐ Yes   ☐ No<br><br>Prior ID number: _____<br><br>Prior ID number: _____ |
| Are you currently serving a term of probation?<br><br>*If "yes", identify the county of current residence, name and phone number of your probation officer.* | ☐ Yes   ☐ No<br><br>County: _____<br><br>Name: _____<br><br>Number:  (____) _____ |
| Are you currently on parole, annual report status, or serving a term of mandatory supervision?<br><br>*If "yes," identify the county of current residence.* | ☐ Yes   ☐ No<br><br>County: _____ |
| Do you have any pending criminal charges?<br><br>*If "yes," attach an explanation page. Place the attachment behind this page.* | ☐ Yes   ☐ No |
| Have you been incarcerated in a federal or non-Texas state institution?<br><br>*If "yes," list all identification numbers. Include the facility name and location.* | ☐ Yes   ☐ No<br><br>ID Number: _____<br><br>Institution: _____<br><br>Location: _____ |

250

## E.  JUSTIFICATION FOR CLEMENCY CONSIDERATION

(1)  State the reasons and circumstances for requesting a commutation of sentence.

Complete this page before attaching any additional page(s). Place any attachments immediately behind this page.

_____

# F.  CERTIFICATION BY APPLICANT

*Please read the following statements carefully and indicate your understanding and acceptance by signing in the space provided.  This application must be signed.*

I hereby give my permission to the Board of Pardons and Paroles or its designated agent to make any inquiry and receive any information of record that it may deem proper in the investigation of this application for clemency; and

I understand that compliance with these requirements is sufficient for the Board's consideration of this application, but compliance does not necessarily mean that favorable action will result.

I hereby swear upon my oath that I am the subject herein named and the facts contained in this application are true and correct.

_____
**Applicant's Signature (Full Name)**

_____
**Date**

COS-10 (R-01/11/2010)        Date: _____
*(Last Name, First and Middle Name)*

_____

# CRIMINAL HISTORY INFORMATION

Provide information on <u>all</u> criminal convictions for which you are requesting a Commutation of Sentence **(list one offense per page)** and the disposition of each conviction. All blanks must be completed for each conviction. Included in this application are two (2) blank "Criminal History Information" pages provided in the event that you have multiple convictions.

**Photocopy as many of these blank pages as needed to list additional convictions.**

---

**Criminal Offense:** _____
*List the offense as it appears in the court documentation.*

---

**Are you requesting a Commutation of Sentence for this offense?**        ☐ Yes  /  ☐ No

---

*Additional Information about the Criminal Offense*

**County:** _____        **State:** _____

**Cause Number:** _____

**Court of Adjudication:** _____

**Disposition/Sentence Date:** _____
Date of sentencing.

**Court Disposition/Sentence:** _____

<u>Examples of possible responses that you may modify to reflect your circumstance</u>:

5 years TDCJ
2 years State Jail Felony
2 years probation

| | | | | |
|---|---|---|---|---|
| **Fine ordered in the Sentence?** | ☐ Yes ☐ No | If "Yes", indicate the amount: | $_____ | |
| | | Was the fine paid in full? | ☐ Yes ☐ No | |
| **Restitution ordered in the Sentence?** | ☐ Yes ☐ No | If "Yes", indicate the amount: | $_____ | |
| | | Was the restitution paid in full? | ☐ Yes ☐ No | |

COS-10 (R-01/11/2010)                    Date: _____
*(Last Name, First and Middle Name)*

_____

# SUBJECT'S VERSION

On this "Subject's Version" page you are providing additional information – your version of events – about the offense that you listed on the preceding "Criminal History Information" page. Describe in your own words the factual circumstances of the offense.

Responses such as "N/A," "Unknown," or "None" are not acceptable for this section of the application. If you do not remember any of the details about this offense you may provide a statement to that effect.

**Criminal Offense:** _____
*List the offense as it appears in the court documentation. The offense should match the wording on the corresponding Criminal History Information page.*

**Location:** _____

**Offense date(s):** _____

**Law enforcement agency involved:** _____

**State in detail events leading up to the offense and the extent of your involvement in this case:**

_____

_____

_____

_____

_____

_____

_____

_____

_____

_____

_____

_____

_____

_____

_____

_____

Complete this page before attaching any additional page(s). Place any attachments immediately behind this page.

## *Court Documentation & Offense Reports*

Place all court documents and offense/arrest reports for this offense after your Subject's Version page(s). Refer to application instruction Page 2 of 2, Procedures for Obtaining Court Documentation, for information on documents to provide with the application.

COS-10 (R-01/11/2010)                                  Date: _____
*(Last Name, First and Middle Name)*

_____

# CRIMINAL HISTORY INFORMATION

Provide information on <u>all</u> criminal convictions for which you are requesting a Commutation of Sentence **(list one offense per page)** and the disposition of each conviction. All blanks must be completed for each conviction. Included in this application are two (2) blank "Criminal History Information" pages provided in the event that you have multiple convictions.

**Photocopy as many of these blank pages as needed to list additional convictions.**

**Criminal Offense:** _____
*List the offense as it appears in the court documentation.*

**Are you requesting a Commutation of Sentence for this offense?**  ☐ **Yes**  /  ☐ **No**

*Additional Information about the Criminal Offense*

**County:** _____        **State:** _____

**Cause Number:** _____

**Court of Adjudication:** _____

**Disposition/Sentence Date:** _____
Date of sentencing.

**Court Disposition/Sentence:** _____

Examples of possible responses that you may modify to reflect your circumstance:

5 years TDCJ
2 years State Jail Felony
2 years probation

| | | | |
|---|---|---|---|
| **Fine ordered in the Sentence?** | ☐ Yes  ☐ No | If "Yes", indicate the amount: | $_____ |
| | | Was the fine paid in full? | ☐ Yes  ☐ No |
| **Restitution ordered in the Sentence?** | ☐ Yes  ☐ No | If "Yes", indicate the amount: | $_____ |
| | | Was the restitution paid in full? | ☐ Yes  ☐ No |

COS-10 (R-01/11/2010)        Date: _____
*(Last Name, First and Middle Name)*

_____

## SUBJECT'S VERSION

On this "Subject's Version" page you are providing additional information – your version of events – about the offense that you listed on the preceding "Criminal History Information" page. Describe in your own words the factual circumstances of the offense.

Responses such as "N/A," "Unknown," or "None" are not acceptable for this section of the application. If you do not remember any of the details about this offense you may provide a statement to that effect.

**Criminal Offense:** _____
*List the offense as it appears in the court documentation. The offense should match the wording on the corresponding Criminal History Information page.*

**Location:** _____

**Offense date(s):** _____

**Law enforcement agency involved:** _____

**State in detail events leading up to the offense and the extent of your involvement in this case:**

_____

_____

_____

_____

_____

_____

_____

_____

_____

_____

_____

_____

_____

_____

_____

_____

Complete this page before attaching any additional page(s). Place any attachments immediately behind this page.

## *Court Documentation & Offense Reports*

Place all court documents and offense/arrest reports for this offense after your Subject's Version page(s). Refer to application instruction Page 2 of 2, Procedures for Obtaining Court Documentation, for information on documents to provide with the application.

# COMMUTATION OF SENTENCE CHECKLIST

***Before submitting your application***, *please ensure that you have complied with all application instructions and have reviewed the checklist information provided on this page. Incomplete applications will not be forwarded to the Texas Board of Pardons and Paroles for voting consideration.*

## Eligibility

Did you review your eligibility for commutation of sentence consideration by reviewing board rules governing commutation of sentences?

## Completing the Commutation of Sentence Application Form

Did you complete the application form as instructed? Review to ensure that you have complied with all instructions, including the following:

(1)  Type or print legibly in black or blue ink;

(2)  Do not alter the presentation of the application by reformatting or rewriting the form, and do not bind or staple the application;

(3)  Respond to all items, if necessary using "N/A," "Unknown," "None," or "Do not remember;"

(4)  For each adult conviction for which you are requesting a commutation of sentence, complete application pages titled "Criminal History Information" and "Subject's Version" as instructed, with a complete and detailed Subject's Version of Offense with location, offense date, law enforcement agency involved, events leading up to the offense and your extent of involvement in the case;

(5)  Sign with your full name the application form with a date of signature.

## Certified Court Documentation

Did you provide appropriate certified court documentation (indictment/complaint/information, judgment & sentence) or clerk statement (fine/restitution paid) for **all convictions** for which you are requesting a commutation of sentence? Refer to application instruction Page 2 of 2, Procedures for Obtaining Court Documentation, for detailed instructions.

## Offense/Arrest Reports

Did you provide offense reports for **all convictions** for which you are requesting a commutation of sentence from the appropriate law enforcement agency? For example, if you were arrested by the Austin Police Department, you must request offense reports from that agency. If you were arrested by the Travis County Sheriff's Department, you must contact that agency.

If you are unsure of the arresting agency, you may access public record information pertaining to criminal convictions by accessing the Texas Department of Public Safety (DPS) Crime Records Service website http://records.txdps.state.tx.us/; or you may contact DPS to request assistance in acquiring criminal history information.

# TEXAS BOARD OF PARDONS AND PAROLES RULES

## Chapter 143. EXECUTIVE CLEMENCY

### Subchapter E. COMMUTATION OF SENTENCE

#### §143.51. Commutation of Sentence

Except in cases of treason and impeachment, upon the recommendation of the board, the governor may grant a commutation of sentence (Texas Constitution, Article IV, §11).

#### §143.52. Commutation of Sentence, Felony, or Misdemeanor

(a)     The board will consider recommending to the governor a commutation of sentence upon a request accompanied by the written recommendation of a majority of the trial officials.

(b)     If the convicted person has the recommendation of two of the trial officials and no written communication is received from third trial official, the board shall give the remaining trial official at least 10 days notice that such a clemency recommendation is being considered by the board (§508.050, Government Code).

(c)     In cases tried prior to the tenure of the present office-holders, the recommendation of persons holding such offices at the time of the trial of the case may be used to bolster and support the recommendation of the present trial officials, if in compliance with the requirements of subsection (d) of this section.

(d)     The requirements of a recommendation of trial officials for commutation of sentence must include the following:

  (1)     a statement that the penalty now appears to be excessive;

  (2)     a recommendation of a definite term now considered by the officials as just and proper; and

  (3)     a statement of the reasons for the recommendation based upon facts directly related to the facts of the cases and in existence, but not available to, the court or jury at the time of the trial, or a statutory change in penalty for the crime which would appear to make the original penalty excessive.

(e)     If the convicted person is not confined in the Texas Department of Corrections, a certified copy of the judgment and sentence must be furnished.

#### §143.53. Commutation of Remainder of Jail Sentence and/or Fine after Reprieve

The board will consider recommending to the governor a commutation of the remainder of the time left to serve on a jail sentence and/or commutation of fine after satisfactory completion of a reprieve of the jail sentence and/or fine.

## List of State Bar Associations

- Alabama Bar Association
415 Dexter Avenue
Montgomery, AL 36104
Telephone: (334) 269-1515
Fax: (334) 261-6310
E-mail: info@alabar.org

- Alaska Bar Association
P.O. Box 100279
Anchorage, AK 99510-0279
Telephone: (907) 272-7469
Fax: (907) 272-0352

- American Samoa Bar Association
P.O. Box 23
Pago Pago, American Samoa
96799
Telephone: (684) 633-1101

- Arizona Bar Association
111 West Monroe, Suite 1800
Phoenix, AZ 85003-1742
Telephone: (602) 252-4804
Fax: (602) 271-4930

- Arkansas Bar Association
400 West Markham
Little Rock, AR 72201
Telephone: (800) 609-5668
(501) 375-4606
Fax: (501) 375-4901
E-mail: arkbar@ipa.net &
arkbar@intellinet.com

- California Bar Association
555 Franklin Street
San Francisco, CA 94102-4498
Telephone: (415) 561-8200
Fax: (415) 561-8228
Los Angeles: (213) 765-1000
E-mail: jonesd@calsb.org

- Colorado Bar Association
1900 Grant Street
Ninth Floor
Denver, CO 80203
Telephone: (800) 332-6736
(303) 860-0608 & (303) 860-1115
Fax: (303) 894-0821
E-mail: comments@cobar.org

- Connecticut Bar Association
100 Corporate Place
Rocky Hill, CT 06067-1894
Telephone: (860) 721-0025
Fax: (860) 257-4125
E-mail: ctbar@ctbar.org

- District of Columbia Bar Association
1225 19th Street, NW
Suite 800
Washington, DC 20036
Phone (202) 223-6600
Fax (202) 293-3388

- Delaware Bar Association
1200 Orange Street, Suite 1100
Wilmington, DE 19801
Telephone: (302) 658-5279
Fax: (302) 658-5212
E-mail: rmarks@dsba.org

- Florida Bar Association
650 Apalachee Parkway
Tallahassee, FL 32399-2300
Telephone: (850) 561-5831
(850) 561-5600
Fax: (850) 561-5827

- Georgia Bar Association
2500 The Equitable Bldg.
100 Peachtree Street
Atlanta, GA 30303-1980
Telephone: (404) 521-0777
(404) 527-8700
Fax: (404) 527-8717

- Guam Bar Association
Supreme Court of Guam, Suite 300
120 West O'Brien Drive
Hagatna, Guam 96910-5174
Telephone: (671) 475-3396

- Hawaii Bar Association
1136 Union Mall
Penthouse 1
Honolulu, HI 96813

Telephone: (808) 537-1868
Fax: (808) 521-7936
E-mail: tkitchen@hsba.org

- Idaho Bar Association
525 West Jefferson Street
P.O. Box 895
Boise, ID 83701
Telephone: (208) 334-4500
Fax: (208) 334-4515

- Illinois Bar Association
424 South 2nd Street
Springfield, IL 62701-1779
Telephone: (217) 525-1760
(800) 252-8908 (toll-free in IL)
Fax: (217) 525-0712
E-mail: info@illbar.org

- Indiana Bar Association
230 East Ohio Street
Indianapolis, IN 46204-2199
Telephone: (800) 266-2581
(317) 637-9102
Voice Mail: (317) 639-5465
Fax: (317) 266-2588
E-mail: isbaadmin@inbar.org

- Iowa Bar Association
521 East Locust, 3rd Floor
Des Moines, IA 50309-1939
Telephone: (515) 243-3179
Fax: (515) 243-2511
E-mail: hshipley@iowabar.org

- Kansas Bar Association
1200 Harrison Street S.W.
P.O. Box 1037
Topeka, KS 66601-1037
Telephone: (785) 234-5696
Fax: (785) 234-3813
E-mail: kansbar5@ink.org

- Kentucky Bar Association
514 West Main Street
Frankfort, KY 40601-1883
Telephone: (502) 564-3795
Fax: (502) 564-3225
E-mail: webmaster@kybar.org

- Louisiana Bar Association
601 St., Charles Avenue
New Orleans, LA 70130-3427
Telephone: (504) 566-1600
Fax: (504) 566-0930
E-mail: infolsba@lsba.org

- Maine Bar Association
124 State Street
P.O. Box 788
Augusta, ME 04332-0788
Telephone: (207) 622-7523
Fax: (207) 623-0083
E-mail: info@mainebar.org

- Maryland Bar Association
The Maryland Bar Center
520 West Fayette Street
Baltimore, MD 21201
Telephone: (800) 492-1964
(410) 685-7878
Fax: (410) 837-0518
E-mail: msba@msba.org

- Massachusetts Bar Association
20 West Street
Boston, MA 02111
Telephone: (617) 338-0500
Fax: (617) 338-0650
E-mail: webmaster@massbar.org

- State Bar of Michigan
Michael Franck Building
306 Townsend Street
Lansing, MI 48933-2012
Telephone: (800) 968-1442
(517) 346-6300
Fax: (517) 482-6248
E-mail: jberry@mail.michbar.org

- Minnesota Bar Association
514 Nicollet Mall, Suite 300
Minneapolis, MN 55402
Telephone: (800) 882-MSBA
(612) 333-1183
Fax: (612) 333-4927
E-mail:
dericson@statebar.gen.mn.us

- Mississippi Bar Association
  643 North State Street
  P.O. Box 2168
  Jackson, MS 39225-2168
  Telephone: (601) 948-4471
  Fax: (601) 355-8635
  E-mail: msbar@msbar.org

- Missouri Bar Association
  The Missouri Bar Center
  326 Monroe St.
  P.O. Box 119
  Jefferson City, MO 65102-0119
  Telephone: (888) 253-6013
  (573) 635-4128
  Fax: (573) 659-8931
  (573) 635-2811
  E-mail: mobar@mobar.org

- Montana Bar Association
  46 N. Last Chance Gulch, #2A
  Helena, MT 59601
  Telephone: (406) 442-7660
  Fax: (406) 442-7763
  E-mail: statebar@ixi.net

- Nebraska Bar Association
  Roman L. Hruska Law Center
  635 South 14th Street
  Lincoln, NE 68508
  E-mail: nsbasn01@nol.org

- Nevada Bar Association
  600 E. Charleston Blvd.
  Las Vegas, NV 89104
  Telephone: (800) 254-2797
  (702) 382-2200
  Fax: (888) 660-0060 & (702) 385-2878

- New Hampshire Bar Association
  112 Pleasant Street
  Concord, NH 03301-2947
  Telephone: (603) 224-6942
  Fax: (603) 224-2910
  E-mail: info@nhbar.org

- New Jersey Bar Association
  New Jersey Law Center
  One Constitution Square

  New Brunswick, NJ 08901-1500
  Telephone: (908) 249-5000
  Fax: (908) 249-2815

- New Mexico Bar Association
  Springer Square
  121 Tijeras Avenue
  P.O. Box 25883
  Albuquerque, NM 87125
  Telephone: (505) 842-6132
  (505) 797-6000
  Fax: (505) 843-8765
  (505) 828-3765
  E-mail: sbnm@nmbar.org

- New York Bar Association
  One Elk Street
  Albany, NY 12207
  Telephone: (518) 463-3200
  Fax: (518) 463-8527

- North Carolina Bar Association
  P.O. Box 3688
  Cary, NC 27519-3688
  Telephone: (800) 662-7407
  (919) 677-0561
  Fax: (919) 677-0761
  NC Watts: (800) 662-7407
  E-mail: NCBA@mail.barlinc.org

- North Dakota Bar Association
  515½ E. Broadway, Suite 101
  P.O. Box 2136
  Bismarck, ND 58502
  Telephone: (701) 255-1404
  Fax: (701) 224-1621

- C Northern Mariana Islands Bar Association
  P.O. Box 504539
  Saipan, MP 96950
  Telephone: (670) 235-4529

- Ohio Bar Association
  1700 Lake Shore Drive
  P.O. Box 16562
  Columbus, OH 43216-6562
  Telephone: (800) 282-6556
  (614) 487-2050
  Fax: (614) 487-1008

- Oklahoma Bar Association
  P.O. Box 53036
  1901 N. Lincoln.
  Oklahoma City, OK 73152
  Telephone: (405) 524-2365
  Fax: (405) 524-1115

- Oregon Bar Association
  5200 SW Meadows Road
  P.O. Box 1689
  Lake Oswego, OR 97035-0889
  Telephone: (800) 452-8260
  (503) 620-0222
  Fax: (503) 684-1366
  E-mail: info@osbar.org

- Pennsylvania Bar Association
  100 S. Street
  P.O. Box 186
  Harrisburg, PA 17108-0186
  Telephone: (717) 238-6715
  (800) 932-0311
  Fax: (717) 238-1204
  (717) 238-7182
  E-mail: info@pabar.org &
  pabar@ezonline.com

- Puerto Rico Bar Association –
  Colegio de Abogados
  de Puerto Rico
  P.O. Box 9021900
  San Juan, PR 00902-1900
  Telephone: (787) 721-3358
  Fax: (787) 725-0330
  Email: abogados@prtc.net

- Rhode Island Bar Association
  115 Cedar Street
  Providence, RI 02903
  Telephone: (401) 421-5740
  Fax: (401) 421-2703
  E-mail: riba@ids.net

- South Carolina Bar Association
  P.O. Box 608
  Columbia, SC 29202
  Telephone: (803) 799-6653
  Fax: (803) 799-4118

- South Dakota Bar Association
  222 East Capitol Avenue
  Pierre, SD 57501-2596
  Telephone: (800) 952-2333
  (605) 224-7554
  Fax: (605) 224-0282
  E-mail: tbarnett@sdbar.org

- Tennessee Bar Association
  3622 West End Avenue
  Nashville, TN 37205-2403
  Telephone: (800) 347-1109
  (800) 899-6993 & (615) 383-7421
  Fax: (615) 297-8058

- Texas Bar Association
  1414 Colorado
  Austin, TX 78701-1627
  Telephone: (800) 204-2222
  (512) 463-1463
  Fax: (512) 463-1475
  E-mail:
  76245.1564@compuserve.com

- Virgin Islands Bar Association
  P.O. Box 224108
  Christiansted, VI 00822
  Telephone: (340) 778-7497

- Utah Bar Association
  645 S. 200 East
  Salt Lake City, UT 84111
  Telephone: (801) 531-9077
  Fax: (801) 531-0660
  E-mail: info@utahbar.org

- Vermont Bar Association
  35-37 Court Street
  P.O. Box 100
  Montpelier, VT 05601-0100
  Telephone: (802) 223-2020
  (800) 639-7036
  Fax: (802) 223-1573
  E-mail: bpaolini@vtbar.org

- Virginia State Bar
  Eighth and Main Building
  707 East Main Street, Suite 1500
  Richmond, VA 23219-2800
  Telephone: (804) 775-0500

(804) 644-0041
Fax: (804) 775-0501
(804) 644-0052
E-mail: vsb@vsb.org

- Washington Bar Association
2101 Fourth Avenue
Fourth Floor
Seattle, WA 98121-2330
Telephone: (206) 727-8202
(206) 727-8200
Fax: (206) 727-8320
E-mail: barchief1@aol.com

- West Virginia Bar Association
2006 Kanawha Blvd. East
Charleston, WV 25311-2204
Telephone: (304) 558-2456
(304) 895-3663
Fax: (304) 558-2467
E-mail: pettyc@wvbar.org &
WVBarAssociation@msn.com

- Wisconsin Bar Association
402 W. Wilson Street
P.O. Box 7158
Madison, WI 53707-7158
Telephone (state): (800) 632-8096
(608) 257-3838
Telephone (nation): (800) 728-7788
Telephone (auto): (800) 444-9404
Fax: (608) 257-5502

- Wyoming Bar Association
500 Randall Avenue
Cheyenne, WY 82001
Telephone: (307) 632-9061
Fax: (307) 632-3737

Raymond E. Lumsden

# About the Author

Raymond Lumsden is currently an inmate in the Texas Department of Criminal Justice, where he continues to fight his wrongful conviction, and unjust sentence.

He is the father of four children, (Anthony, Alyssa, Joshua, and Rylee), and the grandfather of Joe, Rysen, and Aniyah.

He has earned two Advanced Certifications as a Paralegal, and successfully graduated from a correspondence law school curriculum.

He is the author of numerous books, some of which will be available soon. *The Pro Se Section 1983 Manual* is currently available at Amazon, Barnes and Noble and FreebirdPublishers.com.

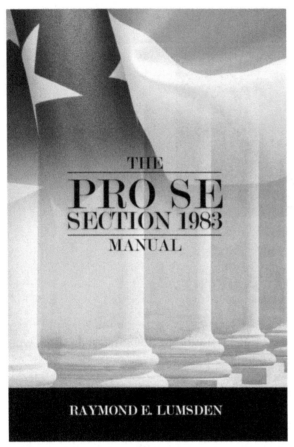

## Thanks for your interest in
## Freebird Publishers!

We value our customers and would love to hear from you! Reviews are an important part in bringing you quality publications. We love hearing from our readers-rather it's good or bad (though we strive for the best)!

If you could take the time to review/rate any publication you've purchased with Freebird Publishers we would appreciate it!

If your loved one uses Amazon, have them post your review on the books you've read. This will help us tremendously, in providing future publications that are even more useful to our readers and growing our business.

Amazon works off of a 5 star rating system. When having your loved one rate us be sure to give them your chosen star number as well as a written review. Though written reviews aren't required, we truly appreciate hearing from you.

☆ ☆ ☆ ☆ ☆  **Everything a prisoner needs is available in this book.**
January 30, 201 June 7, 2018
Format: Paperback

A necessary reference book for anyone in prison today. This book has everything an inmate needs to keep in touch with the outside world on their own from inside their prison cell. Inmate Shopper's business directory provides complete contact information on hundreds of resources for inmate services and rates the companies listed too! The book has even more to offer, contains numerous sections that have everything from educational, criminal justice, reentry, LGBT, entertainment, sports schedules and more. The best thing is each issue has all new content and updates to keep the inmate informed on todays changes. We recommend everybody that knows anyone in prison to send them a copy, they will thank you.

* No purchase neccessary. Reviews are not required for drawing entry. Void where prohibited.
  Contest date runs July 1 - June 30, 2019.

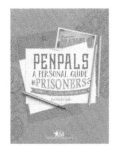

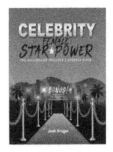

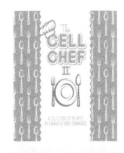

269

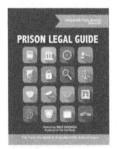

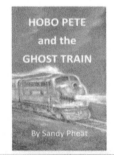

**FREEBIRD PUBLISHERS COMING SOON...**

- **THE PRO SE SECTION 1983 MANUAL**
- **THE HABEAS CORPUS MANUAL**
- **INEFFECTIVE ASSISTANCE OF COUNSEL**
- **POST CONVICTION RELIEF: SECOND LAST CHANCE**
- **POST CONVICTION RELIEF: THE ADVOCATE**

Made in the USA
Columbia, SC
13 November 2020